D0436226

Preferred Lies and Other Tales

Skimming the Cream
of a Life in Sports

Jack Whitaker

Simon & Schuster

SIMON & SCHUSTER
Rockefeller Center
1230 Avenue of the Americas
New York, NY 10020

Copyright © 1998 by Jack Whitaker

All rights reserved, including the right of reproduction in whole or in part in any form. SIMON & SCHUSTER and colophon are registered trademarks of Simon & Schuster Inc.

Designed by Sam Potts
Manufactured in the United States of America
1 3 5 7 9 10 8 6 4 2

Library of Congress
Cataloging-in-Publication Data

Whitaker, Jack, 1924–
Preferred lies and other tales / skimming the cream of a
life in sports / Jack Whitaker.
p.   cm.
1. Whitaker, Jack, 1924–   . 2. Sportscasters—
United States—Biography. I. Title.
GV742.42.W53A3 1998
070.4'49796'092—dc21
[b]   98-21895
CIP

ISBN 0-684-84272-6

All photos courtesy of Jack Whitaker

For my children:
Mary Beth,
Gerry,
Ann,
Jack,
Kevin,
and
Geoffrey

Acknowledgments

Every writer needs a small army of support to finish a book, and I was fortunate to have a strong group to assist me.

I would like to acknowledge Barbara Thomas, Candice Van Houten, and Mary Franklin, whose nimble fingers made neat pages out of my freestyle approach to the word processor.

Peter Sawyer and Ken Kennerly encouraged me and led me to Simon & Schuster. My editor, Jeff Neuman, used his quiet, reassuring manner to shape the book and help me over the high bumps in the road. The copy editor's meticulous checkings saved me from countless embarrassments.

Finally, and most important, I would like to thank Willie Morris, who first encouraged me to write a memoir. Willie believes everyone should write a book and his great love and knowledge of writing are an inspiration to all of us who still believe that the written word is important.

Jack Whitaker
Rancho Mirage, California
March 1998

Contents

Preferred Lies
and Other Tales

plastic glass, half filled, in the hand of someone who is always asking, "Who's going to win?"

The end of the game in that first Super Bowl did not mean that our telecast was over, or that our war with NBC had ended. There was still the postgame show, which was being handled by Pat Summerall for CBS and by George Ratterman for NBC. The show was to consist of Commissioner Pete Rozelle presenting Vince Lombardi with the trophy, and then a question-and-answer period, but there was a snag: Coach Lombardi always kept the press and television out of the Packer dressing room for at least five minutes after all games. That privacy was never breached. I could have warned Pat about this; just two weeks before that first Super Bowl, I had been assigned to the Packer locker room after the championship game against Dallas. About five minutes before the end of the game, I went into the locker room and was watching the game on a TV monitor. Don Meredith was moving the Cowboys down the field for a tying touchdown. It was third down on the Packers' two-yard line with the Cowboys trailing 34–27. Suddenly, Tom Miller, the Green Bay publicist, took those of us who were watching to a small closet at the back of the locker room.

"You'll have to wait in there until the Boss says you can come out," he said. "Shouldn't be more than five or ten minutes."

And, with that, a crew from NFL Films, our CBS cameraman, and myself were herded into this small room and left completely in the dark as Tom closed the door and locked it.

"What am I doing in this business?" I asked myself. "I am forty years old with a wife and six children. What am I doing locked in a dark closet in Dallas on New Year's Day?"

Eventually Tom Miller came and unlocked the door, and out we came, blinking in the bright lights, unaware that the Packers had intercepted a Meredith pass in the end zone to preserve their victory. So it was no surprise to me after the Super Bowl to hear that Pat and George were not going to get into the Packer locker room for awhile. Everyone at that moment was jammed into the corridor that runs the length of the locker rooms at the Coliseum. It was very hot, and we had some time to fill; fortunately, among those waiting was Commissioner Pete Rozelle, standing right behind Pat in that steamy corridor. So, while the Packers and their coach enjoyed their privacy, Pat interviewed the commissioner and the crisis passed.

When the door finally opened, Pat and George Ratterman poured into the room along with the rest of the American sporting press to question Vince Lombardi. One of the agreements that had been made before the game was that in the postgame session, Pat and George would use the same microphone, but that Pat would hold it. The microphone had a CBS decal on it. At one point, Ratterman began asking a question and, in the natural way of things, started to take the microphone away from Summerall. At this point, Bill MacPhail, CBS Director of Sports, who was watching in the remote truck, yelled, "Don't let Ratterman get the mike!" Director Bob Dailey relayed the message in somewhat stronger terms to Pat. What people saw on the screen was Pat Summerall, smiling sweetly at George Ratterman, but slowly and firmly taking the microphone back into his large hand.

CBS won the ratings in that first Super Bowl, and there was great jubilation on Monday morning when the overnight figures were relayed to us from New York. However, there was a very sobering message in those figures. CBS had beaten NBC for two reasons: First, CBS had more stations on their network than NBC did; and second, more people were in the habit of watching pro football on CBS, since we had broadcast the NFL longer than NBC had carried the AFL. So much for who did the better job, or who had the best announcers. Actually, NBC's announcers were darn good. Curt Gowdy and Paul Christman were the voices of the AFL and, as CBS's victory was not due to Ray Scott, Giff, and me, neither was NBC's second-place finish due to Curt and Paul. It was the first revelation to me that announcers are not the most important thing on a broadcast, no matter how much we like to think so.

After Joe Namath and the Jets shocked the establishment in Super Bowl III, and Kansas City defeated Minnesota in Super Bowl IV, the game began getting lost in the surrounding entertainments. It became the reason for a big weeklong party. This presented a problem for the coaches, the players, and the press and television. It was very difficult to focus on the game; there were, and still are, endless press conferences to attend, hourly cocktail parties that endanger human life, and "must-attend" dinners. The Super Bowl was the first athletic contest to transcend its sport and become a festival first and a game second.

After a while, the Super Bowl was not much fun to work, but it was great fun if you had no responsibilities, especially in New Orleans. New Orleans, the town the Puritans didn't settle, the town that care forgot, is the absolute best city for the event. Los Angeles is all right, except that you have to drive two hours on the freeway to get to practice and the press conferences. Miami is fine, but you spend most of your time on the steps of your hotel waiting for valet parking to bring your car around. In New Orleans, everything is in walking distance. No city in America can throw a party like New Orleans can—and that's what the Super Bowl is, a party. The social high point in my Super Bowl travels has been the Thursday night before the game in the Old Absinthe House. In the days when pro athletes used to hang out, the Old Absinthe House on that evening was a collection of sport Hall of Famers, past and present. Football players, baseball players, golfers, all jammed in against the big square bar, mixed with the writers and television people. Only on closing night at Toots Shor's on Fifty-second Street have I seen more quality athletes in one place having a good time.

Where the Super Bowl can leave other cities limp or, even worse, unmoved, New Orleans feels every vibration, dances every dance, drinks every drink. On Monday morning, when the circus has left town, it moves right along, just like the great river it sits on. New Orleans is not as American as apple pie; it is Creole and French by tradition, and a succession of wars and plagues has left a worldly-wise citizenry. New Orleans loves to eat and drink and listen to music, and during Super Bowl week there is a lot of gumbo and jambalaya, bananas fosters, oysters, and red beans and rice. There's also a lot of Dixieland and progressive jazz and fun and laughter. New Orleans takes on the Super Bowl the way it has handled its politicians, pirates, and invading armies—with a wink and a smile.

Yes, the Super Bowl is a party, and I think that's one reason it has become one of the great anticlimaxes in sports. Another contributing factor is that the conference championship games take a lot out of the players. It is difficult to maintain the high level of performance required in those games and carry it over for two weeks into the Super Bowl, and that's reflected in the small number of games that are even worth remembering. Super Bowl I was memorable because it was the first one, Super Bowl III because of Namath and the Jets, and Super Bowl X because it had everything that makes football such a great spectacle. Dallas and Pittsburgh both played superbly, achieving an almost perfect balance between offense and defense. There were only three penalties called, all of them minor ones. In my closing piece I remarked on that fact, and attributed it to the professionalism of both teams. That evening at dinner I sat next to Jack Schneider, the president of CBS, and I told him what I had said.

"Well, you know, of course, they weren't calling holding?"

"What?" I gasped.

"I was sitting in the upper press box just down from the Steeler coaches, and during the first series one of them yelled into his head set, 'They're not calling holding . . . get in there and hold!'"

Now, every time I see an official call a holding penalty that invariably stops a drive and disrupts the rhythm of the game, I wonder why.

21

Super Bowl XXV turned out to be a good game. That time in Tampa was a split-screen week for all of us, coaches, players and the media. We had one eye on the war and one on the game preparations. Not since Super Bowl III had the focus been so much on the game and so little on the amenities. There was almost an air of embarrassment at working so hard on a football game when Americans were fighting once again on foreign soil. It brought home forcibly Duane Thomas's definitive line on this event: "If it's the ultimate game, why do they play it again next year?"

The fact that the game that year came just one week after the championship game helped the Bills and the Giants give us a close and well-played contest. Nothing untoward happened; no one was taken hostage, no sniper had to fire a shot, and Whitney Houston proved forever that the national anthem does not need the help of Air Force jets. But long after the game becomes a dim memory, those of us who were in that production trailer that Friday afternoon will never forget the admonition to "get out of the way." Twenty-five years after Giff and I were scared that we had missed something in the second half kickoff in Super Bowl I, we were confronted by more ominous factors that are among the few things that have grown bigger and faster than the Super Bowl.

Football

"A lot of these players will not be back."

Football entered my life sometime in the 1930s when high schools and colleges owned the game, and professionals were a sideshow. Philadelphia may not have been the "Athens of the East," but it did and does have several top colleges and universities, all of which had football teams in those days. One of my earliest recollections is sitting on the porch of our house on Ogontz Avenue on a Saturday afternoon and watching the crowds coming back from the Temple–Villanova game at Temple Stadium. That was a big deal in those days, and so was the Army–Navy game, played at Franklin Field, home of the University of Pennsylvania. Penn had many good teams, and either tied or led the nation in attendance. Later, when I was in high school, my aunt had season tickets to the Penn games. The seats were in section E-9 in the east end zone, and from there I saw the best teams of the day. The eastern teams that would become the Ivy League were as powerful as any in the country. Yale had players like Clint Frank and Larry Kelley. Army and Navy were ranked nationally. Penn also scheduled other national powers, and during those years in E-9 I saw Tom Harmon of Michigan and Sweet Lelani of North Carolina and most of the All-Americans of the time.

On the Saturdays when I wasn't at Franklin Field, radio was the ticket to games around the country. I remember the awe I felt on those autumn Saturdays, hearing games from such romantic-sounding places as Palo Alto, California, and South Bend, Columbus, Ann Arbor, and Fort Worth. To me, the most intriguing name of all was Champaign-Urbana, home of the Fighting Illini. I have since been to and worked at the stadiums in Palo Alto, Fort Worth, Columbus, and South Bend, and the visits have been a fulfillment of these long-ago Saturday wishes. I have yet to see Champaign-Urbana, and people tell me not to go, to keep my romantic fantasy intact. But I would still like to see it, to connect once more to those boyhood days of the Depression, when so many dreams were born on those autumn afternoons.

In the early 1950s, the opportunity to broadcast from Franklin Field fell my way, first on radio and later on television. It was a great old stadium made for football and the Penn Relays. Its one drawback was the press box, which sat upon the rim of the north side. There was no elevator and the walk up required an effort, even for my young legs. The older sports writers called it Cardiac Terrace. From that press box one year, I was part of the CBS Radio *Football Roundup*. At the time, Red Barber, the best that ever was in describing a sporting event, was head of CBS Sports. During football season, Red would sit in a studio in New York and switch around the country to four or five of the biggest games of the week. At each game, the announcer would give a resume of what had happened, do a few minutes of play-by-play and then throw it back to New York. Among the other announcers were Vin Scully, who handled the games in the Northeast, and Bill Munday, a marvelously purple-prosed southerner, who described the end zone as "the coronation room where the diadem committee was awaiting." He did the Southwest Conference; I was assigned the games in the Middle Atlantic region.

In that time I reported on the Notre Dame teams of Johnny Lattner, the last great Maryland products of coach Jim Tatum, and the buck lateral series of Charlie Caldwells' Princeton teams led by Dick Kazmaier. And, of course, the University of Pennsylvania's teams coached by George Munger. George had coached at Penn before the war and was as much a part of Penn's history as Benjamin Franklin. It was said of George that he was the kind of coach everyone wanted his son to play for, a teacher first and foremost.

In the mid-1950s, with the coming of television, college football began to change. In Philadelphia, the University of Pennsylvania, under the presidency of Harold Stassen, made an awkward attempt to go big time, but cooler heads prevailed and the University was taken into the Ivy League. George Munger resigned during the Stassen years and was replaced by Steve Sebo, who inherited a big-time schedule with Ivy League restraints on scholarships and practice times. A few awful years followed, until Penn's schedule caught up with its principles. My heretical stance on the Ivy League is that I enjoy an Ivy League game more than a Nebraska–Miami showdown. Certainly the Nebraska–Miami game will be the better played game, but it is semipro ball, and the *semi* gets weaker all the time.

As Penn and the Ivy League receded to the shores of common sense, professional football began getting the star treatment in

Philadelphia. This was helped in no small way by the fact that the commissioner of the NFL was a hometown boy. Bertram de Bienville Bell was from a distinguished Pennsylvania family. His brother, John, was the Chief Justice of the Pennsylvania Supreme Court and, incidentally, of valuable assistance to Bert in the growth of the NFL. One day, shortly after he had been elected Commissioner, Bert took his brother to lunch at the Racquet Club. Bert had been reading the by-laws of the league, and he asked his brother to look over a particular subparagraph that intrigued him. Brother John read the subparagraph and said, "Bert, I think this means that you can do anything you want. But give me a few days to think about it."

A few days later, John called back.

"Bert, this by-law means you are a tsar."

With that legal backing, Bert would always have copies of the by-laws for each owner at any meeting where a controversial subject arose, and if there were any objections to the commissioner's ruling, he would say, "Read the by-laws . . . they say I am a tsar."

Bert Bell attended the University of Pennsylvania and played football with Lou Little and Lud Wray. They were a rambunctious group, and football was their passion. Bert never gave up the idea of enjoying the sport after college, and eventually he owned a professional team known as the Frankford Yellowjackets, which grew into the Philadelphia Eagles. He was one of the pillars of professional football.

His face was broad and generous, a pleasant face beneath a wide brow. His dark hair was parted in the middle and combed back, all of which gave him a pugnaciously friendly look. But Bert Bell could be best summed up by his voice. It was a voice whose origins could be traced back to Ned Sparks and beyond. It was a voice that was large and generous, like himself; a voice that could be sarcastic, witty, kind, or wise; a voice that sounded as if the vocal chords were being rubbed sideways against sandpaper beneath a layer of wet gravel. Bert Bell spoke in growls that started somewhere deep within him and exploded upwards as his tongue fought gamely to keep up with his onrushing mind.

Sportswriters and sportscasters were familiar with that voice, especially those around the Philadelphia area. Bert would emcee the weekly Maxwell Club luncheon at the Warwick Hotel. The club was named in honor of Tiny Maxwell, a large former footballer and, later, an official of great reputation and great wit. Once, officiating a college game, he walked off a ten-yard penalty.

"You dope," yelled the offended coach, "there's no ten-yard penalty. That's a fifteen-yard offense."

"The way you're coaching," said Tiny, "that's only worth 10."

And so the spirit of the Maxwell Club was like that of the man for whom it was named. There was an air of irreverence, but football always came first, and that's the way Bert Bell ran the weekly luncheons. A high school, college, and professional player was honored every Monday. There would be highlights of the college games and then an open discussion on rules or whatever Bert wanted to talk about.

Aside from the Maxwell Club, sportswriters and broadcasters were familiar with the Bell voice in a more personal way: The commissioner would call us at home, or at the office, or wherever we might be, to tell us why a certain statement was wrong. Mostly, it concerned Bert's two cardinal rules: Never show or remark about a fight on a field, and never linger on an injury. These were two restrictions that radio and television were trying unsuccessfully to master. Bert insisted on these limitations because he knew the violence, real and potential, that exists in the game, but mostly because the NFL was his life and his love and he would not allow anything to cast a shadow upon it.

When Bert had occasion to call us, he was never angry or arrogant or condescending. He was invariably kind and paternal, as if correcting a favorite child. Occasionally, he would use a gentle needle to make his point.

One hot, humid August evening, Bill Campbell of WCAU was doing a preseason game on radio between the Eagles and the Green Bay Packers in Portsmouth, Virginia. (That was another Bert Bell rule: "They are not exhibition games; everybody is trying to win.") Tobin Rote was the quarterback for the Packers, and he was injured near the end of the first half. Bill, an excellent play-by-play man, dutifully reported the fact. Then an ambulance came onto the field.

"Well, I guess Tobin Rote has been injured more seriously than we thought," said Bill. "Here comes an ambulance on the field. No, they are turning around now, so I guess it's not for Tobin after all. No, wait, there is Tobin and he's getting into the ambulance. Tobin Rote is being taken from the field in an ambulance."

In the second half, Rote came back into the game and threw three touchdown passes to win the game. Bill had just signed off when the telephone rang in the broadcast booth.

"Willie?"

"Yes?"

"Willie," growled the voice, "where did Tobin throw those touchdown passes from, the back of the ambulance?"

Bert took the NFL into the television age and laid the foundation for the great growth that came in the late 1950s and '60s. His successor, Pete Rozelle, built soundly and brilliantly on that foundation, taking the game to its highest level, before Al Davis and his lawsuit seriously wounded the sport and rendered the commissioner powerless—a far cry from Bert's tsar status. Bert's talent for hitting the right note at the right time extended to his death: He suffered a heart attack in Franklin Field, where he had played his college ball, watching the Philadelphia Eagles play the Pittsburgh Steelers, two teams he had owned and coached. Bert knew how to tie up loose ends.

* * *

By 1965, I had been announcing Philadelphia Eagles games for nine years, first as color man with Byram Saam and, after Byram left, as play-by-play man, beginning in 1960, the year the Eagles won the championship. It was an especially rewarding season, not only for the Eagles' organization, but for all of us who had followed the team through the hard times of the 1950s when a record of seven wins in a season was all too rare. In 1958, general manager Vince McNally signed Buck Shaw as the head coach, traded for quarterback Norm Van Brocklin, and moved from Connie Mack Stadium to Franklin Field. The desired results did not happen right away: The Eagles' record in 1958 was two wins, nine losses, and one tie.

On the final day of the season, just before Christmas, on a gray, cold afternoon, Washington beat Philadelphia 20–0 in creaky old Griffith Stadium. The train ride home that evening was not a celebration. A dining car had been set aside for the team, and we all gathered to eat and drink as the dark night sped by in the small towns of Maryland and Pennsylvania. Patches of snow could be seen around the railroad stations, and from every house along the tracks colored Christmas lights twinkled, softening the drabness that would come with the daylight.

Gradually, a few players began to laugh and talk louder as the beers began taking effect. Byram and I sat at a table with Coach Shaw drinking that black, strong Pennsylvania Railroad coffee that always held more than a taste of coal dust.

"Take a good look around," said Buck. "A lot of these players will not be back."

And they were not.

That same night the Green Bay Packers had also finished a dismal season—two wins and ten defeats. In two years Green Bay and Philadelphia met for the championship.

The 1960 season did not begin on a high note for the Eagles. On opening day before a hometown crowd, the Cleveland Browns smothered Philadelphia 41–24. The next week, playing a brand new expansion team known as the Dallas Cowboys, the Eagles were lucky to get away with a 27–25 win. Still, they managed to win nine games in a row, one of them dramatically, in the last moments when Bobby Walston kicked a field goal in the dusky gloom of Cleveland's Municipal Stadium to defeat the Browns, 31–29.

Probably the two most important wins, however, were the two against the New York Giants, in games played on successive Sundays. The first one, played in Yankee Stadium, was really two games. The first half was played in brilliant sunshine and belonged entirely to the Giants. Although New York couldn't score much, their defense kept pushing the Eagles back, and Van Brocklin spent almost every play on the ground. In the second half, the day turned dark and gray, and Charles Bednarik of Bethlehem, Pennsylvania and the University of Pennsylvania volunteered to play both middle linebacker and offensive center.

Immediately, the game changed. With Bednarik at center, Van Brocklin had more time, and began to take the Giants' offense apart. Helped further by a Giant fumble, the Eagles won 17–10. The game is also remembered because of a blind-side hit Bednarik made on Frank Gifford, knocking him out of the game with a concussion. That play ended the last scoring chance the Giants had, and Bednarik, in his exuberance, jumped in the air, waving his fist. Many people thought that Chuck was happy because he had hurt Gifford, and the boos filled the stadium. The truth was that Chuck knew the Eagles had won the game and at the time was oblivious to the injury sustained by Frank. It is nice to report that over the years, Gifford and Bednarik have become friends.

The second game was played in Franklin Field on a sunny, clear day. On the first play from scrimmage, the Giants scored on a seventy-yard pass to Kyle Rote. The next time the Giants got the ball, they marched right back down the field, but had to settle for a field goal. But it was 10–0 Giants and the Eagles hadn't done a thing. Since we didn't televise home games in those days, I was sitting that day with Charley Gauer, the offensive coordinator of the Eagles, and he looked over at me as Don Chandler kicked the field goal and said, "Don't worry, everything's going to be all right."

And eventually it was all right, as Van Brocklin again pulled the Giant defense apart and Philadelphia won, 31–23. A week later in St. Louis, the Eagles clinched their first championship in 11 years, and went into the championship game against Vince Lombardi's Green Bay Packers on a cold but sunny day in Franklin Field. After another disastrous start, Philadelphia managed to hold on, with Chuck Bednarik playing fifty-eight minutes, the last one of which was spent on the back of a squirming Jim Taylor on the Philadelphia nine-yard line. The Eagles were champions of the world of professional football.

It is a pleasant thing to be the announcer of a team that wins the pennant or the World Series or the Super Bowl, and after being with the Eagles in the years when they lost twice as many games as they won, the championship was all the sweeter. Forgotten in the moment of victory against a team that was to become legendary were the lonely rides back from losing ball games when the injuries hurt more and laughter was scarce. Forgotten were those seasons of discontent filled with rumors and bickering. It was enough to bask in the reflected warmth of the moment and to be proud to know men like Van Brocklin and Marion Campbell and Jessie Richardson and Tom Brookshier and all the rest who were, for the moment, the best team in professional football.

But after the 1960 season, the Eagles' fortunes changed drastically. The elegant Buck Shaw resigned as head coach as he said he would, and volatile Norm Van Brocklin retired as a player, as he said he would, and became the head coach for the brand new Minnesota Vikings. In 1961, Philadelphia finished second after a brilliant season by quarterback Sonny Jurgenson and under the guidance of Nick Skorich, the new head coach. Their record was ten and four—but it couldn't last, and in 1962 the erosion became more pronounced. In 1963 the team was sold to Jerry Wolman, who brought in Joe Kuharich as his head coach and general manager, and with him came a whole new cast of assistant coaches and front-office personnel. Since my beginning days in television in 1950 I had been close to the Eagles, through the hard times and the euphoria of the championship season. They were a big part of my professional career. But by 1964 things had changed. New people were in charge and while the team colors were the same, nothing else was. Wholesale trades gave the team an entirely different look and, by 1965, moving from the Eagles to the Giants was not as difficult as it might have been. It was time for a move. And what a move it turned out to be.

Chris Schenkel, the number one announcer at CBS at the time, suddenly left for ABC, which, under the direction of Roone Arledge, was building a sports department that would make ABC a strong and highly competitive network. It was my good fortune that CBS's head of Sports, Bill McPhail, picked me to replace Chris at CBS. At that time, Chris's assignments were the most glittering in all of television sports; they included the Kentucky Derby and the other Triple Crown races, all of CBS's golf including The Masters, and New York Giants football.

A sports team used to get its personality from the coach, the general manager, and the owner, and the Giants were very cordial and polite, if a little uncertain about me replacing Chris Schenkel. Allie Sherman, who had once quarterbacked the Philadelphia Eagles, was the head coach; a nattily dressed, handsome man with flashing eyes, Allie bristled with energy and enthusiasm. The Mara family were just recovering from the death of Jack Mara, and Wellington was assuming the responsibilities of his older brother.

In the beginning years of the NFL on CBS, and up until the late 1960s, announcers were assigned to one team. We became an extension of the club, almost a member of the family. The announcers were approved or at least had the tacit consent of the clubowners. This relationship often made objectivity difficult. The Giant organization was very nice to me, if a little reserved, and I was gradually adapting to the new ways. I no longer drove to Hershey in the humid days of August.

Training camp for the Giants was at Fairfield College in Connecticut on a handsome campus about an hour and a half from my house. Before the first exhibition game in Green Bay, Dr. Sweeney, the lovable team physician, proposed a graceful toast welcoming me to the Giants, and I felt as if I might have cleared the first barrier. But the biggest thing in my favor was that I was working with Frank Gifford.

Frank Gifford was to the Giants and their fans as Joan of Arc had been to the French peasants. The number-one draft choice in the league in 1951, Frank came out of Southern California to join a Giants team that would play a major role in the development of professional football. And Frank, with his movie star looks and great athletic talent, became one of the biggest stars of that team and its fans. New York can't resist heroes and Frank fit the bill; he was Jack Armstrong, out of Hollywood, into the canyons of Manhattan. After a brilliant football career, Frank had taken a job as a sportscaster on Channel Two, the CBS outlet in New York. And, sometime in 1965, Bill McPhail and Bill Fitts decided to team him with me on the Giants' games.

Frank was a strangely shy man with a dry sense of humor and a great love for the game of football. It was a love he shared unselfishly. It is one of many times that I was fortunate to work with a person who so loved his sport that he wanted you to love it the same way, and was determined that I was going to be well-informed.

Since he had only recently retired, Frank knew all the players and coaches on the Giants and they trusted him. So did the rest of the teams in the league. Whatever information he got he would share with me. In those days, most play-by-play announcers would have two big spotting boards, one for each team, which they would place on either side of them. These boards were three deep at each position, with the weight and height and school of the player underneath his name. Next to each board sat a spotter, who would point to the man carrying the ball or catching the pass, and to the man making the tackle. Some announcers still use this system; I had always found it cumbersome and faulty. Cumbersome, because most announcing booths in those days were tiny and cramped enough with a television monitor, two announcers, an engineer, and a cameraman in addition to two spotters. And faulty because it is very dangerous to rely on somebody else when you're calling the plays.

When we first started to work together, Frank would talk about matchups. "What do you mean, matchups?" I asked one day.

"Who's playing against whom," he answered.

And a light dawned. Of course, instead of having the defensive team on one side and the offensive team on the other, what was needed was a card with the defensive team on top against the offensive team on the bottom. Then, not only could you see the matchups at a glance—that is, who was opposite whom on the line and who the linebacker was keying on and which receivers the cornerbacks and safeties were responsible for—but the blocking patterns became easier to see, the pass patterns clearer in terms of what the receivers were trying to do, and it was easier to pinpoint why the offense was working or not working. From that time on, I threw away the spotting boards and, much to the chagrin of several marvelous people, I stopped using spotters. I simply got an index card and put the defensive team on top and the opposing offensive team on the bottom on one side, and reversed the teams on the other side. Then I would memorize the defense first, as if I were the offensive quarterback and was looking out over my center. I don't pretend to say that I suddenly knew all about professional football, but it was the single most clarifying thing that happened, and it increased my pleasure in doing the games tenfold. Spencer Tracy is said to have told a young movie actress that all you had to do was "know your lines and don't bump into the furniture." In announcing pro football, all you have to do is know the eighty players by number and don't bump into your color man. And that is easy enough to do. For several years now, the programs you buy at the stadium have shown the matchups but, back in 1965, it was a new thing for me.

The other thing Frank introduced to game preparation, or at least vastly increased, was the use of film. He would get the films of the team the Giants were playing that week, and we would watch them by the hour, usually on Saturday afternoon or evening. They were the coaching films, broken down into offensive and defensive reels. They were very helpful, especially if the team was one we hadn't seen before.

One cold Saturday night in Chicago, Frank and I were going to dinner with Jack Patera, the defensive-line coach of the Giants, and Harland Svare, who had been the head coach of the Rams. We were up in Frank's room looking at the films of the Bears' defensive team when Harland knocked on the door.

"Are you guys ready?" he asked.

"Come in, we'll only be a minute. We're watching some Bears' film."

"I don't wanta watch any more films," said Harland. "I've seen one hundred hours of them this week."

"Sit down," said Frank. "We'll only be a minute."

Harland sat down on the bed, and we went back to watching the film. In thirty seconds, Harland was on his feet and standing by the screen, which was a sheet we had tacked on the wall.

"Wait a minute," he said. "Run that back again."

So Frank ran the reel back several feet.

"Now watch this," said Harland, pointing at the screen.

"See [Richie] Pettibone there? When he stands sideways and points his left foot forward, that means they're going into a zone. Run it ahead. See, right into a zone."

For the next hour Svare kept explaining the Bears' defense, completely absorbed in a film he had watched all week. And we were an hour-and-a-half late for dinner.

The years I worked with Frank were learning years and good years.

There was a lot more of America to see now, and the country's style and look were changing. Urban renewal was a key phrase. In the football towns the changes were very noticeable. In St. Louis, as in many cities, this urban renewal included a new stadium, and we moved from the Chase Plaza Hotel on the Park to Stouffer's Inn on the river from which we could walk to the stadium. By this time, professional football had fully captured the sporting public.

And television accommodated the public every way it could. One way was to broadcast doubleheaders on certain Sundays. Almost everyone was trying to benefit from the pro football craze. I remember a sunny and warm Sunday in November 1969 at the Stouffer Inn, looking out my window at the Gateway Arch and two old-fashioned riverboats docked just north of the arch, and thinking I had never seen St. Louis look so good. Just down the river from the arch is the Old Cathedral, a handsome edifice built in 1830. The time difference meant a three o'clock kickoff, so I had a leisurely Sunday morning and then walked across the street to the cathedral for the twelve o'clock mass.

Next to the poor box I noticed a stack of circulars. They announced the times of the Masses at the Old Cathedral, with a special word for "You St. Louis Cardinal Fans."

"Come to our ten-thirty Mass," read the circular, "and then have brunch and go to the game.

"Or have breakfast at home, come to our twelve o'clock Mass and walk to the game."

And, finally, my favorite. "Avoid the traffic rush. Come to the postgame Mass. Starts fifteen minutes after every home game."

The bishop was really trying.

In Pittsburgh things were changing, too. We no longer stayed at the Webster Hall Hotel and walked across the street to Forbes Field. The Steelers played at Pitt Stadium while they waited for Three Rivers Stadium to be built, and we now stayed at the Hilton Hotel with its dramatic view of the confluence of the Allegheny and Monongahela Rivers, and watched the new stadium rise on steel beams made in the neighborhood.

Other cities were changing, too, and so were our tastes. Conversations other than football turned to Vietnam and ended often in baleful arguments. But, mostly, life went humming along in a procession of rented cars, credit cards, and expansion teams and new stadiums.

The biggest change that happened to professional football was the end of the war between the AFL and the NFL, which led to the merger in 1966 and to the first Super Bowl in 1967.

They were exciting years. Professional football grew more popular every day and the people involved in the game—the owners, coaches, players, sportswriters and broadcasters—all had a sense of wonderment and delight in being part of this phenomenon. Commissioner Pete Rozelle was leading the way to critical and commercial success. There was time in those days to get to know the players, coaches, and owners, and to form relationships based on trust and respect. There was time to appreciate the hard work and pain required to be a top professional player and to see how short a career could be.

I remember doing a preseason game one August night in Minnesota between the Vikings and the Dolphins. It was a beautiful summer evening just after a rain, and the ground at Metropolitan Stadium smelled as sweet as anything can. As the teams warmed up in the twilight, they were beautiful to look at, smiling, all their uniforms brand new, their helmets shining, the white tape around their shoes blinding. They all had a little Richard Cory about them that evening; they glittered as they walked.

In January, those two teams met in the Super Bowl in Houston. They didn't look the same. They were grimmer, tired and drawn, and they no longer glittered as they walked. Several had been injured, some severely. Injuries are part of the game and the one that is the bête noire of the sport is the knee. The knee was not made to play football; knees were made to say your prayers on, for small boys to play marbles on, for old women to scrub floors on, for altar boys to genuflect with, but the knee was not made to bend sideways, especially not with the help of a 280-pound lineman moving across it at twenty miles per hour. The medial collateral ligament in football is an endangered species. It is to the football player what the thin ankles are to a thoroughbred horse and it seems to afflict the running backs as much as any.

The running back has always been one of my favorites, and the broken-field run is the most exciting play to watch. It is the poetry of this physical game, and along with the pass, it saves football from being merely an exercise of brute strength. When I first started paying attention to professional football, I thought Steve Van Buren was the best I would ever see. Then I saw Hugh McIlhenny and then Jim Brown. Who could be better than Jim Brown? Then here comes Gale Sayers and then Earl Campbell and Walter Payton and Emmitt Smith and Barry Sanders.

But as quickly as they come, most of them go. If the knee doesn't collapse, then the speed goes and so does the rest of the body. I once heard a quarterback and an offensive lineman each acknowledge with a great deal of awe that he could never be a running back because playing that position was like running into a brick wall. Matt Snell used to say that if a running back carried the ball 187 times, then the running back had been in 187 head-on car accidents. The running backs are the incandescent ones, burning brightly for a short time, their life expectancy that of a moth's. Each year a bright new group comes into the league and another four or five limp off to retirement, body and knees scarred, walking like men of seventy-five before they are forty. But while they are here, they light up the game.

And, in another way, so do the quarterbacks with their strong

arms and their capacity for leadership. They are the glamorous leading men in a very unglamorous position. It is a calling in life that requires a strong arm, strong body, strong mind, and a lot of agility to
avoid the concussion-producing poundings of the defensive line-
men and linebackers. And they must be able to win. I am fortunate
enough to have seen many of the great ones, from Otto Graham
and Johnny Unitas to Montana, Young, and Favre. Who was the
best? I don't believe anyone knows. It's impossible to compare different generations because of rule changes, as well as changes in
equipment and training programs. But I would love to have seen
Sonny Jurgenson throw to Jerry Rice. The richness of talent continues to flow into the NFL every year but, instead of serving on twelve
teams as it did in 1960, it now must accommodate 28 teams.

One Sunday night in 1975 in P. J. Clarke's, I was sitting with
Bill Fitts and Kevin O'Malley of the CBS Sports Department. We
were discussing the half-hour pregame show that preceded the
Sunday NFL regional telecasts. Pat Summerall and I were hosting
the show, which had a simple, straightforward format: Pat and I
would stand in front of a bank of videotape machines and talk
about game number one, then either Pat or I would press a button
and the tape reel would start to spin and the director would dis-
solve into tape of the two teams' previous games. There was
plenty of good information in that half hour, but the department
wanted to put a little more excitement into it.

"What we should do," I said that night in Clarke's, "is handle it
like the news department. You should make me the anchorman
in New York, like Walter Cronkite, and then switch around the
country to the game remotes for reports from the announcers doing the games. We would also have a place and time for features
on players and coaches."

Bill Fitts and Kevin O'Malley liked the idea, and so was born
The NFL Today.

"Would you give up doing play-by-play to anchor the pregame
show?" asked Bill Fitts.

"Yes," I said.

I was voluntarily giving up one of the choicest positions in televised sports, that of a play-by-play man in the NFL. The reason I agreed so quickly was that I felt I would be a better anchor man than play-by-play man. I had been doing play-by-play since 1960 and I knew I would not get much better. Also the fact that we would be doing something new and different appealed to me.

Fitts and O'Malley sold the idea to the Sports Department and in 1975, we began *The NFL Today*. It was a hectic first year, but we learned a lot and were in much better shape as the second season approached.

About that time, there was a change in the CBS Sports Department. Bob Wussler came in as the new head of the department and made some changes, and one of them was to bring in Brent Musberger to replace me as the host on *The NFL Today*. Things like this happen all the time in television.

In the broadcast business we all have our gurus, rabbis, and protectors—management people who are supportive. I was more fortunate than most in beginning my TV career at the CBS affiliate in Philadelphia; in a very short period of time in the 1960s, Jack Dolph, Bill Fitts, Frank Chirkinian, and Tony Verna all left that station, WCAU-TV, for the CBS Sports Department. Soon after, Jack Schnieder, who had been general manager in Philadelphia, became the president of CBS. I was well connected in those years under the Schnieder and later the Bob Woods presidencies. When they moved on and were replaced, the new management brought in its own people and some of us lost our friends at court.

That is what happened with *The NFL Today*. It would happen to me again at ABC Sports after Roone Arledge left the Sports Department to concentrate on news. In any cae, as of 1976, I had given up doing play-by-play to host the pregame show, and now I had neither.

I stayed on doing commentaries on *The NFL Today* and at championship games and Super Bowls for a while, but that was really my farewell to football. At first, I missed it terribly, but as the years moved on and the game changed, I found I missed it less and less. I feel that sometime in the 1980s, the NFL began to diminish. With each new franchise, the quality shrunk. In college ball, the exploitation of young men by their universities was not making this the "golden age of learning." Young football players bring in huge sums of money to these educational institutions in return for what is, too often, a bogus college degree. The Knight Foundation Commission on Intercollegiate Athletics points out the correct measures to be taken, but like the Hoover and Grace Commission Reports on our federal government, it languishes because of a lack of will to change the status quo.

Football is a wondrous game with a rich and distinguished history. It has produced some of our very best citizens. It's a game of aesthetic beauty containing grace and cunning, strength and hard contact. But that hard contact has been turned into gratuitous violence in too many instances, and the game is being badly served by our universities and the professional club owners.

There is nothing new about violence in the NFL. Despite the disarming defense that "you must realize football is a rough sport," gratuitous violence like late hits has been a problem in the NFL for a long time, along with controversial calls. Both these problems go back to the same root—the rules of the game. That raises another question: Do coaches and players really want to play by the rules? Are players taught from high school through college and into the professional ranks to obey the rules, or are they taught to break them at every opportunity, as long as they can get away with it? There is evidence enough to support the fact that in many cases the latter is true. Youngsters see all of this and absorb it, and then go to sports banquets and listen to coaches, educators, clergymen and sportscasters tell them that sports build character. My friend Heywood Hale Broun has nailed that one cleanly to the wall; Woody has written, "Sports don't build character, they reveal it."

Professional football has done more than anything else to keep alive the memory of World War II. Young people, who may not know a thing about Pearl Harbor or D-Day, all know what the blitz is, and the bomb. The sport kept coining language that enhanced the picture of violence. Somewhere in the 1960s we began hearing about sacks. To "sack" means to pillage and burn, and the subject of sacks used to be towns and villages; now it's quarterbacks. It is another subliminal way to keep the warfare theme alive. Only with this one, they went well past World War II to the Dark Ages, giving us the impression that linebackers are named Alaric, Attila, and Tamberlane.

I am thankful for the years I spent in football, as a fan and as a reporter, and I am especially thankful for the people I've met down the years in this game. People like Bert Bell and Frank Gifford, Vince Lombardi, Jim Finks, Tom Brookshier, and John Lujack and hundreds more, all of whom had and have a deep love for the game. But until that caring for the sport returns to those who control both the college and professional game, I will be happy to live in an area that does not have an NFL franchise or a Top Ten college team, a place where I can perhaps watch an Ivy League game on an October Saturday afternoon.

Golf, for Beginners

"Would you mind hitting it again? I missed it."

It was a misty, cold morning in January 1944. The *Ile de France* clanged its way up the Firth of Clyde on the west coast of Scotland, moving through the gray waters with assurance, now that her voyage was coming to an end. The elegant liner was carrying American troops to their greatest adventure. She had left New York six days earlier, and without escort had steamed past Montauk Light, south to Bermuda, and then northeast across the wintry Atlantic, outrunning the German U-boats. I had been on guard duty all night. It was a pleasure to be on guard duty, for it got me out of my berth, which was on deck below the water line and a claustrophobic nightmare. It was a chance to move about the great liner. The enlisted men were herded below and ate in a mess hall that was as dingy and loud as the food was inedible. Late at night, the English sailors would come around to our bunks and sell us bologna sandwiches for five dollars apiece. Our first impression of our allies was not favorable. Guard duty at night was a respite from the depths of the *Ile de France*.

As sergeant of the guard I could go wherever I pleased. The upper decks were reserved for officers and were much the same as they were before the war. The officers' mess was in the grand dining salon, and the elegance and luxury of this floating hotel was overwhelming. I had a pleasant surprise one night as I inspected the chapel: There was a plaque on the wall just inside the doorway commemorating the first mass held on board the liner. It had been celebrated by my uncle, Monsignor Joseph Whitaker.

On the last morning of our trip, as my tour of duty ended, I stood on the deck breathing the morning air, glad that we would be landing in Greenoch in a few hours, relieved that the voyage was almost over. I had no idea that I was looking out over some historic countryside. We had just sailed past the Ailsa Craig, the large rock that rises like a mountain out of the Firth not far from the spot where Robert Bruce landed on his way to save Scotland, and beyond which lies the Turnberry golf course, the town of Ayr, and the history of championship golf.

Ayrshire is the birthplace of the poet Robert Burns. There is, in fact, a Robert Burns Memorial Hotel on the banks of the River Doon; it has eight rooms, seven parking places and three pubs, and in all three pubs, the talk is of golf. Just up the A79 from Ayr is the seaside town of Prestwick, whose solid redstone houses peer out to sea with Victorian severity. When you turn off the A79 toward the beach you come out from under the railroad tunnel and find on the right side a gray-brown granite building that looks like the home office of the Bank of Scotland. It is the clubhouse of the Prestwick Golf Club, the place where championship golf began, the site of the first British Open. The year was 1860 and, today,

Prestwick looks like it must have 135 years ago, and, as you look out at the course, down the railway tracks on the right and across the sand hills to the sea on the left, you are overcome with a sense of history.

I did not feel any of that on that January morning in 1944. Looking back, it is surprising to me now that I could ever view the coast of Scotland and not think of the game of golf, even as RAF pilots were stirring in the aerodrome that had been laid down on the fairways of the Turnberry Golf Club. My introduction to golf would come a few years later, and it would become a big part of my life when I began to broadcast tournaments for CBS Sports. I am grateful to the game and to its places. The first broadcast I did was the PGA Championship at Aronimink in 1962; since then, these broadcasts have taken me all over the country and to most of the world. Even now, although things have changed enormously, I can't believe how fortunate I have been. One steamy morning in the Bollinger tent at the British Open at Royal Birkdale, Henry Longhurst looked over the rim of a champagne glass and said, "Remember, Jack, we are skimming the cream."

Skimming the cream for me began when I went to work at WCAU-TV in Philadelphia in 1950, and fell in with a group of golfing buffs. Our number-one personality at the station was the newscaster John Facenda, and his love for the game was deep and infectious. I had just taken up golf and so had Frank Chirkinian, who began working at the station the same week I did. John was a member of Llanerch Country Club, but the rest of us were just starting out and had new families, so we played most of our golf at the Main Line Golf Club, a public facility that straddled Lancaster Pike in Wayne, Pennsylvania. What a grand old place it was, flat on one nine, hilly on the other. It was our training ground and happy playground. But, like Dan Jenkins' Goat Hills and hundreds of other great public facilities, it has long been paved over for motels and shopping centers, which offer nothing to compare to the joys we had trying for the first time to seriously play the game.

Everyone should have the experience of a public golf-course education. There, on the not too manicured fairways and greens, are to be found the true believers. Those golfers are there for only one reason—to play the game—not for social or business purposes. Golf is the only subject and it is pursued with a delightful vengeance. At least, it was at the Main Line Golf Club in the 1950s, where we carried our own bags and dreamed of breaking ninety. In addition to the Main Line Golf Club, we had the great generosity of John Facenda, who would take us to his club as his guest so often we felt embarrassed. And we had George Fazio.

George Fazio was the first touring professional I ever met. He was a local hero from Conshohocken and the leading golf professional in the Philadelphia area. He had lost the 1950 United States Open in a playoff against Ben Hogan and Lloyd Mangrum at the Merion Golf Club. George was a classy player, a swinger rather than a hitter. He had one of the most fluid swings I ever saw, rhythmic and quiet and marvelous to watch. And he was a thinker. He was always planning ahead, thinking up ideas for making money. Once, traveling with Jimmy Demaret in the early days of the Tour, George was going on about some scheme when Jimmy pulled the car up in front of a bank in a small town in West Texas.

"Why are we stopping here?" asked George.

"I want to put all that money we just made in a safe place," replied Jimmy.

George's great hero was Leonardo da Vinci, and there was a touch of the Master in George. He was one of the first touring pros to turn his talents to golf-course design, and he built a great career in that field before it was the fashionable thing to do. His talent has been inherited by his nephew, Tom Fazio, who has built beautifully on George's foundations and taken golf-course design to new heights.

George was compassionate, humorous, stubborn, generous, and intensely loyal and patriotic. At Jupiter Hills in Florida, his favorite of all the courses he designed, he instructed the valet-parking attendants to put all foreign-made cars in the back out of sight; only American-made cars were to be put in front of the clubhouse. Once, a Japanese guest came into the pro shop and inquired the way to the first tee.

"Tell him," George said to his assistant, "if he could find Pearl Harbor, he can find the first tee."

George was the perfect person to introduce us to the wonders of the game and its infinite possibilities. Sometime in 1953, we had an idea—actually, I think it was Frank Chirkinian's idea. I was doing a sports show Monday through Friday between 11 and 11:30 PM on WCAU-TV. John Facenda did ten minutes of news, Phil Sheridan did a five-minute weather show and, after my ten minutes of sports, Ed McMahon, just back from the Korean War, did a five-minute variety program. We asked George if he would come in on Wednesday evenings and give golfing tips. George said fine, and after the first week we knew we had a hit. In all the shows I have ever done, including commentaries on the networks, I have never received so much mail. The response was overwhelming. It was my first indication that golf was on the rise. Most of the mail consisted of questions about the golf swing, which George would answer and demonstrate. In addition, we would have guest pros drop by—most of the top amateurs and professionals from the area, or whoever might be in town. One night, Cary Middlecoff came by. George seemed to know everybody from coast to coast. He had been the professional at Hillcrest Country Club in Los Angeles for a while and was friendly with the Hollywood golfing community.

With this in mind, I went to my superior, Charles Vanda, and asked for an additional ten minutes for the show on Wednesday nights. I cited the great outpouring of mail, and how ten minutes was not sufficient to do the show correctly. I didn't seem to be getting anywhere with Mr. Vanda, who had come to television from Hollywood, so I blurted out the fact that George knew a lot of

Hollywood people and it wouldn't be surprising if Bob Hope or Bing Crosby would turn up one Wednesday evening. Now I had Mr. Vanda's attention.

"You are certainly naive," he sneered at me. "Do you think a star of Crosby or Hope's stature would come on your little golf show? You've got a lot of growing up to do."

I was dismissed out of hand and refused the additional time I had requested. It so happened that the next day I left for West Palm Beach, Florida, to cover the Philadelphia Athletics' training camp. That Wednesday, Bill Campbell, a fellow sportscaster at the station, did the show. Late that night, the phone rang in my hotel room in Florida. It was Bill calling from the Cynwyd Lounge, our hangout after work and the Toots Shor's of Philadelphia.

"Guess who was on your show tonight?" he asked me.

"I have no idea, Bill. Who?"

"Well, here, talk to him."

"Hello, Jack. This is Bob Hope. Sorry we missed you tonight. Fabulous Faz was fantastic."

Fantastic they must have been. Bob Hope had come into town and had called George. George invited him to the show and, for forty-five minutes, they did golf and jokes and the station switchboard almost burned out. I am still sorry I missed it. The only sweet moment was when I learned no one had called Charles Vanda to tell him. By chance, he happened to tune in, but by the time he got to the station, the show had moved down to the Cynwyd Lounge.

Naivete was one up.

Nineteen fifty-three also saw the first nationally televised tournament. It was called the World Championship, and was held at the Tam O'Shanter Club outside Chicago. It ended in a most theatrical way when Lew Worsham holed out a sand wedge from 104

48

yards on the final hole to defeat Chandler Harper by a stroke. The next year, Sam Snead defeated Ben Hogan in a playoff to win the Masters after a swashbuckling amateur from Morgantown, West Virginia almost stole the tournament—Billy Joe Patton became America's newest hero. That same year, Babe Zaharias won the Women's Open by twelve strokes one year after cancer surgery. The U.S. Men's Open was televised nationally for the first time, and a large audience saw Ed Furgol, a man with a withered arm, win the title. Golf was putting on a great show, and television was giving it the biggest exposure it ever had.

After golf and television were properly introduced, it wasn't long before active minds were dreaming up made-for-television events. The first of these was All Star Golf, developed by Peter DeMet in Chicago. It put two professionals head-to-head, with the winner returning the following week against a new player. The prize money each week was three thousand dollars—nice money in 1957, the year Ted Williams became the highest paid baseball player at one hundred thousand dollars. (There is not enough money in all of sports to pay what Williams would be worth in this age of the multimillion dollar complainers.) In 1959, NBC began a series called *World Championship Golf,* and in 1962 Shell's *Wonderful World of Golf* debuted, and for nine years took us to the most famous courses in the world, becoming an integral part of the golfing boom.

All these television shows were filmed, which meant that it took at least two days to complete eighteen holes. This was due to the time-consuming task of setting up each shot, making sure the lighting was right and the framing would show the shot clearly. You never knew what you had filmed until the film was developed. It was also a time for learning the game for some of the technicians, who might have known the esoteric niceties of the film camera but did not know a fairway from a green. The first Shell show was filmed at Pine Valley and featured Byron Nelson against Gene Littler. Byron hit his drive off the first tee and, along with everybody else, was astounded to see the cameraman come running back toward the tee with the ball saying, "Would you mind hitting it again? I missed it."

About this time there arrived on the scene a development that would change television forevermore—sometimes for the better, often for the worse. Videotape came into our lives, and liberated producers and technicians from the time-consuming chores of developing film and the almost-ghoulish task of editing it from the negatives. Now it was possible to tape an event and see immediately what we had; editing became easier, time was saved, and frontiers were pushed back.

Among the first to take advantage of this new technology were Dan Curtis and Frank Chirkinian, the producer and director of the CBS Golf Classic. The format of the Classic was a two-man, better-ball elimination tournament. Sixteen teams were divided into two groups of eight, and the winners of the two groups played a thirty-six-hole final. The players were chosen from the PGA money list. Aside from taping the matches instead of filming them, there was another breakthrough—the Chapman Crane. These motorized cranes had been used to make feature motion pictures for years, but when Frank Chirkinian mounted TV cameras on them, televised golf began to stretch its muscles. By leapfrogging these cameras and using videotape, the matches could be finished in a single day with an hour out for lunch at the end of nine holes. The logistics were simple: When the players were out of camera range on a hole, the crane would move several holes ahead and be ready when the players arrived. Also, TV cameras were changing; instead of having four lenses that had to be changed by hand, they now had zoom lenses controlled by a button. The sixteen matches took sixteen days to complete, weather permitting. And, except for one occasion, weather permitted.

The Classic began life in 1965, three years after I worked my first golf tournament for CBS, five years after Arnold Palmer cemented the marriage between television and golf by winning his second Masters and his dramatic U.S. Open at Cherry Hill. The first half of the draw was played at Baltusrol in New Jersey, the second half and the finals at the La Quinta Country Club in the California desert. Chris Schenkel and Tommy Armour were the commentators. The next year, after Chris had left for ABC, the commentators were myself, Cary Middlecoff, and Vic Ghezzi, and the entire sixteen matches were played at La Quinta. It was there, in November of 1966, that my devotion to the California desert and broadcasting golf matches began—a devotion that continues unabated today.

The first time I had been to the Palm Springs area was in 1960. The CBS *Sports Spectacular* was filming something called the *Baseball Celebrity Golf Tournament* at the Indian Wells Country Club, and it had been a disaster. The show had no format, no competition, and ended with a party scene that degenerated into a food fight when Gene Freese, then a third baseman with the Cincinnati Reds, picked up Mickey Mantle's birthday cake and threw it at the Mick, and Mickey threw it back. This was only my second show on the network, and I was so depressed that I did not appreciate the lures of the desert resort. But in returning for the CBS Golf Classic in 1965, I succumbed completely to the Coachella Valley with its sparkling mornings, dry clear air, and soft fragrant evenings.

We stayed that year at the La Quinta Hotel, which is located across the street from the Country Club. It was built in 1926 in the style of a Spanish inn with individual cottages for rooms, each with a fireplace, set among citrus trees. In the heyday of Hollywood, it had been a retreat for the more venturesome stars who traveled beyond the El Mirador Hotel and the Racquet Club in Palm Springs. Director Frank Capra spent a lot of time there and eventually died at the hotel; he wrote the screenplay for *Lost Horizon* at La Quinta, and as you smell the orange blossoms and look up at the Santa Rosa Mountains, you can see where he got his inspiration. In 1965, there was the hotel, the golf course, and, a half a mile down the road, a small village. If you stepped off the fairway you were in the desert. It was quiet and peaceful; the only noise at night was the mournful cries of the coyote. Today, La Quinta has eleven golf courses, thousands of homes and condominiums, and one of the lowest unemployment rates in the country. The hotel is still there, bigger now, with two large conference centers, but you can still smell the orange blossoms and look to the Santa Rosa Mountains and beyond, and appreciate what it must have been like sixty years ago.

It was in this idyllic setting that my secondary education in golf began. The mood at the Classic was more relaxed than at a regular tournament. We were close to the players all day, and most evenings we would have dinner with them. Over the years, many long-lasting relationships were forged.

That year we had a celebrity-filled gallery. The Hollywood desert community loves its golf as much as it does a good review. One morning I was sitting in a golf cart making notes on the match, when a tall, familiar figure approached. He was immaculately dressed and carried a walking stick.

"Young man," he said to me, as sternly as a minister rebuking the town drunk, "you show too much putting on television. You might not know it, but there is a lot more to golf than putting."

And with that he walked away. It was Randolph Scott, probably the best golfer among the Hollywood stars and, at that time, the only actor ever to be admitted to the Los Angeles Country Club, a place that looked upon acting as disreputable. When Randolph Scott proudly told Phil Harris that he had been accepted for membership, Phil said, "The board of directors must have seen some of your old movies on television."

On the days when Bo Winneger was playing, Frank Sinatra, Yul Brynner, and their group would be on hand to root for their favorite Las Vegas professional. It was a gaudy sixteen days. The tournament was won by Bob Charles and Bruce Devlin, who defeated Tony Lema and Bobby Nichols because Charles sunk about a hundred yards of putts—which, to Mr. Scott's dismay, we had to show on television.

The *Classic* moved the next year to a brand-new spa and golf-and-tennis resort north of San Diego. La Costa wanted people to see its lavish facilities and hoped that exposure on CBS would help. One of its selling points was the weather: "The best in the country," they said, "mild and temperate." Most of the time that is true, but the year the *Classic* was played at La Costa, rain made one of the greatest comebacks in the history of weather. For eleven days and nights the rain came down on San Diego County, and it came down nonstop. It fell on the golf course, on the tennis courts, and on the roof of the spa and all the new condominiums. It brought mudslides, washouts, and frustrations. Production was halted for eleven days. Schedules were interrupted and changed. Plans were drawn up to build an ark. But, somehow, we muddled through and had a memorable finale as Dave Marr and Tommy Jacobs defeated Raymond Floyd and Bobby Nichols when Jacobs holed out from the bunker on the final hole. The *Classic* seemed indestructible.

Indestructible, but not stationary. The next year, it moved again. The Firestone Tire and Rubber Company became interested, and off we went to the famous South Course of the Firestone Country Club in Akron, Ohio. The shooting dates were changed from November to October. Akron, Ohio! How could "they" do that to us? How could "they" take away a two-week working vacation in Southern California and drop us in Akron, Ohio?

We stayed eight years in Akron and never lost a single day to weather. Waking up in a motel room in downtown Akron is not quite the same as waking up to a glorious California morning among the citrus trees, but over the years Akron endeared itself to us and we came to attach ourselves to this hard-working town. There were then four billion-dollar corporations in Akron. It was the "Tire Capital of the World." Every morning on our way to the course, we would drive by those factories, which were teeming with activity. It would give us pause, if only for a moment, to real- ize how fortunate we were to be going to work at a golf course. The people were friendly and very much golf-addicted; even on the most dismal mornings, when it might be drizzling a little, in upper-forty-degree temperatures, there would be five or six hun- dred people there to watch the matches. Most of the time the weather was superb. Autumn in the northeast is a great show and autumn golf is exhilarating. The grass is never greener than it is in October, and the fairways and greens at Firestone were deep emerald against the bright yellow, red, and russet leaves of the South Course's magnificent trees. These were the years of my in- ternship, of learning some of the finer points of the game. And I had two very fine teachers.

The first was Cary Middlecoff. The "Golfing Dentist from Memphis," the press had dubbed him, since Cary flirted with den- tistry before deciding he would rather drill a four-iron than a tooth, and before he became the first amateur to win the North-South Open. He became a professional in 1947. He won two U.S. Opens and lost a third in a playoff. He was a Masters champion and three- time Ryder Cup player. Cary is tied with Walter Hagen at seventh on the all-time list of PGA Tournament winners; they both won forty times. The tall Tennessean with the hesitation at the top of his swing set this brilliant record against that great array of postwar players that included Hogan and Snead, and against the new hun- gry Californians led by Casper, Venturi, and Littler. A chronic bad back shortened Doc's career but, in its short span, it was brilliant.

He was great company, a man with a quick mind and a sense of humor wrapped around a Tennessean drawl. And, like all the best golfers, he had a deep knowledge of the game, and was very gen- erous with that knowledge. One day we were sitting in a golf cart at the second hole at Firestone, an uphill par-five. Sam Snead had hit his drive into the right hand rough; he took out a three-wood and hit his second shot onto the green. Cary shook his head in awe. "Only Sam could have hit that shot," he said. "He has the greatest wrists and hands in the game. Most of us would have taken an iron from that lie and laid up."

Cary was a good storyteller, and listening to him talk about the tour and other golfers was a fine learning experience. You could pick up on little things that gave a real picture of professional golf in those days. The rookies were always tested by the veterans. Cary said the first time he played with Ben Hogan, the Hawk "walked" on him. I asked what he meant.

"Ben had the honor, and after he hit his tee shot, he walked off the tee and down the fairway before I had hit my ball. So, I just teed it up and put one right past his ear. He never walked on me again."

The only thing that could dampen Middlecoff's spirits was the subject of bunker shots. Cary looked at sand the way children look at brussels sprouts. He often had trouble in bunkers, the one weak spot of his game, and one wonders how many more tournaments he might have won if he had mastered that shot. It makes his record all the more brilliant. He was also an avid baseball and football fan, Ole Miss's number-one booster and the maker of the perfect martini. He was a true southern gentleman.

I was very surprised when CBS decided they would not renew Cary's contract. Someone wanted a change and Cary, true to his code, did not whine or complain. He asked me if I could find out why he was let go so that he would not make the same mistakes the next time. Cary never went any way but first class. And so did the man who replaced him. When the job was offered to Ken Venturi, his first call was to Doc. He told him that he would not take the job if Middlecoff still wanted it. Cary told Ken to take the job and not to worry about it. It is a nice feeling, knowing people like that.

The best story I know to explain Ken Venturi happened one day on the driving range at Mission Hills golf club in Rancho Mirage. The two of us were hitting balls and, for once in a blue moon, I was hitting them straight and true.

"Isn't it funny," I said, "that when you're hitting the ball, you automatically have good rhythm and tempo. You don't have to think about it."

"Absolutely," said Ken. "You can't hit the ball without the proper tempo."

"How do you find it when you lose it?" I asked.

"Work. Work hard," said Ken. "You know, Bobby Jones once told me that when his timing was off, he would hum 'Limehouse Blues,' and that would get him back in the groove."

There was a pause, and then Ken's eyes suddenly gleamed.

"My song must be 'Jazz Pizzicato.' "

And how true that is. Ken rushes through the days plucking away on the strings of life at an exhausting tempo. He does many things very well—making martinis, playing the drums, doing card tricks, driving racing cars and hitting the golf ball. All "Jazz Pizzicato."

The first year that Ken worked on the *CBS Golf Classic*, Frank Chirkinian asked him to tape some golf lessons. The first was a demonstration of the pitch shot from less than a hundred yards. The eighteenth hole at Firestone was chosen, and Ken dropped a ball about seventy yards from the hole. After demonstrating the stance and the swing, he hit a shot that bounded on the green and ran right into the hole. Al Loretto, the cameraman on the crane, was following the ball and when it disappeared into the hole, he let out a loud "whoop" and threw up hands—and the camera, out of control, drunkenly swept the sky.

"You're going to have to get used to that, Al," said Ken. "I do that all the time."

I was playing with him one day and he said, "Watch this. A little knockdown eight. It will take three bounces and go to the left."

He quickly swung at the ball and there went this crisply hit eight-iron onto the green. It took three bounces and then went to the left and stopped.

"Now," he said, "here's a two-bouncer going right."

Again, a crisply hit ball flies to the green, takes two bounces, and then goes right and stops. Subsequently, I have seen him hit those shots many times and enjoyed the look of amazement that appears on the faces of those who see it for the first time.

One does not easily forget a round of golf with Ken. A round that takes more than three hours is anathema. He drives the cart like Mario Andretti when the caution flag has just been taken down. He cannot abide being held up; consequently, it is a rare occasion indeed when you play the holes in sequence. He is forever leapfrogging the holes to get ahead of people. We were doing just that at Firestone one day after one of the matches. Almost the entire crew would play in the afternoon if the matches were over in time. We would play until dark and then head for the Diamond Grill in Akron for a Boston strip steak, sliced tomatoes, onions, and cottage-fried potatoes. Every professional golfer in America knows the Diamond Grill.

On this particular day, I was riding in the cart with Kenny Andretti, and we were crossing the tenth green to the ninth tee. The path cuts right in front of the eleventh tee. Standing there was Al Loretto, the cameraman who had missed Kenny's pitch shot going into the hole. We waited while Al hit his tee shot, which seemed to go off in the general direction of the thirteenth green. The look on his face was heartbreakingly melancholy.

"Kenny," Al moaned, "what am I doing?"

Kenny immediately bounded out of the golf cart, ran up onto the tee and said to Al, "Take your stance."

Al took his stance. Ken moved his right hand over on the club, told Al to change his left foot, and moved his right shoulder so that he was squared away.

"Now swing," said Ken.

Al swung, and the ball went straight and high and far, landing in the middle of the fairway about 240 yards away. Ken was back in the cart. He didn't say a word and off we went to the ninth tee as Al stood looking after us and crying out, "Kenny, tell me what I did. It feels so uncomfortable."

Ken is firmly in the annals of American golf with his dramatic victory in the 1964 U.S. Open, conquering the course and the heat with tremendous willpower. In 1956, he stunned the Masters tournament with an opening round of sixty-six. When he reached the tenth hole on that windy Sunday afternoon, he needed only to shoot a forty on the back nine to win. He missed by one shot as Jackie Burke, Jr. edged him out. His final round eighty would have been enough to mark a downturn in people's careers; that Ken's best years were still ahead of him on that April afternoon marks him a true champion.

On that ill-fated final round, the tournament did not, as was customary, pair Venturi, the leader, with Byron Nelson. Because of the close association of the two as pupil and teacher, it was decided to break tradition and not have Nelson play with the third-round leader. Ken drew Sam Snead as his partner, and, down the years, the legend grew that Sam never spoke to Venturi, and that the silence unnerved the amateur.

Several years ago, at a golf dinner in New York at which Ken received an award, he put that story to bed. Speaking directly to Sam, who was in the audience, Ken said, "Sam Snead could not have been nicer to me that afternoon. He was thoughtful and courteous and never upset me or my game. And, Sam, I want to take this opportunity to say this to you publicly, after all these years: You were a perfect gentleman that day."

Ken's life has been sunshine or shadow. Never the gray light for him. Through the good times and the bad, it has been his deep love of golf that has kept him intact. Most of the time, there is a smile on his face, whether he is pulling the nine of hearts out of the icebox, hitting a knockdown eight-iron, or sampling a bottle of Mouton Cadet. Occasionally, there is a moody silence as he recharges his batteries.

When Ken was still a young amateur with a mixed bag of clubs, he was paired at the Masters with his hero, Ben Hogan. On the first green, Hogan walked over to him and said, "Ken, go ahead and putt out ahead of me. This gallery will stampede to the next tee when I putt out, and the noise would distract you."

Well, thought Ken, isn't that nice. I've made a new friend.

On the fourth hole, the par three, Ken, hitting first, put his three-iron on the green as Hogan watched intently. Then Ben hit a three-iron that was short and in the bunker.

"Let me see that bag," Hogan snarled. "A mixed bag of clubs. Serves me right for watching an amateur. When we finish today, give me your address and I'll send you a matched set of clubs."

"I made a friend on the first hole and lost him on the fourth," Ken would say later.

The scene shifts now to the 1973 British Open at Troon. Ken is paired the first day with a skinny young Welsh professional in khaki pants, a tattered sweater, and a mixed bag of clubs.

"When the round is over," said Ken to the young Welshman, "give me your name and address and I'll send you a matched set of clubs."

That's Ken Venturi, and his "Jazz Pizzicato" style helped make the CBS Golf Classic years pleasant ones.

After those years in Akron, the Classic finally came to an end. The regular tour was beginning to prosper, and there were tournaments on television almost every week, especially in the winter months when the Classic used to air. It would have been competing against live tournaments, and so it died a natural death. It had been a marvelous learning experience for all of us; I had the opportunity to observe the best golfers of the day up close, to know them personally, and to learn an awful lot about golf, life on the tour, and to understand not just the glamorous aspects of professional golf, but the downside—the travel, the suitcase living, and the weeks away from home.

They had been years of eight in the morning on-camera openings at the first tee, of heavy, starchy luncheons after the first nine holes, of golf in the late afternoons, and Boston strip steaks, tomatoes and fries in the evenings. Cholesterol was unknown to us in those far-off days, and most of us smoked and had a drink or two, but we all felt good and worked hard and enjoyed every minute.

In one of the last years of the show, during a dreadful heat wave, sixty-one-year-old Sam Snead shot a sixty-six over the South course at Firestone in a first round match. He lost to twenty-three-year-old Lanny Wadkins, who had fired a sixty-three.

"Flippy-wristed college kid," Sam growled. "His putting ought to be illegal."

But the kids were coming. New players were arriving every week. Things were changing. Professional golf was on a great roll, and the early made-for-television shows were giving way to live broadcasts of PGA Tour events on the networks. CBS was right in the middle of this golfing transformation. The Masters was its centerpiece and, for a while, it did the PGA Championship and a dozen or more regular tour events. The tour events of those years tended to run together. I remember the places more than who won. Only the major championships, which I'll describe in a later chapter, stay in my mind.

The CBS golf schedule was a great paid vacation. We began, for many years, at the Phoenix Open. It always fell on Super Bowl week, often was delayed because of frozen greens, but had the greatest tournament organizers on the entire tour. The Thunderbirds know how to put on a golf tournament. After Phoenix, it was up to Pebble Beach for a week at the Lodge, then down to San Diego for the Andy Williams San Diego Invitational, then to Riviera for the Los Angeles Open and five days at the Bel Air Hotel. From there, we went to Miami for the Doral, to Ft. Lauderdale for the Jackie Gleason, to Hilton Head, and then into Augusta for the Masters. The winter was over.

At Pebble Beach, I worked the seventeenth hole, that flat par-three that has had so many famous moments. From the back tee across the road that leads to the Beach Club, you hit to a green lying like a sideways figure eight on the edge of Carmel Bay. In the middle of the figure eight is a ridge, and trouble awaits you if you are on the wrong side of that ridge. Phil Harris sunk a very long putt from the wrong side to win the Crosby with Dutch Harrison in 1954. Someone asked him how long the putt was.

"I don't know," said Phil. "But I wish I had that much real estate on Wilshire Boulevard."

"Was it fifty feet?"

"Hell," said Phil, "it broke further than that!"

It was here that Jack Nicklaus hit the flagstick on his way to winning the 1972 U.S. Open, and it was here ten years later that Tom Watson won his Open championship when he holed out from the left rough with one of the Open's most memorable shots. You are aware of all this history as you sit in the tower behind the green, the tower that sits almost on the eighteenth tee on the edge of the water. And, yet, there is a scrimlike veil over the golf action as you gaze out over the most seductive scene in golf.

To the right is Stillwater Cove, with more than an occasional sea lion lying on its back, cracking open a mollusk for lunch. Farther off to the right is the mouth of the Carmel Valley, its hills purple and green, looking more like a Scottish glen than a California valley. To the left stretches the five hundred and forty-two yards of the eighteenth hole, and the pebble beach that gave its name to this special place. All of this, accompanied by the crashing surf and the cawing of sea gulls. It was often difficult to concentrate on golf.

Helping one's concentration was the presence of Frank Chirkinian. It is not too difficult to assess Frank Chirkinian's impact on television golf: It has been tremendous. Its effects will be felt for many years. His innovative style has been absorbed by a new generation of producers and directors; some have improved on them and found their own voice, but as all golf writers came from Bernard Darwin, so all golf directors and producers come from Frank Chirkinian.

I first met Frank in September of 1950, on the third floor of the WCAU building on Chestnut Street in Philadelphia. He was standing by the water cooler drinking from a paper cup. His head was covered by a helmet of jet black, curly hair, and his nose would have made even Caesar envious. He wore a tan, suede vest with F.C. in script over the left breast, and he looked like Akim Tamiroff's youngest son. Both of us had just started working in television at the CBS affiliate; I was doing a five-minute newscast in the morning and Frank was a production assistant, one of whose jobs was to be a sanitation engineer on a circus show called *The Big Top*. He followed the elephants. In a few months, I was doing the sports on the six o'clock news and Frank was a director. By 1952, we had both moved to the eleven o'clock news. Since we were on the night shift, we would frequently play golf in the mornings, and thus began those wonderful times at the Main Line Golf Club, learning to hit three-woods off hardpan.

Frank was always experimenting. Videotape was still in the future and we did our nonlive TV on film. There was a process known as *stop action*, with which you could stop the film frame by frame. At the beginning of the George Fazio series, Frank used this technique to illustrate George's lessons—but Frank knew more than how to use the tools; he became a truly fine student of the game and the players. He learned the idiosyncracies of the golfers, how many times this one waggled the club before swinging, how many tugs at his golf glove another would make before he was ready, how long this player would stand over a putt. So, when he would cut away from a player who looked like he was ready to play, you could bet your house he would get back in time for that shot or that putt.

Both sides of the camera would merrily have run through a brick wall for Frank. The technicians would go to extra lengths to make sure everything was in perfect order. Frank had a great rapport with these men, who belonged to one of the strongest unions in the land. Cameramen would fight to give him great pictures, always looking for that extra something to make the show better. Most viewers don't realize how important those technicians are to a show. One of the many good things that happened to me was working with and getting to know these marvelous artisans. They work long and hard and take great pride in their work. And Frank knew how to tap into that pride.

He was equally adept at handling announcers. He knew when to flatter and when to use the lash. Ah, the lash! It was a stinging combination of irony, sarcasm, and pseudo-anger, and the ridicule one suffered after making a mistake was something we all tried to avoid like a three-putt green.

We also had Bob Dailey as a director. Most of the golf crew had worked with this tall, goodlooking New Yorker many times. He and I had shared the early days of the CBS *Sports Spectacular,* the Sugarman summers in Europe, and the NFL. Bob was great company. He had a quick wit and laughed easily. He had come to the sports department after directing the *Person to Person* series at CBS, and was not overimpressed with celebrities. He was a good tennis player but, like the rest of us, was carrying on an unrequited love affair with his golf game. He also gave most of us our nicknames. Pat Summerall was "The Kicker" because of the field goal he kicked in the snow to beat Cleveland that gave the Giants the 1962 Eastern Conference title. Frank Glieber was a remarkable sportscaster from Dallas who had a rich deep baritone voice. Frank also loved to eat—anything, anytime—and his physique reflected his passion in an ample way. Bob dubbed him the "Mound of Sound." Ben Wright was, of course, the "Limey" or the "Englishman," and I was simply "Whit," until one fateful day at the Houston Open.

The Woodlands, where the Houston Open was played, is one of the few places on tour where we stayed right at the golf course. After Sunday's final round, I got into my yellow rental car, put the key into the ignition and turned it. The key would not move. Several more tries brought two parking attendants over. They were large football players from the University of Houston. They tried, too, and, although the key fit perfectly, it would not budge. Pat Summerall came by, but even his melonsized hand could not move the reluctant key. Finally, Bob Dailey appeared carrying his garment bag over his shoulder. I showed him that the key fit perfectly but would not turn and, in utter frustration, I looked up at him. In a French accent, he said, "Inspector Clouseau, 'zis is my car. Why do you not try your own automobile?"

And, indeed, I was in the wrong car. My car, the same make and color as Bob's, was in the next parking space. But it was too late; from then on, I was "The Inspector," or "Clouseau," in honor of the Peter Sellers character. I must admit, the nickname was not far off the mark. I had a great talent for leaving passports and traveler's checks behind, raincoats in hotel rooms and airplane tickets in desk drawers.

Once, at the Western Open in Chicago, I sent a pair of slacks to be dry cleaned. Too late, I remembered I had left my car keys in the pocket. I raced down to the lobby, but the laundry and cleaning had already left. Frantically, I called the cleaners. They could not help me. Dejected, I hung up the phone. What a ribbing I was going to take on this Clouseau caper. At that moment, coming out of the coffee shop across the lobby were Frank Chirkinian, Bob Dailey, and Ben Wright. I decided the best policy was to tell them immediately. The sooner the insults began, the sooner they would stop.

"Frank," I said, "you won't believe what I've done."

An unsmiling Chirkinian held up his hand.

"Don't say a word."

"But, Frank . . ."

"Whatever you have done, it cannot compare with what this idiot Englishman has done."

Now Bob was grinning like the Cheshire cat. I looked at Ben. He had a silly expression on his face and the face looked a bit askew. He looked, in fact, like a crude peasant who had been rescued from a pig farm in Yorkshire rather than the middle-class product of a public school he purported to be. His upper mouth had collapsed. In an enthusiastic spell of regurgitation, his dental bridge had disappeared into the depths of the hotel's plumbing system, never to be seen again. And there he stood, just hours before we were going on the air, toothless as a nonagenarian, his beautiful English enunciation reduced to sibilant slurping.

Necessity does make doers of us all. Frank called the tournament director. No problem. One of Chicago's leading dentists was a member of the tournament committee. Dr. Fu immediately opened his office and made Ben a temporary bridge with which he was able to speak reasonably well that afternoon. A crisis was averted. Dr. Fu was inducted into the CBS Golf Hall of Fame and, for the rest of the year during rehearsals, Ben would be represented on screen by a set of chattering false teeth as his Feldstone School accents described the golf hole he was covering.

One year at the Sammy Davis, Jr., Greater Hartford Open, we all found a brand new set of golf clubs and a golf bag in our rooms, courtesy of our host. Sammy loved golf and gave very generously of his time to the tournament. He put on a show that had more energy than a hurricane, and his presence on the golf telecasts kept everybody loose and smiling.

Jackie Gleason was also a gracious host when his delicate condition was under control. One night, he invited us all over to his house, which had a beautiful poolroom, with the table sunk in the middle and comfortable chairs placed so everyone could see the action. That evening, he and Ken Venturi put on an exhibition that was absolutely remarkable. Minnesota Fats and the "Jazz Pizzicato" kid were amazing to watch.

Those years, most of the announcers and Frank and Bob Dailey would have dinner together every night. There was a great feeling of camaraderie that I've never experienced anywhere else. There was a lot of good-natured needling and a lot of laughs. We all knew it was time to go home when Ben Wright would begin his imitation of a Scottish bagpiper playing "Amazing Grace," accompanied by Pat Summerall's shouting "Suey, Pig!" Life was good, and it was summer all year long.

Those were the prime years, too, of Johnny Miller and Tom Weiskopf, of Lee Trevino and Tom Watson, and the generation that came charging in on the heels of Arnold Palmer. In 1960, when Arnold won his Open championship, there were forty-one tournaments with a cumulative total purse of $1,335,000. In 1995, it was forty-four tournaments for $62,250,000. Golf had become the darling of corporate America. In a remarkable marketing move by the tour and the networks, tournament sponsors were required to buy seventy-five percent of the television time in order to become the title sponsor. The relatively low ratings are of little consequence since the sponsors are reaching nearly one hundred percent of those who will buy their products. And the networks make money on most tournaments.

In 1981, my relationship with the middle management of CBS was less than marvelous, and when Roone Arledge made me an offer to come to ABC, I was more than happy to accept, even though it meant leaving some very close friends. The move provided the opportunity to work the U.S. Open and the British Open, two championships I had longed to broadcast. ABC also did the PGA Championship at that time, so they had three out of the four majors. In addition, the network covered the U.S. Women's Open, the U.S. Men's Amateur Championship, the Ryder Cup, and the Walker Cup. There were great times ahead.

Traveling the Globe on the
Sugarman Express

"Who's the blond-haired guy with Marvin?"

A good argument can be made that track and field is the purest of all sports. It is a contest against time and distance, and has been affected less by technological advances in equipment than any other athletic pastime. In the late 1960s, it was one of the few truly international sports. It was not as popular in the United States as it was in Europe, but it had a loyal and sizable following in America in those days. It seems that the more people began running for exercise and entering marathons, the less interest they took in competitive track meets. Thirty years ago, however, the sport enjoyed a healthy existence, aided somewhat by the rivalries with the Iron Curtain countries, especially the confrontations with the Soviet Union.

One warm, blustery May afternoon in 1969 at Villanova Stadium, just two blocks from where I used to live, CBS began televising a series of track meets sponsored by the Amateur Athletic Union (AAU) that would span the years between the Olympics. In seeking programming that would keep the CBS Sports Department active in the summer months, Jack Dolph had made a deal with Marvin Sugarman, whose production company had secured the rights to all AAU events.

Marv Sugarman is a tall, slim, bespectacled man who could sell a life-insurance policy to those 120-year-old Ukrainians who are always eating yogurt. He is energetic, hard-working, charming and compassionate. Marvin was first associated with the Captain Kangaroo program, and then branched out to become a producer of sports shows. His working companion was Lou Tyrell, who was the line producer, director, editor, father confessor, and vital force behind the shows. Lou had white hair, and a round, pleasant face that more often than not wore a smile. He needed his good temperament and sense of humor and his unending vitality to make everything work.

Also working on the show as an announcer was Dick Bank, a Los Angeles businessman who was the country's number-one track fanatic. Dick was a slightly built, bespectacled young man who could give you split times on any race over the last twenty years at the drop of a flag. The third member of our announcing team that first year was Ralph Boston, the 1960 gold medalist in the long jump and many times world champion. Ralph is a tall, lithe man with a big, big grin, a marvelous sense of humor, and a mind as quick as his feet.

Doing a track meet live on television is like walking across Niagara Falls on a tightrope while blindfolded. Disaster lurks with every step. That is because a track and field meet resembles a three-ring circus; most of the time, more than one event is going on. When you try to do one live, you're bound to miss something important. Also, while the timing of a track meet varies, the last event is usually the pole vault and it can take forever to complete. Indeed, on that first program in which Marvin Sugarman and CBS collaborated, the pole vault went on forever as the contestants, vaulting between gusts of wind, would wait and wait until the moment was right. Actually, that first show had all the earmarks of a disaster: We missed the finish of a couple of events and the delays by the pole vaulters almost forced us off the air before the event was even completed. It held nothing of the promise of what the series eventually would become.

During the four years of the series, a pattern of travel developed that, except for minor changes, never varied. We would first broadcast five or six meets in the United States, mostly in California, leading up to the AAU Championships. The United States National Team was made up of the first two finishers in each event in that championship. Then we were off to Europe for nine or ten weeks. The basic stops in Europe were Oslo, Stockholm, and Stuttgart. Then, each year, another city would be put on the schedule to replace one from the year before. We went to London, Paris, and Leningrad once each; Warsaw twice; Malmo, Sweden twice; Aarhus, Denmark and Augsberg, Germany once each.

After that first outing at Villanova, we taped the rest of the shows, with the exception of the 1969 AAU Championships in Miami and a United States–Russia dual meet in Los Angeles. My job was quite a simple one on the taped shows: I would open the show, run down the competitors in the running events, interview the winners, and then close the show. Dick Bank and Ralph Boston did the play-by-play and, later, Bill Toomey would join them. I didn't have to stay around waiting for the editing to be done; that chore fell to Lou Tyrell, who not only directed the field events, but edited the tape into the wee hours of the morning. He and his associate producer Lucretia Scott and the technicians would put in twenty-two-hour days sometimes; so would Ralph Boston, who would have to wait until the tapes were ready. Then he would go, most of the time, into the front seat of a Volkswagen at three in the morning and, holding a microphone, do commentary on the picture he was watching on a portable Sony black-and-white TV set that was leaning against the windshield. Compared to the sophistication of CBS's studios, this was almost primitive. Still, if the track meet ended at nine Saturday night, it was edited and on the air Sunday afternoon. If the meet finished at eight Friday night in Helsinki, it was edited and back in the States in time for its Sunday airing. The Sugarman people were scrupulous at meeting their deadlines and never missed one.

After the shaky start at Villanova, I went west for the second show in the series. We were covering the California Relays in Modesto, and I was apprehensive. I was the only CBS talent on the show aside from a director, usually Bob Dailey or Tony Verna, who handled the running events. There were compensations, as I found out on this second show. I was going places I had never been. I had been to San Francisco many times and to Oakland, but never east beyond the Bay. I would now go beyond many bays.

On this Friday, a perfect Northern California spring day, I went south on the Bayshore Freeway from the airport to the San Mateo Bridge. Not as historical as the Oakland Bay Bridge, nor nearly as tall, the San Mateo Bridge sits close to the water and, as I looked to the left up the large expanse of bay, San Francisco gleamed white in the clear sunlight. I drove through Hayward and Castro Valley, and then due east through brown hills with green trees that looked like camel-hair coats with mink collars, through Livermore with its green golf course on the right, down a sweeping, turning hill into the San Joaquin Valley, vibrant with spring, and finally into Modesto and the Sun Dial Motor Inn, where in the morning we had strawberries as big as plums and the Coors beer flowed cold and clear from the tap.

It was a part of the country I had never seen before and it was pretty and rich-looking and clean, and the road signs pointed to Stockton, Sacramento, and Merced. It was the heart of the California League, and one could not help ponder over the infinite variety of this state that is much more than Beverly Hills and smog and esoteric religious cults.

The California Relays is one of the most difficult events to cover because of all the high schools that are entered, and because a relay is the most difficult of all play-by-play challenges. The atmosphere was relaxed and easy though, and I was beginning to enjoy that special feeling of outdoor track meets, a feeling of joy and excitement. I would look back later and think that one of the most pleasant things to experience is a late spring afternoon in California at a track meet when the shadows are beginning to lengthen and everything is over except the pole vault. You sit in the infield with the rest of the athletes who have finished for the day, the runners and the jumpers and the throwers. They sit relaxed and smiling, talking quietly among themselves, applauding the vaulters, their graceful figures draped carelessly on the ground. Track-and-field athletes are some of our finest people. Some are introspective individuals, and all participate in a pastime that is the basis of all sport. They sacrifice more than other athletes, and 30 years ago there was really no professional payoff for them when they graduated. They are smarter than most of us because they devote their time to the simple tasks of trying to defeat time and distance and appreciating spring afternoons.

The week after Modesto we were back in California for the first annual Kennedy games at the University of California at Berkeley. Here, in the last year of this turbulent decade, there was a remembrance of things past: On Friday, thirty thousand protestors flowed through the streets of Berkeley. For a moment, it looked as if they would push through the gates and overturn our TV equipment under Edwards Stadium. Suddenly, the anger and the sullenness dissipated, and there was no confrontation with the police. On Saturday the campus looked like it might have looked twenty years earlier. The campanile still stood, the bookstores and shops did a Saturday business, and Edwards Stadium was clean and suavely groomed for the track meet.

At 12:20 P.M., the hammer throwers began their whirling heel-and-toe dance, flinging the sixteen-pound ball in the general direction of downtown Oakland. The crowd began arriving, and the first big hand of the day went to Hal Connally, still unretired, still amazing in the speed of his spins. The running events began slowly, with the trials in the 120 hurdles, but suddenly the afternoon picked up speed. The women's 100-yard dash was won by Nationalist China's Chi Cheng, a soft, lovely-looking lady who made one think of Cathay and Marco Polo. She beat Barbra Ferell in 10.5 seconds and gently said in the interview, "Happiness is winning."

Willie Davenport, with a bandaged left knee, won the 120-yard hurdles. He started slowly, came on, and knocked over the last hurdle as if it were a blade of grass. Then, suddenly, the games were over. It was 5:15. Mist shrouded the hills above the stadium beyond the campanile and the football field. It had been a pleasant day for all of us, a spring afternoon to remember when winning becomes difficult.

The AAU National Track and Field Championships were held at Dade Junior College in Miami that year, and we broadcast the events live. I can't remember anything going wrong. The most memorable and disappointing thing was that Jim Ryun dropped out of the mile run. Every sport needs stars, and Jim Ryun was one of the biggest, and there was now a question of whether or not Ryun would ever compete again. Certainly, he had not qualified for the U.S. Team that would go to Europe.

The United States track team's travels in Europe are the sport's answer to the Grand Tour. Track meets abound on the Continent and Scandinavia, and the American stars are very much welcomed and very well known. Ralph Boston, although he was in the early stages of his retirement, was mobbed everywhere he went through Scandinavia and Europe, as well known over there as our football or baseball stars are known in the United States.

Our first stop that year was Malmo, Sweden, just across the

Oruk Sund from Copenhagen, once the number-one town in the old Hanseatic league. From there it was on to Stuttgart, famous for being the home of the Daimler-Benz Motor Works, manufacturers of the Mercedez Benz. It was heavily bombed during World War II, and rebuilding was still going on back in 1969. This workingman's town is dominated by the Central Railroad Station, a monolithic, massive, gray building that sits in the center of the city like a Rocky Mountain, massive and implacable. It seems to be an anchor that keeps the city on the floor of the valley.

We stayed in three different hotels in the years we stopped at Stuttgart: The Graf Zepplin, which is Old Germany; The Schlosstgarten, which is New Germany; and the hotel in the railroad station, which is Fortress Germany. And three things remain in my mind from our visits to Germany, two of which happened in Stuttgart and the other down the road in Augsburg.

The first occurred on our first visit to Augsburg. The hot, humid weather was broken a bit by some rainstorms on both evenings in Rosenheim Stadium. On the second evening, the highlight of the competition was the decathlon event. In 1968 in Mexico City, twenty-nine-year-old Bill Toomey had defeated West Germany's Kurt Bendin for the gold medal. In the World Championships that same year, Bendin defeated Toomey. So here in Augsburg, in the rain, was the rubber match between these two great athletes.

The two were pretty much even after the first five events on opening night. On the second night, the German was pulling ahead. Then, Bill did one of his worst pole vaults, his weakest event of the ten, and one which he approached with all the confidence of a shoplifter trying to vault over an electric eye. Bendin had a sizeable lead. There remained only the javelin and the fifteen hundred meters.

The rain began to fall more steadily. Toomey, shaken by his performance in the pole vault, confronted the javelin. It was dark now, and the rain came down silver against the arc lights as Bill

Toomey, from the depths of his character, unleashed his career best in the javelin and put himself in a position to win the event if he could win the fifteen hundred meters.

There is a forty-minute wait between the javelin and the fifteen hundred meters, and on this night, all the other events had been concluded by the time the javelin was over. Fifty thousand German track fans sat in the rain, not daring to move until the event was over. As the decathletes lined up for the start of the race, those fifty thousand German fans took up the chant:

"Ben-deen! Ben-deen! Ben-deen!"

Faster and faster, louder and louder, fifty thousand voices thundered through the rain.

"Ben-deen! Ben-deen! Ben-deen!"

They chant well in Germany, much better than in the United States. There is a rhythm and a discipline to it that raises goosebumps.

"BEN-DEEN! BEN-DEEN! BEN-DEEN!"

You don't know what it is to play an away game until you are in a foreign country and hear the entire stadium shouting,

"BEN-DEEN! BEN-DEEN! BEN-DEEN!"

Bill Toomey was up to the task. In the forty minutes since the javelin, he had rested and psyched himself up, and he made easy work of the race, winning it handily to capture the decathlon as the shouts of Ben-deen, Ben-deen, Ben-deen receded in the night, and gave way to a smattering of applause. That remains one of the most memorable events I have covered.

The second thing happened in Stuttgart. It was not as athletic but, for a moment, it was almost as dramatic as Bill's victory. We arrived one year at the stadium to find that the meet was going to be telecast throughout Europe and Scandinavia, as well as behind the Iron Curtain. There were thirty or thirty-one different countries broadcasting. The Germans had developed a special unit, one that would be used in the Munich Olympics in 1972; it was like a school desk, on which was fastened a television monitor complete with a headset and a microphone. Every country had one assigned to it, except the United States. We had no facilities at all.

"Goddamn it," yelled Dick Bank. "I'm going to reach five million people on Sunday afternoon and I have no facilities, while Albania, who has ten television sets in the whole goddamn country, gets everything!"

"Okay, Dick," said Lou Tyrell, "I'm trying to do something about it."

"Well, these damn Krauts are so stubborn, they won't listen to anybody."

Lou went and talked earnestly to one of the committee members. The German remained impassive to all of Lou's pleas. He kept repeating that no one had made any arrangements for the American broadcast. Lou kept telling him that there had been conversations and showed him some letters. Still, the German remained adamant.

"See that?" wailed Dick. "We're not going to get on the air with this meet."

Now Lou was beginning to get mad.

"You Americans don't know how we work," said the German. "You've never been here before."

With that, Lou exploded.

"Oh, yes, I have been here before, you bastard; I dropped ten thousand tons of TNT on those railroad tracks over there in 1944, and if we don't get some facilities for this track meet, I'll blow this stadium up."

With this, the German's jaw dropped. He pulled himself up and almost saluted Lou.

"Just a moment," he said.

Ten minutes later we had facilities for Dick Bank. They were not as fancy as Albania's, but we were in business.

The other memorable thing that occurred in that stadium by the railroad tracks happened on a pleasant summer evening. It was the year Chancellor Willi Brandt of West Germany was attempting to establish a detente with the Soviet Union. It was a major news story in Germany, and had become a very controversial matter. On the eve of the chancellor's departure for Moscow, he came to the track meet in Stuttgart. He was seated halfway up the stands in the middle of the track.

When I first put on my headset, Bob Dailey, our director, said, "Willi Brandt's here," and showed me, on my TV monitor, where he was sitting.

About half an hour later, Bob put the interrupt key down.

"Marvin wants you to interview Brandt."

"What?" I shouted.

"He's going to try and bring him over to you."

My position for the meet was on the first turn, on the grandstand side, about forty yards down from where the chancellor was sitting. I watched on my monitor with admiration and disbelief the little drama that followed. First, Marv took a seat in the first row of the aisle where the chancellor was. In a few minutes he moved surreptitiously to a seat halfway up to the chancellor's row. Then, in a sleek move, he managed to sidle into the same row as Mr. Brandt, but on the end of the aisle. Next, there was a lot of shaking of hands and then, beaming and smiling from ear to ear, there was Marv, sitting right next to the chancellor and talking non-stop.

"Here they come," said Bob Dailey.

And, indeed, here they came, the Chancellor and Marvin, walking down the stairs and onto the track, followed by photographers and reporters. Majestically they made their way down toward me. Bob was taping the entire thing, and we all thought of the old story and everyone was shouting the punch line:

"Who's the blond-haired guy with Marvin?"

I couldn't believe it. CBS News couldn't get to the chancellor on this night, but here was Marv Sugarman delivering Willi Brandt to me to be interviewed at a track meet. What do you ask a head of state in this situation? Luckily, there had been a very thoughtful piece in *The New York Times* the previous Sunday. It had been written by Robert Lipsyte, I think, and it had to do with international sports competition. The thrust of the essay was that those competitions, especially the Olympics, increase nationalism and therefore do more harm than good. As I stood looking at the chancellor's rugged face, pleasant and smiling in the late sunlight and heard Bob Dailey say, "Tape is rolling. Stand by," I happily thought of the article.

"Mr. Chancellor," I began, "there are some who think that international competitions such as this track meet only fan the flames of nationalism and, therefore, should be abolished."

That was as far as I got. The chancellor broke in.

"No, no, no," he said, and launched into an impassioned and earnest defense of international sports competition. "It is the only sane way for nations to compete against each other in this world that cannot afford another war." He went on for about three minutes, his handsome face intense, his eyes glinting as he pursued his thoughts. There was no need to ask another question.

"Thank you, Mr. Chancellor," I said. And with that, the entourage turned and made their way back to their seats, photographers and newsmen moving along in a sloppy circle around Mr. Willi Brandt and Mr. Marv Sugarman, producer, entrepreneur, and friend to the leaders of the Western World.

So Stuttgart has become a memorable place in my travel folder, and my manner of leaving it the last time was also unforgettable. We were departing Stuttgart for Munich, where we would spend the weekend before catching a plane for Leningrad. I decided to drive to Munich. But when I got to the Hertz Rent-A-Car office, the only car they had available was a brand new Porsche. Now I am not quite the equivalent of Bobby Rahal; I am hardly the best driver in the world. I gratefully accepted the automatic transmission years ago. If pushed, I can operate a gear shift, but I knew that a brand-new Porsche might be a little beyond me. The Hertz girl came out and gave me a demonstration of how the gears worked but, in my increasing nervousness, I retained very little of what she was saying. Thankfully, the car was parked facing downhill, and I got away in low gear, but at the bottom of the hill I shifted incorrectly and the car bucked and coughed and made those horrible sounds, like a wounded water buffalo. Starting over, I couldn't find first gear and then, moving forward, I somehow shifted into reverse, and a terrible grinding noise filled the streets of Stuttgart. By now, the good burghers of the town had turned and stared at me, first, with utter contempt and then with open hostility. Then they began to yell and scream and gesture wildly with their arms, and to whistle, which is the Teutonic equivalent of the Bronx cheer.

In total disgrace, I managed somehow to get up the hill and, at long last, gratefully onto the Autobahn before the citizens laid hands upon me.

That first summer in Europe (1969) was filled with new experiences, new people, and new places. From Germany we went to London, where we broadcast the last track meet held in White City Stadium. Then to Oslo, a town I would grow to love. And from Oslo we were going to Warsaw, my first trip behind the Iron Curtain.

It rained almost the entire week we were in Oslo, and we ran out of daylight the first night of the meet in Bislet Stadium. But we didn't mind too much, since Oslo was a comfortable town, clean and clear-aired, even with the rain. Most of us were looking ahead to the following week in Warsaw. Because the Polish Government had issued only a group visa, we all had to go into the country together and all leave the same day, arriving on Monday and leaving the following Saturday. So we were all up at 6:15 Monday morning for a 7:30 flight to Copenhagen. After a three-hour wait in Copenhagen Airport, we boarded a Lot airliner and were off to Warsaw.

The Warsaw airport in 1971 was a modern, bright, and sunny place. We arrived there in the late afternoon and were met by an English-speaking guide from Intourist who would be the official interpreter, guide, and spy for our stay.

She was an attractive brunette of about twenty-five, with a melancholy look forever on her pretty face, and a tendency to nag everyone like an older sister who has been left to raise the family. While we waited for an interminable time to be processed through customs and passport control, Ralph Boston and I started having a catch with a frisbee. Most of the Polish people had never seen one and were fascinated, but not "Big Sister."

"Stop that," she said in a voice we all recognized from school days. "It is not dignified to do that in a public place."

Finally, we were herded onto an ancient bus and moved into the city. The athletes were staying at one hotel and the television people at another. Our hotel was only five years old. It was built of gray stone, had a large concrete canopy over the three front doors, and was falling to pieces. On our way in we were besieged by men trying, we found out, to see if we had any American money to trade. The official rate at the time was 24 Polish zlotys to the dollar, but these black-market speculators were offering ten times as much. It reminded me of Berlin right after the war.

The rooms in the hotel were small and the place had a grim institutional look about it. As soon as we washed up, we all met in the dining room for supper. It was a big room, the grand ballroom and dining room combined. There was a five-man dance orchestra with a saxophone, trumpet, drums, bass, and piano. It was very warm, and a few of them were in their shirt sleeves as they played Glenn Miller arrangements of World War II tunes. There was something quite touching about seeing these middle-aged Poles in shirt sleeves, and listening to the slightly off-beat and thin-sounding strains of "String of Pearls."

The soup was as thin as the music and everyone was feeling a little let down. We would be here for four days and could not leave until Saturday because of the group visa.

On further inspection, the hotel turned out to have three bars at which, for a stiff price, you could get scotch, vodka, and champagne, and all three of the bars were filled with women. Their

79

price was more reasonable, and if you had any American money, you were a king. It was hard to put it all together—the hustling of money and girls in a government hotel in an Iron Curtain country.

Fortunately, among those staying at our hotel were Bob Dellinger and his wife. Bob was from California and was making a movie of our track team with Bob Seagram, the pole vaulter. He introduced us to the American cultural attaché and United States Information Officer, Michael Eisenstadt, who invited Bill Toomey and me to dinner the next evening. We went to his house first for a few drinks and he and his wife gave us a crash course on Polish folkways and mores vis-a-vis the government:

"By all means, don't touch the black-market money changers or the women in the bars. The government might use it for black-mailing purposes."

The Eisenstadts were very kind and open people and their company was a delight. They had been in Dubrovnik before Warsaw and were quite at home in the Eastern bloc countries. They took us to an Hungarian restaurant that night where we ate well and drank some very passable Hungarian wine and listened to gypsy violins. Warsaw was beginning to brighten.

The days passed slowly, and our athletes were complaining about their hotel and the food they were getting. We finished the track meet on Friday night and were all ready to leave the next day. The group visa stated that all of us must leave on the same day but, as far as we knew, not on the same plane. Most of our group were leaving on a 7:00 A.M. plane for Paris. One of my first rules is never catch a plane before noon if you can help it, and there was a flight to London in the early afternoon. Dick Bank and Roger Stephenson, our engineer, and I opted for the later plane.

On Saturday morning at seven o'clock, I was awakened by a phone call from a distraught Lou Tyrell.

"You guys have to get out to the airport right away. They won't let us take off until you get here."

Dick, Roger, and I, half-dressed, got a cab and hurried to the airport where we found our Intourist Big Sister guide in a tizzy.

"Come, come, where have you been? Get on in there. You are holding the entire airplane up."

"Lou," I asked, "does she mean we're to get on the plane?"

"That's the general idea," said Lou. "They have delayed this flight forty-five minutes for you guys."

"But we're going on the later plane."

"No," said Big Sister. "You all must go on the same plane."

"We went all through this yesterday with your people. They said it would be all right to take the later plane."

"No. No," said Big Sister. "You are on a group visa. You must go on this plane." She was terribly distressed.

After another fifteen minutes of arguing it was decided that the plane would be allowed to go and we would be allowed to take the later plane—but we had to surrender our passports to Big Sister and return to the airport at eleven o'clock.

This we did, and we immediately began to feel naked and insecure in this Iron Curtain country without a passport. When we returned to the hotel I called Michael Eisenstadt, and he sent a young man from the embassy to meet us at the airport.

When we returned, Big Sister was there looking terribly woebegone. I imagine she was going to be reprimanded by her superiors. At any rate, she was relieved to see us, and we her, for she had our passports. With Big Sister and our young friend from the embassy translating, we got through customs and had everything stamped and official, and then sat for a few minutes in the coffee shop. Finally, it was time to get on the bus that would take us to the plane. There was an armed guard at the door leading to the bus, and when he looked at our tickets and papers, he barred the way, motioning for us to go back inside. My heart dropped. What could possibly be wrong now? Finally, after more haranguing by our embassy man, the guard allowed us to pass. For some reason, Dick Bank was behind us, and as Roger and I took our seats on the bus, we looked up to see the guard stopping Dick, and Dick, his eyes popping out, shouting plaintively, "Don't leave without me."

Again, our man from the embassy straightened things out and we were, at last, away, airborne, on our way home to a home we now appreciated more than ever.

The next year when we returned to Warsaw, things were quite different. The government had relaxed many regulations and there were no longer people trying to buy American money, nor were there girl-filled bars. The city was more lively and European, and we passed in and out of the country with relative ease. We renewed our acquaintance with the Eisenstadts who took us to a marvelous country inn for dinner; we discovered the old town and much of the awakening charms of this battered capital whose citizens have given the world so much beauty.

Warsaw was the last stop in Europe that year and it was home for the last time, back to football and the 11 o'clock news. I was tired of transatlantic airplanes and resolved to rent a place in Europe for the next summer.

We would be in Europe for nine weeks in the summer of 1970, from the middle of July to the first week in September. Through some very nice people in New York, I was able to rent an apartment in Nice right on the Promenade d'Anglaise. Jean Claude Pujol runs a marvelous French restaurant in New York called Les Pyrenees. Through Jean Claude, I met his father who vacationed every year in Nice; he found an apartment for me for the month of August.

The track-and-field year began again at Villanova. Then it was on to the California Relays at Modesto again, and to Berkeley and Orange County and, finally, to the AAU Championships in Bakersfield, California, hometown of Frank Gifford and Dennis Ralston, and where Ralph Boston said, "The heat hits you in the face like a fist."

The first two finishers in the Championships again made up the National Team and went on the European tour. In the first year of the series I had gotten to know the athletes of the 1968 Olympics: John Carlos, Lee Evans, Marty Liquori, and, of course, Bill Toomey, who was now part of the announcing crew. They were all marvelous interviews—I was comfortable with them and looked forward to another group of track meets in Europe. But there was change in the air and it became evident in this championship.

On the first night, John Carlos pulled up lame and Willie Davenport was defeated in the hurdles. On the second night, Lee Evans was beaten in the 400 meter and Marty Liquori was beaten in the mile. There would be some new faces on the national team this year. Ivory Crockett would replace the lame Carlos and John Smith, and Wayne Collette would dominate Lee Evans in the 400, while Thomas Hill and Marcus Walker would be making it tougher for Willie Davenport in the hurdles.

The team with the new faces and the usual CBS Sugarman team left for Europe in the second week in July. At the last minute, my wife Bert decided it would not be right to leave our children for nine weeks, so she was not going. This left me with a lease on the apartment and only me to live there. Then Tony Verna, who would be directing most of the shows in August, said he would share the cost with me, and off we went.

Our itinerary that year was Paris, Stuttgart, Leningrad, Stockholm, Oslo, Cologne, Malmo, Helsinki, and Warsaw. The lease on the apartment did not begin until August. After the show in Paris, I went up to St. Andrews for the last two days of the British Open. It was my first trip to St. Andrews, and I had brought my clubs with the idea of playing the Old Course on Sunday, but it was not to be; Doug Sanders tied Jack Nicklaus for 72 holes and on Sunday there was an eighteen-hole playoff. I was slightly disappointed, but the pain was eased by having a first-row seat for the playoff on the world's most famous course.

From St. Andrews I went to Stuttgart and after Stuttgart, in that ill-fated Porsche, I drove to Munich, where we all spent the weekend at the Byersherhoff resting up for our week in Leningrad. After our experiences in Warsaw, everyone was apprehensive. On Monday we all boarded a seven o'clock plane from Munich to Copenhagen and, like the year before when we went to Warsaw, we had a layover of several hours. The Copenhagen Airport is one of the main crossroads of the world, and if you're there long enough you are bound to see someone you know. On this particular day, Tony Jacklin, the British golfer, passed through, as did several people who knew me from Philadelphia, and a man I had been in the Army with said hello. The chimes that announced a departure or arrival tinkled over the loudspeakers, and we passed our time reading and shopping the duty-free counters laden with rich Danish chocolates and whiskeys. We should have bought the place out. Finally, we boarded our flight that would make one stop in Helsinki and then on to Leningrad.

It was late afternoon when we landed at the Leningrad Airport and almost immediately our education began. We could only spend rubles and, at the end of our stay, they would not exchange what rubles we had left over for dollars. When the Russians play at home they are tough to beat. Then there was an interminable wait for our luggage. We were made to wait sitting in buses that looked as if they had come straight from the scrap heap. After an hour and a half of waiting we were on our way into the city, accompanied by three Intourist gentlemen who spoke English and had the same puritanical mien as Big Sister had in Warsaw.

The next bit of bad news was that they had changed our hotel. We had booked into the Astoria Hotel, the best in town, but for reasons they never told us, the Russians moved us to the Sovietskia.

"The most modern hotel in Europe," said one of the guides.

"Yes," I answered, "but is it the best?"

It was a distinction the guide ignored, refusing to answer.

One of the many disparate people I had met in P. J. Clarke's in New York over the years was Victor Shuderhov, the official interpreter for the Soviet heads of state. He would come into Clarke's whenever he was in New York, and Danny Lavezzo, the owner, and he had become friends of a sort. Danny had taken him to a couple of Giants games and had asked me to be sure and ask for him when I got to Russia.

"Do you know if Victor Shuderov will be at this track meet?" I asked, without trying to sound pretentious. There was no answer from our Intourist chaps. No recognition of my question, nor the name Victor Shuderhov.

"Do you know if Victor Shuderov, the interpreter for Comrade Breshnev, will be here?" I asked again.

"I never heard of the man," said Intourist number one.

The bus pulled up to the side of Hotel Sovietskia, a tall white building on a side street. There were no porters and we all carried our bags to our rooms. In addition to my luggage, I had one of the few sets of golf clubs ever to be seen in downtown Leningrad, and I received more than a few puzzled stares. My room was small; it had a single bed against the wall and a window that looked north across the canal to St. Isaac's Cathedral, its big golden dome dominating the skyline, the tallest building on the horizon except for the TV tower beyond.

After stashing our luggage, we all met downstairs in the bar and huge dining room of the hotel. At the bar, the only drink you could buy was a disastrous-tasting champagne cocktail. The dining room was large and bright with a big window at the far end through which the late-evening summer sun shone. There was a dance floor and, except for our party and a group of Jewish tourists, the room was filled with Russians. There was a heavy sprinkling of Navy personnel, since Leningrad is the Annapolis of Russia and the fleet was in. The food was as appealing as the champagne cocktail, thin soup, gray meat. We could feel a long week coming. As we finished dinner we noticed an increase in the amount of noise in the room. People were talking louder and faster and the music was getting louder and people were dancing with determined gusto, if not joy, grim-faced and, for the most part, terribly drunk. On this disturbing note, we called it a day—a long day—a day that saw us go farther in ten hours than Hitler had in 20 years, from Munich to Leningrad, where we were staying in the most modern hotel in Europe.

The first thing we heard the next morning was that our television truck was not on the premises. It apparently had been stopped at the Finnish-Russian border. Marv Sugarman, the friend of Willi Brandt, was riding shotgun on the trip and we became a little concerned. The track meet was scheduled for Thursday and Friday evenings and the truck should have arrived on Monday.

Tuesday was a clear, cool day—perfect for sightseeing, which we all did. It was reassuring to see the track team wandering through the streets of Leningrad in sandals, blue jeans, and their dark blue warm-up jackets with USA on the back. It was a sobering kind of sightseeing, for even on this bright, sunlit day there was a melancholy, almost tragic, air about this city that has remnants of great beauty. But I had yet to hear laughter or see a smile. How much of this sadness and dreariness came from the government and how much from the 900-day siege in the forties? I don't know. I would suspect that the latter is more responsible. Beyond the Winter Palace and the monuments to Lenin, the most impressive thing in this city that Peter built is the cemetery where 670,000 people lie in mass graves, part of the million who died from 1942 to 1945. Now, two generations later, the effects are still felt.

That evening Bob Dailey and I went over to the Astoria Hotel and met Neil Leifer, then one of the leading photographers at *Sports Illustrated* and an old Leningrad hand. We got a decent drink at the bar of the hotel and then he took us to an Intourist restaurant where we could get a good filet and ice cream, excellent coffee, and a dry red wine that was a little bitter, but so very good after the wretched champagne cocktails at our hotel. We knew now that we would make it through until Saturday.

The next morning, our TV truck had still not arrived. It was another clear, cool day, and Bob Dailey and his wife, Jeri, and I hired
a car and an interpreter and went down the Moscova Prospect past
the airport to Pushkin. It is the village of the poet and the site of
the palaces of Catherine and Alexander. It was unbelievable, too
much really, too opulent, too much splendor. Restoration was going on while we were there. One could understand the Revolution
a little better after seeing this home of the tsars.

When we returned to the hotel we heard that Marvin Sugarman had safely brought the TV truck to Leningrad after charming
the Russian border guards and arguing his way south.

While all this was going on, our track team was having its own
experiences. Their hotel was the Hotel Sputnik but it was not out
of this world. When Wayne Collette finally saw hot water pouring
out of the bathroom spigot in a rich, dark-brown color, he called
to his roommate, John Smith: "Hey, John, come look at this, the
sink is bleeding."

The food was a problem, in quality and quantity. The men
were hungry all the time.

Ralph Mann, the hurdler, said, "We keep getting the same
meat every day for lunch. I've never had anything like it before.
And there were no cats or dogs around, either."

Although the Russians were staying at the same hotel, they ate
in a different dining room and the Americans suspected that their
food was different and much better.

At the last minute the Russians decided to put a new track surface in Lenin Stadium. It was an asphalt surface and it was put
down on Wednesday, the day before the meet. The work was
done by a group of women in their sixties and perhaps older.
These hard-working souls did their best and worked all through
the morning hours of Thursday painting the lane lines by hand.

Pat Putnam of *Sports Illustrated* wrote, "They came up with
400 meters of unbelievably bad road. It looked like a tar road in
Minnesota after a hard winter."

It was against this background that the meet began on a cold, rainy Thursday night. A sellout crowd cheered and cheered as Valeri Borzov, with a premature (what they call a rolling) start—illegal, but never questioned on this night—won the 100 meters, beating out Ivory Crockett and Ben Vaughn. It was an upset and the beginning of Borzov's international prominence that eventually resulted in two gold medals in the 1972 Olympics.

We had an upset of our own on that cold, rainy night as Frank Shorter and Ken Moore finished one-two in the ten thousand meters against Russia's two favorites for the event. Friday, the weather was perfect, but the United States, although fighting all the way, came up short, losing to the Russian men for only the second time in nine dual meets. The women were also beaten by the Russians. It was an exciting meet to telecast. We encountered some difficulties, but not as many as our athletes. First of all, we wanted to do an opening with me standing on the top row of the stadium with the dome of St. Isaac's Cathedral behind me. But the Russians said no; the Russian Navy was in the Neva and could theoretically have been seen on camera. We tried to explain that our picture would not show the ships at all, just the skyline behind the stadium.

"Nyet!"

Then, on the first night, that cold, rainy, chilly evening, Dick Bank found his announcing booth on the top of the stadium. It was primitive to say the least. Dick found his microphone and headset, but little else. There was no table, chair, or other amenities. And Dick, never one to hide his feelings, let go.

"These goddamn Russian bastards, they couldn't run anything right. Look at this, no goddamn table or chair, what the hell am I supposed to do? Those Commie sons of bitches!"

All of Dick's comments were being heard over the loudspeaker in the TV truck. And in the TV truck at the time were the three chaps from Intourist who had never heard of Victor Shuderov. They sat impassively in the back of the truck. As soon as Dick began his tirade, Bob Dailey put down the interrupt key and said, in a soft singing way, "Dick, we have company."

But Dick was in full bloom. "These Russian assholes. What are we doing here anyway?"

"Dick, we have company," sang Bob.

"These people don't deserve a good track meet. This whole country stinks. I can't wait to get out of this hell hole."

"Dick, shut up or you'll never get out. We have company in the truck."

Finally, it dawned on Dick that he was being heard by the Soviet Marx Brothers and he took off his microphone. There was no reaction from the Intourist people. It was as if they had not heard a thing.

The next day was sunny and fresh, as we headed for the airport and a plane that would take us to Stockholm. At the airport there were a few anxious moments. We couldn't exchange our rubles for dollars and customs took a little time, but finally we were all cleared and on our way to the airport. Everyone except Dick Bank. Poor Dick. While we waited aboard the SAS plane, the Russians opened every piece of luggage he had and painstakingly went through every item of clothing, questioning him sternly. After twenty minutes or so, they let him come aboard, shaken by his ordeal, as any of us would have been. Those chaps from Intourist don't miss much.

As we took off, I looked over the city, this town of Pushkin and Tchaikovsky and Roskolnikoff and the tsars and most of all Lenin, whose mark almost obliterates the decades before 1917. It could be the fairest city east of Paris, but as we headed out across the Bay of Finland toward the Swedish coast, I still had not heard it laugh.

After the Stockholm meet I went home, finally ridding myself of those golf clubs that I used once, when Ralph Boston and I played in Stockholm. Then back to Oslo and from there finally to Nice to take up residence in the apartment.

Tony and I met at the airport in Nice and with only a little difficulty located Jean Pujol, who took us to our apartment. It was on the Promenade d'Anglaise, on the fifth floor, with a living room and balcony that faced the Mediterranean. Two bedrooms and two baths and a kitchen. It was furnished art deco style and was bright and airy. Our concierge was a jolly, fat lady about sixty years old, and in my compound-fractured French I told her that we would like breakfast at ten o'clock.

After she had left, Tony said, "We are either going to have breakfast for two at ten o'clock, or ten for breakfast at two o'clock."

It was breakfast at ten o'clock as everything worked out well with the apartment, and the south of France, although hardly what it must have been years ago, still had the perfect weather, fresh seafood, and a variety of places to ease our boredom, if not to cure it. I had been in Nice once before and I was glad to be back.

That prior visit came shortly after the end of the war in Europe, when those of us who were not going home immediately were given furloughs on the Riviera. Officers were sent to Cannes, the enlisted men to Nice, and for once the Army did things right and everyone went first class. It was a heady time for a twenty-one-year-old. The morning we had left I had been on guard duty at the Second Armoured Division's headquarters in Wölfenbuttel. My post was the house in which Marlene Dietrich was staying as a guest of the division and my partner and I had actually gotten a glimpse of her. Now, on the afternoon of that same day, we were discovering the enchantment of the south of France, the sparkling spring weather, the endless array of freshly cut flowers, the Mediterranean natives who were beginning to put zest back into their lives after six years of war. One of our first stops was a bar near the old section of town. We came in to the dark room from the bright sunshine and found we were the only people in the place. The bartender was a large stout man of about forty years who looked at us four American G.I.s with a cold indifference that momentarily put us off. Then he turned on the radio on the shelf behind the bar and the room was full of Glenn Miller. He asked us what we wanted.

We ordered our drinks and decided we wanted a livelier place to launch our holiday. There were two price lists behind the bar; the more expensive list had "Avec Music" at the top, and the prices were about twice as much as the other list.

Tech Sergeant John Shrednitz, our leader, asked for the bill, and in a loud outrage and fractured French said, "You've charged us double . . . where is the music?" pointing to the empty band-stand and the tables piled with chairs. A Gallic shrug and a tilt of the head toward the radio was the only answer. *Vive la France!*

We found a much nicer and more friendly place on our second evening. It had a terrace and a small lounge with an oval bar. It was crowded and noisy every night and we thought it was the most chic place we had ever seen. We became friends of the proprietor and the piano player. There was a brand new song called "C'est Finis," a marvelously sad French song that later became a hit in America under the title of "Symphony," which was probably the G.I.s' pronunciation of "C'est Finis." At any rate, it was our own private song, being played by our new friend. The same people were there every night and we soon became friendly in the way of saloon people all over the world. Most of the crowd were service-men like ourselves, but there were a few civilians, and they told us that our friend the piano player had been a hero with the French Underground. This impressed us very much. He reluctantly ad-mitted the fact to us, but would not talk about it, thereby giving himself an aura of mystery. And then one night we found out that he carried a gun, a small automatic, and for us his character was complete. The dashing, romantic resistance hero with his own se-cret sadness. I can't believe how impressed we were when we dis-covered he had a gun. We, who had fired much heavier things like mortars and Thompson submachine guns and howitzers, who had been fired at by German eighty-eights, screaming neubleweffers, and the 240-millimeter railroad gun that sounded like the end of the world, were terribly impressed with the piano player who carried a small automatic. In 1970, Tony Verna and I

had a drink on the terrace. The place looked the same, but no
one remembered the piano player.

In 1970, we enjoyed our weeks by the sea. We traveled from Men-
ton to St. Tropez and got plenty of sun. But even in such a romantic holiday setting, boredom was just a step away. Sometimes,
the highlight of the day was waiting for the *Paris Herald Tribune*
to be delivered at the store on the corner. Still, it was better than
hanging around the towns to the north, and it was with some sadness that we said goodbye to the concierge and the apartment at
the end of August. We were on our way to Warsaw, and then
home.

The next summer we did not go to Europe until the end of July
and then stayed only five weeks, and in 1972 we did only three
meets in Europe beginning in August. Nineteen seventy-two was
an Olympic year and the United States team scheduled those
three meets in Europe as warm-ups for Munich. They opened at
Bislet Stadium in Oslo, and two young men from Finland, Lasse
Viren and Pekka Vesala, won the 5,000 and 10,000 meters, a feat
they would repeat at the Olympics. The United States team
seemed disorganized and desultory.

The next meet was an invitational at Viareggio in Italy. Viareggio is a resort town and that week it was crowded with Italians on
holiday. We stayed just to the north in a place called Forte dei
Marmi, in a hotel that used to be the estate of the Agnellis. It was
a lovely place and Marv Sugarman gave a wonderful lunch on the
lawn under a grape arbor, and later we all went to the beach and
rented paddleboats and took them out beyond the breakers, where
turning around we could look up at the mountains and the quar-
ries of Carrara in Tuscany and, seeing the white marble through
the summer haze, wonder how in the hell those 15th Century
boys got the marble from there down to Rome for Michelangelo.

The track meet was well attended by the expressive Italians and, once again, except for our 4×100 relay team, the Americans seemed flat. Later that night, in a spot on the beach across from the hotel, Ralph Boston, Bill Toomey and I were having a few drinks.

"This team's in trouble," said Bill. "They don't give a damn."

"Well, we've had a few injuries," I said, "Rod Milburn and . . ."

"That's not it, Jack," said Ralph. "These kids just don't seem to want it. Why, hell, I saw a kid miss qualifying for the team and you know what he did? He just smiled and took his girl's hand and walked away. Why, man, if that had been me I'd've been so mad I wouldn't have smiled for two weeks. No, the whole attitude is bad."

Our next and last stop was the Hans Braun International Track and Field Meet in Munich. From Viareggio, we drove to Florence where we spent a night and then took the train to Munich, and the comfortable Byersherhott Hotel. There was much to see on this trip to Munich. The entire town was higher than the Octoberfest. The Olympics were in the air. We went out and got a firsthand tour of the facilities. The Germans did not seem to have missed a thing. They were jovial and hospitable and confident that they would have one of the finest Olympics ever staged.

One of the people who arranged our tour was Hans (Jonny) Klein, the public information head for the organizing committee. He and Bill were old friends, and he asked Bill if he would attend a meeting that night. Jonny was running for the Bavarian Senate and wanted to introduce Bill to some of his potential voters. Bill said yes, and asked if he could bring me and Atis "Pete" Petersen, a track coach and old friend. Jonny said yes, and so it was that on another one of those golden summer evenings we were speeding down the Autobahn from Munich to Salzburg.

After an hour's drive, we turned off the Autobahn and soon pulled up in front of Jonny's house, a two-story wooden structure set in a green field with a view of the mountains behind.

He introduced us to his wife, and after two beers and some

cheese and sausage we were off to the meeting. It was held in a small village about twenty minutes from Jonny's house, and about three hundred members of the young Catholic Democrats were in attendance. Jonny made a short speech and then introduced Bill, and then me and Pete Petersen. Then he asked for questions. Soon, the youngsters were asking if the Olympics were necessary, if the money should not go to other things. Bill and Pete and I took turns in answering.

One smiling young blond boy asked how we Americans could say that we were for the Olympics because the games promoted peace when we were killing defenseless people in Vietnam. Then he asked us why we were so hypocritical, that the Olympics were hypocritical and a waste of time. We tried to answer the best we could with Jonny doing the translating. But the smiling young man kept at it. Americans and the Olympics and sports were all wrong. All of a sudden, Pete Petersen, who was sitting on my right, spoke up.

Atis Petersen and his family were born in Riga in Latvia, fled from the Russians during World War II and, after many hardships, made it to the United States. In time, young Pete became a track athlete and then a highly respected coach; his father became an ardent fan of American football. Pete told this audience the whole story of his family's flight and of their putting down in the United States and how much track had helped him. With deep emotion, before Jonny could make the translation, Pete told the smiling young blond man and everyone in the room that, as far as he was concerned, neither the United States nor the Olympics were hypocritical and that the money spent by the German government on the Olympics would do more good than harm.

On that note, the rally broke up, with Jonny and a few other Germans apologizing for the questions asked by the smiling young blond boy. His questions, in retrospect, seem very relevant and become more so with each passing Olympics. But that evening was one of the first times I had been questioned about my government's actions while in a foreign country, and that can be a frustrating and maddening thing, especially on such a controversial topic as the Vietnam War.

From the rally we headed back toward Munich. We stopped at a country inn on a hilltop where we ate wienerschnitzel and drank the good dark German beer. Jonny was in high spirits. He told us how the Germans had financed the Olympics with a special coin they had minted, how Munich would be better off with the Olympic facilities after the games were over and, most important—and his eyes gleamed as he spoke—how the 1972 games would erase the stigma of Hitler and show the world the good side of the German people.

The next night, through heavy rains, we taped our track meet. It was seventy-two hours before the Opening Ceremonies of the Olympics, and I stood in the early evening rain with the Olympic tower over my shoulder, to wind up the series. This not only marked the end of the summer but, for all practical purposes, the end of my participating on the Sugarman shows. We had been with this track-and-field team since 1969; I had gotten to know most of the athletes and I hated to leave them on the eve of their biggest experience. But such are the ways of television networks; ABC had the rights to the Olympics and I was going home to watch them on television.

That year we spent the Labor Day weekend with some friends in Warwick, Rhode Island, and it was while driving home early in the morning that we heard the report on the car radio of the hostages being taken in the Olympic Village. It is difficult, even today, to describe the feeling I experienced later as I watched Jim McKay, program interrupt in his ear, tell us all that the hostages had been killed at the airport. The man who was providing the information to Roone Arledge who relayed it to Jim through the earpiece was Jonny Klein.

For me, the Sugarman Express had come to a halt. Four years of California springs and European summers were over. It was time to do something else. Time for a change. It was time for a change in the Olympic movement, too.

The Olympic movement did change, finally breaking the bonds of the Avery Brundage's hypocritical tyranny, the "throw Eleanor Holmes off the team, the games must go on at any cost" mentality that ruled the movement for so long. The Olympics enthusiastically embraced the world of corporate underwriting and television windfalls. The stunning job done by the Los Angeles Organizing Committee in 1984 rewrote the way the games are mounted. Professionals have entered some arenas and the event has moved farther away from the intent of the founding father, Baron Pierre de Coubertin.

As the Olympics changed, so did track and field. Athletes are paid now and can earn handsome sums as professionals. This, of course, is an improvement, but it has brought a new set of problems. Arguments over appearance fees produce "no shows," and some record holders duck natural confrontations that would help the sport because a loss might endanger their commercial value. In addition, over the entire sport hangs the dark cloud of performance-enhancing drugs. There is nothing new about this. The problem is just bigger and there are newer drugs. Steroids and other potentially harmful products endanger the essence of this basic sport. The first time I heard of anabolic steroids was in 1968, the first year of the Sugarman shows. The weight-lifting athletes, the discus throwers, and shotputters all knew about them and were convinced many Russian and East German athletes were taking them, and the Americans felt disadvantaged. Now the virus has spread to runners and swimmers with new enhancers coming from China. Unless some kind of worldwide recognition can be effectively introduced, the integrity of track and field and all sports will be compromised.

If the world of running, jumping, and throwing has changed, so has the way in which we televise it. In those Sugarman years, after an all-night edit and voiceover session, the tapes were hand-carried to New York and delivered to the CBS broadcast center.

How different is it today? Well, in the mid-1980s, Marty Liquori and I did the Rotterdam Marathon in what used to be called a "same-day turnaround." Because of the five-hour time difference between New York and Rotterdam, we had time to edit the two-and-a-half-hour race down to an hour and send it to New York by satellite for same day broadcast. As Marty and I came out of the remote truck after finishing the voiceover session, I heard our chief engineer, Chris Johnson say, "Damn it." I asked what was wrong.

"The Atlantic satellite is down," he said.

"What are we going to do?" I asked, thinking that all our work might have been for nought.

"Well," said Chris, "we are going to send it from here to a ground station in Germany, then up to the Indian Ocean satellite, then down to Hong Kong. From Hong Kong up to the Pacific satellite, then down to Los Angeles and from there by line to New York."

"My God, Chris, how long is that going to take?"

"About two and a half seconds," he said, walking away.

Two and a half seconds! More than halfway around the world in two and a half seconds! Then I was hit with another thought: When the signal came down in Hong Kong it would be early Sunday morning in the Crown Colony. And when the signal reached New York, it would be the previous Saturday afternoon. Time and distance are relative, except in the world of track and field where I hope youngsters still sit in the infield on late spring afternoons watching the pole vaulters finish up.

The Majors

"That's the second time
that son of a bitch has done that to me."

The ultimate satisfaction in covering golf tournaments is working the four major championships. Any golf tournament is a pleasure to report, but those four, each with a different personality, are the standard by which we measure greatness and they stand apart. My years with ABC broadcasting the U.S. and British Opens and the PGA Championships, along with my CBS years at the Masters, gave me the complete set.

The Masters is the only one of the four that is conducted by a private, nonprofit club. The Augusta National Golf Club is beholden to no one except its members. It was very late in changing its rules to allow African-Americans to play and to admit minorities to its membership. They have strong opinions about what TV announcers can say and what is shown on the telecast. These are indisputable facts, but to dwell entirely on those negative aspects is to ignore the very positive effect the Masters has had.

It is very likely the best sporting event in the world. The ticket allotment system is a marvel. Once you get on the list, you had better behave or your subscription will not be renewed. Accommodations for the public on the golf course are the best of any of the major tournaments. The refreshment stands are numerous and discreetly painted green and set among the trees. The television towers are permanent structures, also painted green and set back in the trees—a far cry from the ugly pipe-and-canvas towers that are found at other golf tournaments. Everything is done to protect the great beauty of this former nursery for the pleasure of the gallery and the players. Free pairing sheets are put out daily, and everything is done to protect the integrity of the game. At the Masters, the tournament comes first.

Corporate entertaining is done in private homes away from the course, not in tents set up on the eighteenth fairway. Incidentally, that is not true at that other major sporting event conducted by a private club; at the Wimbledon Tennis Championship, the corporate tents are as numerous as the tennis courts. At the Masters, money is never mentioned out loud. It is the last place, perhaps, where the golf tournament is the first consideration and the aim is to make it better every year.

The Masters field is small but it is one of the most elite in golf. Its quality is insured by thirteen different criteria that can earn a player the invitation that the overwhelming majority of players crave passionately. The best players in the world come to Augusta and the winner knows he has beaten the best. The Masters also gives a lifetime exemption to its champions, which other major tournaments do not. They are welcomed back for as long as they want, to play or merely to attend the champions' dinner and sit on the veranda of the clubhouse. It is another grace note that sets the Masters apart.

And so does the telecast. Because the late Tournament Chairman Clifford Roberts demanded from CBS that commercial interruptions be held to a minimum, the network and the sponsors agreed. Equally or even more important to the uncluttered look and sound of the telecast is the absence of the usual network promotional announcements—another concession the club obtained. The results have been some telecasts of quiet dignity that enhances the dramatic moments that have occurred with incredible regularity over the years.

My first Masters telecast was in 1963 and I worked the seventeenth hole. That was the year that Nicklaus won his first Masters. The next year, I worked either fifteen or sixteen when Palmer beat Nicklaus and Dave Marr, and, finally, in 1966, I was the anchor at eighteen, a treasured assignment I received when Chris Schenkel departed for ABC.

Ah, 1966. A three-way playoff occurred among Jack Nicklaus, Gay Brewer, and Tommy Jacobs. In those days, the Masters, like the United States Open, held an eighteen-hole playoff on Mondays. Playoffs on Monday are to television what a triple-bogey finish is to a golfer; the audience is minuscule, the network loses the revenue of its regular programming, and should the play be slow and go beyond six o'clock, it invades the sacred precincts of local news programs, which makes the affiliate station managers less than jolly good fellows.

On this particular Monday, for a reason lost in time, the three players teed off at an hour that would never get them to the eighteenth hole by six o'clock. CBS went on the air at 4:30 and it was forty-five minutes before we had a player on camera. For three-quarters of an hour everyone on the broadcast danced as fast as we could, ad libbing, pulling up tapes on earlier rounds until, finally, like a squad of lost infantrymen, the players and their caddies came into view. Now we had no chance of finishing before six o'clock, and new pressures began to build as we realized the players might not finish before the daylight died and, unthinkable thought, before Walter Cronkite and the *CBS Evening News*. (If local news was sacred, Walter was the "Untouchable.") Well, we made it, but barely. Just as I said, "And Jack Nicklaus becomes the first man to win back-to-back Masters Championships," the *CBS Evening News* was right on top of me. That was some tough Monday.

The following March, on a cold, rainy night in Manhattan, I was riding in a taxi with Jack Dolph, the Assistant Director of CBS Sports.

"You're not going to work the Masters anymore," he said.

"What!!!" I gasped.

"You called the gallery a mob and didn't mention there would be a green coat ceremony on the putting green after the players checked their cards."

"Jack," I said, "I didn't call the gallery a mob. I said there was a mob scene at the eighteenth green." And there was, since in the fading light, all the spectators stampeded up the eighteenth to try to get a view of the green.

"No matter," said Jack. "You're off the Masters."

It was a difficult moment for both of us. Jack had always been a champion of mine but, in those days when the Masters was involved, CBS became obsequious to an embarrassing degree. Mr. Paley loved the tournament on his network and Mr. Clifford Roberts and the Augusta National was accommodated in every way. I was shocked and, with the demons of insecurity grabbing at me, completely crushed. The 1967 Masters was a difficult time for me, but soon I began getting sympathetic pieces written about me in the press and people were generally very supportive. I have always been a little suspicious of the reasons given for my dismissal. A few years ago, someone told me that they had just watched a kinescope of a Masters telecast where Jim McKay had called the eighteenth green a "mob scene" and no fuss was made. I think they just didn't like my work. As the years went by, the incident became more of a plus for me than a minus, and it was another reminder never to use a cliche. Perhaps if I had described the scene at eighteen that evening as "a heaving mass of humanity," I would never have been fired. But I doubt it.

I didn't go back to the Masters until 1973, when CBS invited me to visit. One of the most endearing places in the world is the second floor of the clubhouse at Augusta National during Masters Week. It gathers the elite of the golfing world who sit at small tables over breakfast and lunch and from time to time get up and go out on the veranda to check the scoreboard between the tenth and eighteenth fairways. I was sitting at one of those tables that year having a late breakfast with Cary Middlecoff and listening to some wonderful stories being told by Claude Harmon, when Frank Chirkinian came by and told us that Henry Longhurst had just been taken to the hospital and that CBS wanted to put me on the sixteenth hole for the telecast.

"Come on, we've got to see the Old Man."

The Old Man was Clifford Roberts, the terror who made CBS tremble and who had me thrown off the Masters telecast. Now he would pass judgment on my parole. We were ushered into his office down by the pro shop off the first fairway.

Frank said, "Mr. Roberts, here is Jack Whitaker."

The terror stood up, put out his hand and smiled warmly.

"Young man, we are very fortunate that you are here."

And just like that, I was back at the Masters.

The sixteenth hole at Augusta, as even some citizens in Ulan Bator know, is the comely par three with water and a hill full of spectators on the left side. It is called Redbud, and it was known as the private domain of Henry Longhurst, former Conservative Member of Parliament for Acton, former low-handicap golfer, golf writer for the *Sunday Times* of London and BBC commentator. The sixteenth hole at Augusta was Henry's sacred plot, his sceptered isle, his jewel set among the Georgia pines. Henry had made the sixteenth and himself part of the Masters' lore. The gallery would applaud him as he ascended the steps to his perch, and George Drago, for many years the cameraman at sixteen, would always have fresh flowers and liquid of the proper kind waiting for Henry on his desk. That year I was as much in awe of Henry as I was of the tournament. Fortunately for Henry and the rest of us, he was back the next year and I drifted onto the thirteenth hole.

The thirteenth hole is probably my favorite to broadcast. It is a par five reachable in two shots, with a large left-to-right sloping green. Some very dramatic things happen there at the end of Amen Corner. Aside from that, the TV tower is set back beyond the creek, hidden away from the galleries. In the moments in between groups, it is quiet and you can enjoy the peaceful setting without distraction. One year Dick Siderof, the amateur from Connecticut, reached the thirteenth in two shots and made his birdie. Playing behind him was Ben Hogan. As Siderof watched from the fourteenth tee, Hogan, who had driven just about where Dick had, laid up, got on the green in three and sunk a putt for his birdie. After the round, Siderof asked him why he had not gone for the green in two since he had driven the ball far enough. Hogan looked at Siderof for a moment and then said, "Oh, I didn't need a three."

It is always an entertaining if impossible task to define the most exciting event that you have ever covered, but certainly in my years at the Masters, 1975 must rate very high. The tournament began that year with a light rain falling and mists swirling about the top of the pine trees. Augusta National had the look of Transylvania about it that Thursday. Bobby Nichols shot a sixty-seven to take the first round lead on a day when the course was as easy to play as it has ever been. On Friday, the rain was heavier in the morning but by noon the sun was out. Jack Nicklaus ripped through Amen Corner with birdies at eleven, twelve, and thirteen on his way to the 36-hole lead, five shots ahead of Tom Weiskopf.

On Saturday it was sunny and cool with gusting winds. Johnny Miller responded with six straight birdies on the front nine to thrust himself into the tournament. He shot a brilliant sixty-five, making up eight strokes on Nicklaus, who had a seventy-three. Tom Weiskopf, with a birdie at eighteen, led the tournament and Nicklaus by one shot, Johnny Miller by three shots, and Tom Watson by five.

Sunday was a perfect day, sunny and warm with little wind, as four of the world's best golfers teed off for the final round. As they turned for home, Weiskopf and Nicklaus were tied at eleven under par and Johnny Miller, after a thirty-two on the front nine, was just two shots behind at nine under par. They started the last nine holes, shimmering as they walked, club shafts flashing in the spring sunshine, linotyping golf history as they went, each in eye contact with the other. The excitement never let up and the vignettes were plentiful. Weiskopf's face when he put his second shot in the water at eleven: The handsome countenance was long and solemn as he controlled his marvelous temper and took a bogey and then watched Nicklaus birdie the twelfth to take the lead from him.

I was working the fourteenth hole that year and Nicklaus, after a par at thirteen, inexplicably putted through the green at fourteen and took a bogey to drop back into a tie with Weiskopf. Tom came right behind him, striking a perfect iron close to the pin for a birdie and the lead. Miller, in the meantime, had birdied thirteen to draw closer to the leaders. At fourteen, he hit his drive to the left where it hit a tree. His second shot also hit a tree. His third shot hit the flagstick and stopped inches away for a miraculous par.

At this point a lusty yell rose from the fifteenth green as Jack Nicklaus hit a heroic one-iron for his second shot to reach the par five in two. He two-putted for a birdie and once more was tied for the lead. But Weiskopf and Miller both birdied fifteen and Tom went into the lead once more as the drama moved to the sixteenth. Weiskopf, arms folded against his chest, stood quietly on the sixteenth tee with a one-stroke lead, watching Nicklaus, who was on the green after hitting a mediocre tee shot that left him forty feet from the hole. His putt had to go uphill across two slopes. Jack's caddy, Willie Anderson, attended the flagstick. Jack walked around the putt, reading it from different angles. Finally he took his stance, knees bent, head tilted. Silence, long and deep, fell around the course; it reached from the sixteenth green back along the gallery by the pond and up the hill to the sixth tee. Even the Georgia pines dared not move as the sun splashed through them to throw lengthening shadows across the green. Nicklaus drew back his hands and the putt was on its way, up the hill, breaking right, now left, and then, as if being led by a radio beam, it disappeared into the cup.

Willie Anderson jumped as high as he ever did in his life and Nicklaus jumped even higher, turned in midair, and then ran across the green as the silence was shattered by a mighty shout. Nicklaus was once again tied for the lead. On the sixteenth tee, Tom Weiskopf looked on, seemingly impassive.

Now it was time for Tom to play, and for once on this magical day, he played a very poor shot, forty-five yards from the hole short of the green. His pitch shot was almost perfect but not quite, and a bogey four was the result. Tom fell one stroke behind Nicklaus, who parred seventeen and eighteen, and now waited to see what Weiskopf and Miller would do. Weiskopf parred seventeen, but Miller birdied it to draw even with Tom, just one stroke behind Nicklaus with one hole to play. Given the circumstances of time and place, both men hit magnificent shots to the home green, shots of incredible courage and talent that both players and all of us who saw them will remember with gratitude. Miller put his twenty feet from the hole, Weiskopf seven feet. Miller's putt, a downhill right-to-left terror, was stroked boldly, and for a brief moment it looked as if it might find the bottom of the hole. Then, in the last few inches, it slid away. Now Weiskopf. The moment the putt left the blade it looked good. It was rolling surely and with the right speed, dead on line and right on time for its rendezvous.

But then, in the last cruel April moment of this tournament, the ball rebelliously broke off to the left. Jack Nicklaus had won his fifth Masters title.

In a way, Weiskopf and Miller had won something too. That Sunday afternoon, an event of great theater and emotion took place, an event that went into another dimension, unforgettable because of the great talent on display and for the feelings it stirred and the memories it still evokes. Tom Weiskopf and Johnny Miller will always be a part of one of the great golf tournaments of all time.

Perhaps above all, the Masters is a place of reunion. It is here that all the members of the worldwide golfing community gather for the first time since the PGA Championship or the Ryder Cup the previous year. It celebrates the coming of spring and the passage of another winter. The lawn in front of the clubhouse is sprinkled with golf-course architects and equipment salesmen, with tournament chairmen and sponsors, with agents and clothing manufacturers. On the second floor of the clubhouse and on the adjoining veranda, golf writers and television people mingle, gathering at one table that grows larger as each new person appears. There is a wonderful waiter named Charles. Across the room you might see Claude Harmon with Cary Middlecoff, and next to a table by the window, Alistair Cooke and Pat Ward Thomas of the Manchester *Guardian*. They could quite possibly be talking about Henry Longhurst, on whom they kept a compasionate eye.

"Henry's life," Alistair would say, "ended the day he came down from Cambridge."

This was a reference to Henry's confession that on the evening of the day of his last match for Cambridge, he cried unconsolably in his bed at the Bell Hotel in Sandwich.

Henry seldom came to the second floor until after the telecast. One evening, all of the broadcast crew except Henry were assembled at one table and Bob Dailey, our director, was giving the order for celebratory drinks.

During the broadcast, Bob would cue the announcers when he was going to switch the picture to another hole by saying, "Throw it to fifteen," or "Throw it to eighteen."

Now as he was concluding the drink order, Henry, who had worked the sixteenth hole, arrived. Sizing up the situation in a flash, he cried out, "I say, Bob, throw it to sixteen will you."

The first order of business on the second floor was the horse races. The horse races were an ingenious game of chance in which you and a partner would put up a hundred dollars apiece and then choose four or five pairings for each round. The Masters always sends the players off in groups of two, and the idea was to pick the pairings you thought would score the lowest. The team would pick in turns decided by pulling a number out of a hat.

Each day there would be a race for the lowest aggregate score of a pairing, another race for the lowest single score of the day, and the lowest total of all the pairings you had picked. There were prizes for first, second, and third. This had the effect of keeping you deeply informed and interested in all the players in the field, not just the first ten on the leaderboard, and gave you a deeper knowledge of the tournament. It was wonderful discipline and great fun.

The horse races were very different from the Calcutta. For years, the Calcutta was held at a CBS house on Wednesday night and the drinks flowed freely. Bob Drum was the auctioneer and would goad the bidders with outrageous statements.

"What am I bid for this three-putt, choking idiot? Does anyone fancy this charlatan who couldn't win on the LPGA tour?"

One year he concluded the bidding but had forgotten one player. John Derr, one of our more astute members, asked if he could buy any player left over for a dollar.

"No!" thundered Drum. "You know the rules. It'll cost you five dollars."

"I'll take him for five," said Derr.

The player he bought for five dollars that Wednesday evening was Bob Goalby, who won the tournament Sunday when Roberto DeVicenzo signed an incorrect scorecard. It was the best bargain in the history of the Calcutta.

Each year the Calcutta got bigger and richer. Big-time rollers began to infiltrate, and as always, big money dampened the fun. The old CBS Calcutta was discontinued around 1987.

Sometime in the mid-1970s the Jerry Danford Award was established. This was given to the person whose behavior during The Masters was deemed by his peers to have been the most bizarre. It was named for one of the best and freest of spirits among TV sales executives. The award was presented a week after the Masters at Mike Manuche's restaurant. I am a recipient of the Jerry Danford Award. In my defense I offer the old adage, "No good deed goes unpunished."

One evening it was decided to visit one of the less elegant saloons in downtown Augusta. It was a smoky-dim room frequented by the G.I.s from Fort Gordon, where they served drinks in small glasses that looked like they might have contained Kraft cheese in another life. After the first round, several of us wanted to leave, but we had no transportation. We came in two cars, and one of our party who wanted to stay on offered his keys to Bill Brendle, the sports publicist for CBS. Bill, Pete Axhelm of *Newsweek*, and I left. On the sidewalk I said to Brendle, "Bill, you look a little wobbly. Give me the keys. I'll drive."

"Okay," said Bill, and he got into the front seat. Pete stretched out across the back seat. I was driving up Walton Way when a traffic light changed very quickly from yellow to red and I slammed on the brakes, knocking Pete to the floor.

"Sorry, Pete. You all right?"

"Yeah, I'm fine."

The next traffic light turned yellow as I reached the intersection, and this time I accelerated through in order to keep Pete on the back seat. Those lights were quick, but not as quick as the police car that pulled out behind me, lights flashing, siren blaring. I pulled over to the curb. The policeman, a flashlight in my face, snarled, "Get out of the car!"

I got out and he immediately spreadeagled me against the car, frisked me, and removed my wallet and took my belt.

"New Yorker, huh?" he sneered.

"Yes."

"Yewall don't know how to drive, do you, sonny?"

Now he told me to empty my pockets. At this point Axhelm and Brendle were protesting.

"He didn't do anything, officer."

"Shut up," said the cop, "or you'll be going where he's going."

At this point a patrol wagon pulled up and I was ushered in as Pete and Bill told me not to worry. The patrol wagon made one stop on its way to the police station to pick up a poor derelict. The driver said to the arresting officer, "Got another one of those stupid Yankees in the back. Cheap son-of-a-bitch, only had thirty dollars on him."

"What did he do?"

"Ran a red light. Hope we get a dozen more of those assholes tonight."

By the time I was put in the detention room behind bars with the evening's collection of drunks and felons, Brendle and Axhelm and most of our group were on hand. The duty officer was the former head of the vice squad, and he was listening intently as one of Augusta's more prominent madams explained who I was and what I was doing in Augusta. In minutes I was free, my thirty dollars and my wallet returned. An apology of sorts was offered, along with a request for some tickets to the Masters. Doesn't it always depend upon whom you know?

Bill Brendle and Pete Axhelm had rounded everybody up and

they were all very supportive. For the moment, I was the hero of the group. As we left the police station, the owner of the car I had been driving when arrested kept hurrying us along.

"Come on, let's get out of here," he said.

After we were safely on our way home, I asked him why he was in such a hurry.

"Jack," he said, "I've got some marijuana in the trunk. If they had searched the car, we'd have all been gone for a while."

It was the closest call I'd had since World War II. I was too embarrassed to accept the Danford Award that year. Now I am embarrassed that I didn't.

It has been part of my sweet fortune to have played Augusta National a few times. Members of the media were extended the privilege of playing on the Monday morning after the tournament with the course set up as it was for the final round on Sunday.

You are very much aware of the place as you move over these storied holes. My first impression as I stood on the first tee was that the golf course looked very big. The first fairway spread out before me like the wide ocean, and I wondered if I could get my tee ball halfway up the hill. The fairways are big and wide, the greens are big and undulating, the hills are big and steep, and all this bigness is deep green, trimmed in flaming red and creamy white. In addition to this physical beauty is the fact that you are walking over ground every inch of which has been the scene of golfing lore. Augusta National is one of the few places in sports that matches the hyperbole of its reputation.

I remember only one shot from my rounds at Augusta. I hit a four-iron two feet from the hole at the par three twelfth hole. It wasn't until later that Jack Nicklaus told me it was the improper shot with the hole cut on the right side.

"On Sunday at the Masters at the twelfth hole," he said, "you never aim at the flag stick."

Nevertheless, I exult in my birdie two. It was ten shots better than the twelve made there in 1980 by Tom Weiskopf when he put six balls into Rae's Creek.

The Masters is not perfect. There is that soft arrogance of the very rich and successful that can, at times, annoy, and occasionally, as beautiful as they are, you hope you never see another azalea bush or dogwood tree. But the tournament has grown into something special and it has changed with the times, slowly perhaps, but surely.

The Masters continues to hold the golfing public around the world in thrall. Springtime in Georgia, Bob Jones, and the Augusta National golf course have helped this smallest, youngest, and most private of the four major championships make its mark. The United States Open, by contrast, is an older, larger, and more public championship played on a different course every year. It is our most prestigious championship, and the one that provided the greatest incentive as I moved from CBS to ABC.

"Whitaker," screamed a voice in my headset, "get down there and interview Nicklaus."

It was the strident tone of Chuck Howard, the producer of ABC's golf coverage. It was on a gray, cool day at Pebble Beach, a day to sit by the fire and read a book. It was also the final round of the 1982 U.S. Open, and my first golf outing with ABC after twenty years at CBS. And it was different, very different.

At CBS, Frank Chirkinian and Bob Dailey ran what we called "quiet trucks." They sat at their consoles in the remote trucks and called their shots and talked to the cameramen and announcers on headsets, but there was very little yelling coming through the headsets. Both men had a quiet, sarcastic way of letting someone know they had made a mistake. Screaming was held to a minimum, but not at ABC.

Chuck Howard screamed and yelled like a man possessed. It

was a double shock to me, first because it was so different from CBS and, second, because Chuck Howard was one of the most organized of men. He was one of the pioneers of ABC Sports. Along with Jim McKay and Roone Arledge, he had led the way in sports coverage that made ABC a major influence in broadcasting. In the years at CBS when I would take a vacation at the British Open, it was Chuck who was the gracious host, securing me credentials and a room. One year at Turnberry he brought his father along and the three of us had a great visit one evening before dinner. Chuck at home with his family could be like Robert Young in *Father Knows Best*, but in a remote truck he became Charles Foster Kane destroying the bedroom at Xanadu. It was like a chemical reaction. When the show was over and it had gone well, Chuck was all smiles and congratulations, a concerned and caring producer.

Whatever it was it worked, because over the years Chuck produced many historic events with style and flair—from major golf tournaments, big-time college football games, and Triple Crown races to the Olympics—and to my knowledge never lost a friend.

Not all of ABC's producers were screamers; Doug Wilson and Ken Wulff, to name two, were composed, but there was a common thread of fear in the department that manifested itself most clearly in the treatment of the production assistants, known as P.A.s. CBS had P.A.s, but their role was not as highly (or lowly) defined as it was at ABC. At ABC, the P.A. was the lowest form of life. They were last in line. They were all bright young men and women who aspired to become directors and producers, but before they could move up the ladder they were severely tested. They picked up directors, producers, and announcers at airports, made hotel accommodations, went for coffee, arranged for interviews, and tended to a hundred and one things, worked fifteen hours a day, and got yelled at a lot.

In my first year at ABC, I had an assignment at the Indianapolis 500. That year the network did a tape-delay broadcast of the race in prime time. It was the year Gordon Johncock won by a mere .100 of a second, one of the closest of all time. After the show was over, one of the P.A.s, a lovely young woman named Garland Peete, was standing in the compound outside the remote trucks. One of the producers was screaming at her, almost out of control. Jim McKay and I were standing nearby looking on.

"You know," said Jim, "Garland was on the staff of a senator from North Carolina and was one of the most popular young women in Washington before she came to ABC. Now look at her, being yelled at in a muddy field in Indiana."

But such was the thrall that TV held for bright young people in those days. They lined up for the jobs, and the discipline they learned as an ABC sports P.A. or associate producer stayed with them as they moved up the ladder and began yelling down at the new group of beginners. To this day Terry Jastrow, the former producer of ABC's golf coverage and president of Jack Nicklaus Productions, reverts to his early days: He is forever picking up our suitcases or helping with dinner reservations and the like so that we have to say to him, "Terry, you're the producer now, not the P.A."

I don't know who instituted this reign of terror but it was, at least in the short run, effective. All of the people Chuck excoriated over the years were at his memorial service, recounting with affection and respect all those screaming moments. All of them are now successful producers or presidents of production companies.

When I heard Chuck screaming at me to go down to interview Nicklaus, I was not upset. I was in seventh heaven. This was a week I had waited for since a long-ago June afternoon in 1950.

That day was a gorgeous affair that June often arranges. At the time I was working at a radio station in Allentown, Pennsylvania, making thirty-five dollars a week, going nowhere, my young career becalmed in the backwater of a thousand-watt radio station. I was frustrated and concerned that maybe broadcasting was not for me, or me for broadcasting. The glorious late-spring day depressed me more, for I felt I should be somewhere else doing something else. I was living at the YMCA, and as I came out of the bright sunlight into the dreary lobby after lunch that day I happened to look up at a small television monitor above the desk. There I saw Bobby Cruickshank putting out on the eighteenth green of the Merion Golf Club in the final round of the 1950 United States Open.

It was one of those moments when everything becomes clear and sharp. It was almost a vision. At that moment I heard myself saying, "That's where I should be today, back in my hometown at Merion, broadcasting the U.S. Open on television."

On Monday I quit my job and went home to Philadelphia. In September, I began working at the CBS-TV affiliate, and within a year I had fallen in with those coworkers who took to golf with a passion only slightly less than preteens feel for rock stars. Furthermore, George Fazio, who had lost that 1950 Open in a playoff to Ben Hogan, was a friend.

In 1954, the U.S. Open was held at Baltusrol, and on the Friday of the tournament a group of us drove over to follow Fazio. This was my first exposure to the championship, my first glimpse of Jimmy Demaret, Sam Snead, Ben Hogan, and all the other golfers we followed each week in the newspapers. It was an exhilarating experience and I thought that, along with the World Series, it was the best sporting event of the year. It was also my first taste of VIP treatment. After his round, George Fazio took us onto the terrace of the clubhouse where we mingled with the players. Sitting off to one side alone on a glider swing was a man with a withered arm. "Ed Furgol," said George. The next day Ed Furgol won the championship and I had become a U.S. Open addict.

Over the next twenty-seven years I followed the championship from afar. It was with a wistful yearning that I watched ABC telecast the Open those years and listened as Jim McKay, Dave Marr, and Bob Rosberg told the stories of those times: of Arnold's win at Cherry Hills, of his inexplicable collapse at Olympic; of Hubert

Green and the death threat at Southern Hills; of Nicklaus' fourth title at Baltusrol. So it was with a great deal of elation that I accepted an offer to join ABC Sports in 1982. Finally, I would get to work a U.S. Open.

Here I was—then—behind the 18th green at Pebble Beach. It had taken me 32 years to go from the lobby of the YMCA in Allentown, Pennsylvania, to the edge of Carmel Bay at the U.S. Open. But I had made it and now I was about to interview the best golfer of his time on the brink of a record fifth Open title.

The final round had been another Nicklaus classic. He had been three shots behind the third-round leaders Tom Watson and Bill Rogers when he teed off for the final round at 12:38 on this gray day. A bogey on the first hole had put him four back. Then he gathered himself and fired off five straight birdies before a bogey at his favorite par four in the world, the eighth, slowed his charge. But he was now running with the leaders. A birdie at fifteen tied him with Watson, and when he putted out for a closing round of sixty-nine, they shared the lead.

When Jack finished checking his scorecard, he came over to where I was waiting. We both looked down at a television monitor on the ground and watched as Watson hit his tee shot at the par-three seventeenth into the rough left of the green. While Tom was walking to his ball, I interviewed Jack. His eyes were bright and you could almost hear the adrenaline pumping but, as always, he was controlled and focused. He had played extremely well that day, he said, and would be happy to take his chances in a playoff with Watson even though at that moment Tom appeared to be in trouble. We concluded the interviews and I threw it back to Jim McKay in the tower. Then Jack and I watched as Watson chipped the ball into the cup for a birdie and a one-stroke lead in the championship. It was an incredible moment, an incredible shot. For an instant Jack sagged like a fighter who has taken a heavy body shot.

Very softly and ruefully he said, "That's the second time that son of a bitch has done that to me."

That was a reference to a long putt that Watson had made from the edge of the fifteenth hole at Turnberry in the 1977 British Open that beat Jack by one stroke for that championship. And on this day, at that moment, Nicklaus sensed that, once again, Watson had pulled off a dramatic shot that would give him the championship. Fifteen minutes later, after Watson had been presented the winning trophy, Jack was gracious and sincere in congratulating Tom on his win. You would never know if, or how much, it hurt. It was a stunning finish to my first U.S. Open.

It was difficult to top the 1982 Open for dramatics and leaderboard value. Watson almost repeated next year at Oakmont, but Larry Nelson took that one when Tom hit his approach shot over the green on the last hole. The final holes were played on Monday after a violent thunderstorm on Sunday scared everybody off the course. Nineteen eighty-four was special for me since the tournament was held at Winged Foot, where I had been a member since 1966. It was made memorable by Greg Norman, who made three of the most amazing pars I have ever seen to force a playoff with Fuzzy Zoeller. He missed the green to the left at sixteen and was on a bank in high grass; somehow he managed to pitch the ball six feet from the hole and he made the putt. At seventeen, he pushed his drive into the trees on the right. He pitched out to the fairway. His third shot landed ten feet from the cup and he converted. At eighteen, he pushed his approach shot into the grandstand. He got a free drop and his third shot left him on the collar of the green with a long downhill left to right putt. I was standing nearby waiting to do interviews, and I watched Greg as he stepped up to the putt. He and Fuzzy were tied at this point and Fuzzy had driven into the middle of the eighteenth fairway. Greg needed the putt to have a chance at a tie. He seemed fearless; there was a look of utter confidence upon him as he stroked the ball smoothly into the hole. He later said he saw a mark in the green which gave him the line. When the putt dropped the crowd at the green exploded into cheers and shouts. Fuzzy, waiting in the fairway, waved a white towel in mock surrender. It was great theater. The next day, Fuzzy shot sixty-seven to Greg's seventy-five and, as they walked up the eighteenth, Norman took out a white towel and waved it.

The Open that came closest to 1982 for me was 1986 when, for the first time in ninety years, the championship returned to Shinnecock Hills in Southampton on the eastern end of Long Island. Shinnecock was one of the founding clubs of the USGA and hosted the second U.S. Open in 1896. Its most memorable moment came when a group of professionals signed a paper saying that they would not play in the tournament if John Shippen, an African-American, and Oscar Bunn, a Shinnecock Indian, were in the field. When the paper was presented to USGA President Theodore Havermeyer, he told the group that the Championship would be held if Shippen and Bunn were the only players in the field. Everybody played the next day. However, since that July day in 1896, little attention was paid to this resort-area course. It was redone in 1931 by William Flynn and became a quiet little gem of a golf course, rolling over the hills that rise between Shinnecock and Peconic Bays.

The USGA, urged on by their Executive Director, Frank Hannigan, took a big gamble in selecting Shinnecock. Not because of the golf course—they knew it was of Open quality. They had a successful Walker Cup there in 1977. The problems lay outside the golf course. There were no hotels in the vicinity, the main access road to the club was a two-lane highway, and the club could not supply enough volunteers. Most of the problems were solved beautifully. The local police put in a sensible traffic plan. The Long Island Railroad put on special trains from New York City, and the USGA limited ticket sales to twelve thousand a day. It was the most comfortable Open I have ever seen, and everyone enjoyed themselves. The players loved the course, the spectators loved being there. I had been a member at Shinnecock for almost ten years, and I was delighted at the reception the club and the course received. It was a splendid tournament.

The first round was played in winds that gusted up to forty miles per hour. Bob Tway was the only player to shoot even par seventy. Half the field did not break seventy-five. Then the wind slackened, and the last three days were sunny and calm and the scores began to drop. On Sunday afternoon, on the back nine, there occurred the fiercest battle for a major championship I have ever witnessed. At one point, nine players were tied for the lead: Greg Norman, Lee Trevino, Ben Crenshaw, Bob Tway, Mark McCumber, Payne Stewart, Hal Sutton, Chip Beck, and Lanny Wadkins.

It was a frenetic time in the TV truck and Chuck Howard was in full flight. We went from live coverage to tape coverage trying to chronicle every player as he tied for the lead. Once we didn't know which was live and which was tape. Judy Rankin was probably the most victimized by this nine-man rush to the top. Judy was one of our on-course commentators that day and they kept moving her from one group to another. Just as she would reach the Mark McCumber group, Lee Trevino would birdie to tie, and back Judy would go to the Trevino group, only to be told to go ahead to Ben Crenshaw who had just made a three to tie for the lead. Judy must have walked thirty-six holes that afternoon.

It was a glorious hour-and-a-half of madness before Raymond Floyd birdied the sixteenth hole to get clear of the madding crowd. Pars at seventeen and eighteen gave him a 279 total, the only man in the field to break par. It was an emotional moment for this ruthless competitor, and his tears of joy and the laughter of his family gave an additional lift to this quite remarkable championship. It had been a magical week.

* * *

The saddest moment in all the Opens I broadcast occurred at Oak Hill in 1989. Tom Kite had a three-stroke lead after four holes in the final round. We had a hookup in Austin, Texas with Harvey Penick, Tom's teacher, anticipating a win for Tom and a reaction from his old mentor. But at the par-four fifth hole, Tom came apart, scoring a triple bogey seven, and he eventually tied for eighth behind Curtis Strange. It was, therefore, very gratifying to be at Pebble Beach in 1992 when Tom tamed that treacherous course on a wild and windy Sunday. The winds turned Carmel Bay into the North Atlantic in March, and on that final day only four players broke par. Kite, helped by an incredible chip-in at the par three seventh for a birdie two, beat out Jeff Sluman and Colin Montgomerie to take his first major title.

The Championship in 1994 at Oakmont was won by Ernie Els in a playoff against Colin Montgomerie and Loren Roberts. The story that year was Arnold Palmer's farewell appearance in our National Championship. He had played in thirty-two U.S. Opens, five of them at Oakmont, close to his home in Latrobe. His final walk up to the eighteenth green on Friday was an occasion that had "moment" written all over it. It was like Churchill's last appearance in the Commons, Sinatra's last concert, Ruth's last at bat. And, as with all such affairs, it was a strangely bittersweet occasion. The applause was lusty and the cheering full-throated, but there was an undercurrent of sadness as we watched the familiar figure stride up to his last Open green.

Part of that sadness was the awareness of our own mortality and the sense that an age was ending and, with it, some very good times. Arnold was so overcome he could hardly speak on television or in the pressroom. The moment was so overwhelming that the golfing press, a group that treats sentiment and clichés with utter disdain, were reduced to head shaking and throat clearing.

That was my last Open as a broadcaster. The USGA had awarded the television contract to NBC and my employment at ABC ended. It was a wonderful way to go out, with Arnold

Palmer, the man who led professional golf into the Platinum Age.

I did not have as long a run at the Open as Arnold did, but the thirteen I covered for ABC along with fourteen British Opens and nine PGA Championships were rewarding years, especially those times when Dave Marr was sitting next to me in the booth. I have been very fortunate in my golfing teachers and broadcast partners. George Fazio, Cary Middlecoff, Ken Venturi, and Dave Marr constitute an all-star faculty. They were all generous with their knowledge. I call Dave the all-time greatest shortstop. He could head off or correct mistakes I would make in a way that softened the offense to the point of making it disappear. He had a nicely developed sense of humor that he worked beautifully into his commentary and he never panicked. His soft-spoken style was a perfect match for the game. ABC Sports made one of the worst middle-management decisions in history when they cut Dave, and since then their golf coverage has never been the same.

When Dave won the PGA Championship at Ligonier in 1965, his life took a big turn. But he was ready for the changes. He came from a rich Texas golfing background, and made himself a well-read person with many interests. All of that mingled with a warm personality and sense of humor, and endeared himself to all who worked and played with him. His deep competitiveness and, at times, his temper were always controlled by his courtly manner and a genuine concern for those around him. His too-early death has left an unfillable gap in the golfing world.

It was also a treat to work with Bob Rosberg. He was the first and remains the best of the on-course commentators. He has a quick mind, sharp humor, and, glory hallelujah, speaks in complete sentences, even daring to use an adverb, thus proving that they used to teach English grammar at Stanford. He can quickly size up a shot, plotting out the distance, wind, and hazards, and when he says, "He has no shot," believe that, nine times out of ten, the player has a problem. If he happens to put the ball on the green, it is a miraculous shot.

Rossie always says what he thinks, and if you don't know him very well, you might suspect he has a negative outlook on life. Once we were all sitting around at a golf tournament and naming our favorite hotels on the Tour; one by one we nominated our choice. When it was Bob's turn, he said, "I don't know which one's the best, but I'll sure tell you the worst one."

Bob Rosberg, like Dave Marr, won one major tournament, the PGA Championship. But Rossie's record in the U.S. Open is quite sparkling. In the eleven-year period from 1959 to 1971, he had six top-ten finishes, including two seconds and a third. He lost by one stroke to Billy Casper at Winged Foot in 1959 when Casper, the most underrated player of his time, had four of the best rounds of his career. Rossie missed tying Orville Moody in 1969 by a stroke when he, one of the best putters in the game, inexplicably missed a three-footer on the final hole. He missed tying Nicklaus and Trevino at Merion in 1971 by two shots, and that one must have hurt the most.

At the eighteenth hole in the second round, his drive hit a tree and disappeared. Nobody saw where it went. He was hitting a Titleist 4, and one was found after a brief search. But as Rossie was surveying his second shot, a USGA official told him it was not the correct ball. The official had found another Titleist 4 in a ditch to the left of the fairway and declared that to be Rossie's ball. Bob argued, but to no avail. Now he had what he might often say about other players on television: "He has no shot." All he could do was get the ball up onto the fairway.

When they reached the ball on the fairway, they saw it was stained and faded, indicating that it had been in that ditch for some time. Bob finished the hole with a double-bogey six. He reported the incident, but the USGA backed their official who claimed he had seen where the ball went.

In 1963 at the Orange County Open, Rossie and Tony Lema were tied at the end of 72 holes and were on the first tee getting ready for a playoff. This was before the young man from San Leandro had become "Champagne Tony." In fact, things were not going well with him on the Tour, and he had told Rossie during the last round that if he didn't win this one, he was quitting the Tour and getting a club job. Whereupon he hooked his drive on the first hole of the playoff into the trees. They found his ball just in bounds, and from there Tony went on to win the playoff. He stayed on the Tour, and became one of its biggest stars until his death in an airplane crash in 1966.

Thirty years after that playoff, a man approached Rossie while he was working an ABC golf tournament. "You remember that playoff with Lema back at Mesa Verdi?"

"Yes," said Rossie.

"Well, you know his ball was out of bounds on that first hole of the playoff. I kicked it in. I was a great Lema fan."

"If you hadn't done that," replied Rossie, "he'd still be alive."

All those traveling years at ABC golf were enjoyable because of Dave Marr and Bob Rosberg.

I have always been attracted to the U.S. Open since that day in 1950 when I watched Bobby Cruickshank putt out at Merion. There is an aura about this championship that is hard and unsentimental. There is not the soft, green look of Augusta about the Open, nor the gray, windy aspect of the British Championship. The U.S. Open has a stern and daunting visage of narrow fairways, penal rough, and slick greens. It is usually played in hot, humid weather. The players' faces are tense and their bodies sag with fatigue. This is our national championship, and it is a grueling seventy-two-hole examination.

In 1977, ABC began eighteen-hole coverage of the third and fourth rounds of the Open. This was a new experience for me when I joined them in 1982. There is a distinct advantage in covering the leaders from the first hole; it is easier to tell the story of

123

the tournament and you don't miss any of the dramatics. In 1982, Jack Nicklaus made five birdies on the front nine and we saw every one of them and knew immediately that he was mounting a charge. At Oak Hill in 1989, we saw Tom Kite self-destruct at the fifth hole in the final round to take himself out of contention. Golf is an eighteen-hole game, and great shots or mistakes happen equally on the front and back nines. CBS has yet to show all eighteen holes at the Masters, but the time will come.

The BBC, on the other hand, covers all eighteen holes on all four days of their championship from early morning to almost close of play. It is a marathon performance, indicative of the great interest there is in Great Britain for the oldest golf championship in the World. The British Open, or "the Open," as it is called, like the Masters and the U.S. Open, has its own look and feel. The look, of course, is that of the links, those treeless tracts near the sea with hidden bunkers, large sand hills, and black-and-white flagsticks usually bending into a strong wind.

The Open Championship has given me many pleasant memories, from the first one I covered in 1982 when Tom Watson edged out a young man named Nick Price at Troon. I stood behind the 18th green under the grandstands with Tom and Linda Watson waiting to see if the young Zimbabwian could hold on to force a playoff. But the par three seventeenth hole caught him up, and Nick couldn't birdie eighteen and Watson won his fourth British Open.

The seventeenth hole has been a major factor in many British championships. At Turnberry in 1977, a birdie at the seventeenth for Watson and a par for Nicklaus was the difference. In 1984, at St. Andrews, Watson, in a tight fight with Seve Ballesteros, hit his second shot over the green at seventeen, the infamous Road hole. The ball came to rest next to a stone wall and Tom was powerless as Seve went on to claim the victory.

Then there is the seventeenth hole at Muirfield, a par five reachable in two shots. There in 1972, Lee Trevino in an almost lackadaisical manner chipped into the hole to deny Jack Nicklaus a chance at the Grand Slam. In 1987, Paul Azinger allowed Nick Faldo to steal the championship when he could not birdie the seventeenth. Nick Faldo won again at Muirfield in 1992 when John Cook did the same thing that Azinger had done, parring the hole when a birdie was needed. Faldo then made his par at 18 to win by a stroke. As he sank the putt, an audible sigh, full of anguish and sorrow, escaped him and he almost collapsed from the stress. At the presentation ceremony, in a rather indelicate manner, Faldo told the press what they could do.

For seventeenth-hole heroics, however, it is hard to beat the performance of Constantino Rocca at St. Andrews in 1995. His second shot landed on the road that gives the hole its name. Whereupon the resourceful Italian used his putter to pop the ball up onto the green from where he made par. Then, at eighteen, needing a birdie to tie John Daly, he scuffed his second shot, leaving himself a long putt through the Valley of Sin. Now trembling with frustration over his clumsy second shot, he made the putt and the gallery erupted with a sound seldom heard at the main altar of golf as the joyous Rocca flung himself onto the hallowed ground. John Daly defeated Rocca in the playoff, but the Italian's play at seventeen and eighteen will be remembered deep into the twenty-first century.

That Open was remarkable for another reason: John Daly. John added to his stature as a mythic figure during this championship. A Paul Bunyon with long hair and a metal-headed driver, he did what mythical figures are supposed to do. He slew the beast that was the windy Old Course at St. Andrews, and he did it in a manner few golfers ever try and fewer still succeed: He overpowered the oldest golf course in the world. He used his great length off the tee, a dangerous concept on these historic fields, to subdue the subtle dangers of St. Andrews.

There has been some concern that the new technology and long-hitting players are rendering the Old Course obsolete as a venue for the Open. I think not. When the wind is up, as it was for the final round in 1995, the Old Course is a formidable foe, and John Daly's win enhanced the reputation of both.

There were some bizarre incidents on our British Open broadcasts. At Royal Birkdale in 1983, Hale Irwin whiffed a putt. He completely missed the ball to lose the championship by a single stroke. I had never seen that before. As a matter of fact, I still haven't. I was anchoring the broadcast at the time and was checking some scores when Hale committed his gaffe. When I looked up, he was tapping in and I was about to give him a par on the hole, but Dave Marr, with his acute sense of anticipating that his partner was to make a mistake, put a hand on my arm and made the correct explanation.

In 1982 at Troon, Bobby Clampett set the course on fire the first two days, shooting sixty-seven, sixty-six to take a five-shot lead over the field. Then he wandered around hopelessly in the final two rounds, turning in scores of seventy-eight and seventy-seven. Bobby's face as he putted out on the final hole was that of a man in shock, drawn and ashen, looking older than his caddy. Ironically, the last time I had seen that stunned look, I was sitting next to Bobby Clampett in the Butler cabin in Augusta on an April Sunday afternoon in 1979. Bobby had finished the Masters as the low amateur and was waiting for the closing ceremonies. I was composing a piece about what a great champion Ed Sneed was going to be. Bobby and I watched in alarm as Ed bogeyed the last three holes to force a playoff, which Fuzzy Zoeller won. As Ed's winning putt refused to drop on the final hole, the look on Ed Sneed's face was the same mask of despair Bobby Clampett wore at Troon.

Telecasting the British Open is a different experience from broadcasting in the United States. First of all there is the time difference—five hours to New York, eight to California. If you are a British Open fan and live on the West Coast, you have to get up early in the morning to see the broadcast. In the past, ABC used to do a tape delay of the final two rounds, but for several years now the broadcasts have all been live, which I think is much better.

The other difference is that we use the pictures (the video) of the BBC. ABC has several cameras of its own for interviews and features, but the bulk of the action coverage comes from the BBC, and this occasionally has caused problems. The BBC, freed from the strictures of commercial programming, wanders leisurely around the golf course, covering every hole from morning till night. They focus, of course, on players from Great Britain, their colonies, and Europe. For example, we might see Tiger Woods about to hit his second shot from a gorse bush at the eleventh hole, and in the middle of his backswing, the BBC might cut away to watch the third putt of the Mid-Surrey Amateur champion at eighteen. In the early days when something like that happened, the ABC anchorman would say, "These pictures are coming to you from our good friends at the BBC."

These differences have been narrowed in recent years through the wonderful cooperation of the BBC, and the fact that good golfers come from everywhere now; today, that Mid-Surrey Amateur Champion might well be in contention. Then, too, there has always been a bit of the BBC in the ABC broadcasts. Those BBC stalwarts—first Henry Longhurst, and now Peter Alliss—lend the sound of the moors and the comfort of a tearoom in Berkshire to the shows. Their more relaxed approach to the game is most welcome.

There have been many great performances and moments in the Open Championships I have covered. Seve pumping his fist in the air at St. Andrews in 1984; Seve with his magnificent chip shot on the last hole at Royal Lytham and St. Anne's in 1988; the winning putt by Sandy Lyle after a flabby chip shot at Royal St. George's. But I think I would choose as the best performance during the years I worked at the British Open Greg Norman's victory at Royal St. George's in 1993.

That was the year we got our first glimpse of Ernie Els, the year Nick Faldo and Payne Stewart shot record sixty-threes, the year the best golfers in the world were at the top of their games in that third week in July. On Monday and Tuesday, the golf course was hard and bouncy and the players all looked troubled during the practice rounds. Then, on Tuesday evening, it began to rain and the rain continued through Wednesday. The result was to cool down the fairways and to soften the greens. Presenting a professional golfer with soft greens is the greatest blessing you can bestow upon him. When the greens are soft, professional golfers smile and tell jokes, buy presents for their wives and talk engagingly to the media.

So, on Thursday, the excitement began as Greg Norman ripped off five straight birdies on his way to a sixty-six and a tie for the lead with Peter Senior of Australia, Mark Calcavecchia and Fuzzy Zoeller. On Friday, Nick Faldo got in the middle of things with that sixty-three and, by Saturday night, the leader board was crowded with the best golfers in the world. Bernhard Langer led at two hundred with Faldo, Norman, Pavin, Els, Couples, and Price right behind.

Sunday the wind was up and the course was returning to its hard, fast condition. And here is where Greg Norman stepped out. Playing steadily and putting beautifully, the Australian held everyone at bay. When Langer hit his drive out of bounds at fourteen, it was Greg's tournament to win or lose. And win it he did. This time, no one holed out a sand shot on him, no one chipped into the hole. This time it was solid golf on Norman's part, an inexorable march down those five final holes to the championship. He beat the best golfers in the world playing at their best that week down by the shores of Sandwich Bay.

All of the venues for the British Open have glorious golf courses, but few have enough first-class accommodations for the invasion of spectators and media that descend upon this oldest and most commercial of our major championships. St. Andrews is able to house most of us comfortably, and Muirfield, too, and, if you can afford it and can get a reservation, there is nothing better than the great white hotel at Turnberry. But, elsewhere, the lodgings are less than alluring, especially to the spoiled American. You might find yourself in one of those hotels made out of three rowhouses in the Albert Road in Blackpool. It will have a romantic name like Le Mediterrania, be fully licensed, full of people wearing tank tops and tattoos, the walls a dirty tan, the rug bile green, and the bathrooms down the hall.

We were able to avoid this problem several times by renting private homes for the week. Depending on the number of bedrooms, four or five couples would share the cost, and over the years we've stayed in everything from comfortable bed and breakfasts and stately homes to minicastles. Our first venture was in 1977, the year of the great Watson–Nicklaus battle at Turnberry. The home was almost a castle and was owned by a Scottish nobleman. It was about forty-five minutes down the coast from the golf course in Cairn Ryan. It was as comfortable as an old golf glove. It also came with a marvelous cook. We lived like royalty that week. The most fascinating and enjoyable of the places we rented over the years was down among the barley and wheat fields of Kent when the Open was held at Royal St. George's. In 1985, the mother of all den mothers, June Jenkins, helpmate of Dan Jenkins, found an estate that dated back to Elizabethan times. Knowlton Court is a manor house deep in the countryside, with six hundred acres of farmland, cattle and sheep, just twenty minutes from the golf course. It is owned by the Fox-Pitt family, descendants of Charles Fox and William Pitt, the British statesmen and political rivals. Here, on this historic estate, we had a taste of a lifestyle that is fast disappearing. There were wonderful half-day side trips to take from Knowlton Court: up to Canterbury to the cathedral, or a ferry ride across the channel to France and lunch at Boulougne or Calais.

When the Open returned to St. George's in 1993, June again

arranged for a stay at Knowlton Court. It hadn't changed, and we had another weeklong house party built around the golf tournament. This time we visited Leeds Castle and had a pub lunch in the village of Chilleton and went over to Sissinghurst Castle to see the magnificent gardens planted by Sir Harold Nicolson and Vita Sackville-West, in which she and her friends sat at lunch on the afternoon of September 23, 1940, as the R.A.F. knocked the German Luftwaffe from the skies above them.

That year, they were hard at work on the tunnel under the English Channel that now connects Britain with France. We went down to Folkestone to see the construction. There was a kiosk there with literature on the project. Someone noticed in one of the pamphlets that the machine that burrowed under the channel to form the tunnel was invented by a man named Whitaker. It was called The Great Whitaker Boring Machine. I'm still hearing about that.

Next to St. Andrews, Royal St. George's is my favorite site for the British Open. That is due in great part to Knowlton Court, but also to the Kentish countryside and the abundance of history, golfing and otherwise, that lies about. The Open Championship has visited this part of England many times, at Deal, at Prince's, and at Royal St. George's, which returned to the rota in 1981 after a thirty-two-year absence. Prince's, which abuts Royal St. George's, was the site of a fascinating golf/war story that Ben Wright told me. This was Ben's version:

Laddie Lucas was one of England's outstanding amateur golfers, a lefthander and Walker Cup player who became an R.A.F. fighter pilot during World War II. His spitfire was hit one day over France, and he turned and headed for England. He could not make it back to his base but he thought he could land the plane on one of the fairways at Prince's, a course he knew by heart. He managed to crash land on the course, climbed out relatively unhurt, then went into the clubhouse and had tea with his father who was the secretary of the club.

When I heard Ben tell the story I thought it was a great yarn, one that might have been in one of those Hollywood war movies with C. Aubry Smith and Reginald Gardner. A stiff upper lip, British pluck, understated "cream or lemon," and all that. I knew that most English golfers knew the story, but Americans might not have heard it, so I asked Terry Jastrow if I could do the piece for the telecast in 1993. He said yes, so over to Prince's I went with producer Jim Walton and a camera crew to tape the story on the site where Lucas had crashed his plane. We introduced ourselves to the secretary of the club and told him we would like to do the Lucas story. "Too bad, you just missed him," said the secretary. "He was here yesterday."

Oh, damn, I thought, what a great opportunity we missed. It would have been so right to have Mr. Lucas tell the story himself.

"Is he still around?" I asked.

"No," said the secretary. "He went home. Can I help you?"

"Well, we'd like to set up our camera at the spot where Mr. Lucas crashed his plane."

"That might be difficult," said the secretary.

"Why, didn't he land on the fairway?"

"No," said the secretary. "Suppose you tell me the story you want to do."

So I told him the tale as Ben Wright had told me, ending with "and he went into the clubhouse and he had tea with his father who was secretary of the club."

"Ahhh," said the secretary. "Not quite."

"Not quite?"

"No. Mr. Lucas' father had been secretary here, but Prince's was closed during the war. Used it for artillery practice."

With a sinking feeling, I asked, "Didn't Mr. Lucas land his plane on one of the fairways?"

"Oh," the secretary replied. "He tried. He wanted to land on the fifth fairway over there but he overshot it by about half a mile and landed out there near those trees just off the course."

My heart sank even further.

"As he was being helped out of the cockpit, he said, 'Never could hit that fairway with a driver, don't know why I thought I could hit it with an airplane.'"

Ah, a punch line! The true story was as good as or better than the Wright version. And that's the way we told it, standing in the rain on the terrace of the clubhouse and gesturing to the fifth fairway and to the place where the plane had crashed. If only we had been there a day earlier.

In retrospect, I should have known something was amiss in Ben's version. I knew that Prince's was closed during the war because of a quote from Lord Barbizon, who, when told that Prince's was to be used as an artillery range, shuddered and said, "That's like throwing darts at the Mona Lisa."

Prince's was also the place where the sand wedge was introduced. In 1932, Gene Sarazen brought his new invention to Prince's for the British Open. He put it upside down in his golf bag to avoid detection in case it was illegal. It wasn't. Gene won the Open and the wedge became a friend to man.

Yes, there is an abundance of stories along this stretch of Kentish coast and weather that varies from that of "obscene malignity," as one St. George's member put it, to a fine spring day, "with the sun shining on the waters of Pegwell Bay and lighting up the white cliffs in the distance, it is nearly my idea of heaven as to be attained on any earthy links," as Bernard Darwin put it.

When the Championship is played at Muirfield, outside Edinburgh, you are presented the opportunity to sample Scottish golf at its best. Muirfield may be the finest course on the rota. There is not a single tree to be seen and the holes are routed so the wind helps on some and is against on others. Since the course lies on the Firth of Forth, the wind is usually present. The first nine holes proceed clockwise, the last nine counterclockwise, and bunkers abound. It is a handsome and graceful place, marred only in past years by a couple of secretaries who were as rude as clerks in a Gucci store. For years, Muirfield's secretary was a retired English officer named Paddy Hamner who had an Olympian talent for boorishness, if all the stories about him are true. His churlish behavior to Americans wanting to play Muirfield is legendary. I never met the man, but his reputation as a Charlie Dickens villain was enhanced by a story Jo Anne Carner told me.

She and her husband Don Carner and Carol Jo Skala and her husband were on a golfing holiday in Scotland and Muirfield was their last stop. They had arranged to play it on the day they were flying back home.

"We arrived at the club," said Jo Anne, "and Paddy Hamner greeted us, invited the men into the clubhouse to change shoes, while Carol and I changed in the parking lot. We were running a little late when we reached the seventeenth hole and I lost a ball in the rough. We didn't want to miss our plane. I knew Hamner was watching us through his binoculars, so I turned my back and dropped another ball down the front of my body. After walking around a few seconds, I said, 'Here it is' and played on in.

"When we had finished the eighteenth, the men were invited into the clubhouse for a drink. Carol and I changed our shoes in the parking lot. The men came out with the secretary and we said goodbye. As we were getting into the car, Mr. Hamner asked me what I had shot. 'Seventy-five,' I said. Then, with almost a leer, he said, 'Pity about the ball at seventeen, wasn't it?' "

Mr. Hamner's successor had that same streak in him. At the Open in 1987, I was standing in front of the Secretary's office with a group of golf writers talking with Paul Azinger. Paul was having a wonderful tournament; he almost won it, coming up short at the par five seventeenth hole on Sunday and losing by one shot to Nick Faldo. There we were talking away with Paul when I felt a sharp jab and a push in my back. I turned around to see the Secretary, a small bespectacled man in brown, snarling loudly, "Would you mind not coffee-klatching in front of my office."

I may have missed a twinkle in his eye, but I truly feel this was the unreconstructed arrogance of the Empire in full flower. And I was appalled that a speaker of the Queen's English had stooped so low as to make a verb out of a noun.

Despite nonsense of this kind from ill-mannered Secretaries of the Honorable Company of Edinburgh Golfers, Muirfield still ranks just behind St. Andrews and St. George's among my favorite venues for the Open.

St. Andrews is the number one choice simply because it is an awesome place like Mecca, the Vatican, or Independence Hall. It is quite possible that Shakespeare did not write all those plays, and it is just as possible that golf did not originate in Scotland. However, there is no doubt that the Scots took the game as their own. St. Andrews was not the first organizer of the game; that honor goes to the Gentleman Golfers of Edinburgh who wrote the first rules in 1744. Ten years later St. Andrews adopted the same rules and, since then, it has been the official center of the game. Golf has been in St. Andrews at least since the fifteenth century and the Links of the Old Course is the game's eldest golf course. It was formed by wind and rain and the ministrations of the R and A. The course is older than Shakespeare, the piano, and the printing press. It grew out of ninety-five acres of sandy soil by the North Sea and the River Eden and when you first see it you wonder what all the fuss is about. The second time you play it you think it just might do, and the third time you are a committed convert.

You cherish the memory of each bunker, of the Road Hole, of the Swilcan Bern and the King William IV Bridge that was built before Columbus sailed for India. The Old Course is ancient, but when she dances with the wind she is as stiff a challenge to today's high-technology millionaires as it was to the gutta percha players of the last century and to the shepherds before them.

St. Andrews is a remarkable place. It has been a university town since the Middle Ages and today the pursuits of academia along with the lore of the ancient game give off a tranquil air that softens its violent history. The origins of St. Andrews are as indistinct as the origins of the game of golf, but it grew into the educational and ecclesiastical capital of Scotland though its history is as violent as a Sylvester Stallone movie. When Mary, Queen of Scots, and her subjects were bunting the ball around the Links of St. Andrews, the Catholics and Protestants were killing each other in the name of God and heresy. Burnings at the stake and other delightful pastimes were held frequently, supervised by whatever religious group was in power at the time. And then it was off for a round of golf on the links, but never on the Sabbath.

It was a happy coincidence for me that the first British Open I attended was at St. Andrews. It was in 1970, and I was covering the United States track team in Europe. I was able to get away for the weekend of the championship. I came into St. Andrews as most people do, on the road from Cupar. Ahead are the eighteenth fairway and the stone clubhouse of the R and A with the town stretching away to the right. That day it was a surprising sight, not quite like the old prints of the same scene. Down the right side of the first fairway was a tall grandstand, the first I had ever seen at a golf tournament except for a much smaller one at the fifteenth green at Augusta National. Off to the left was a collection of small tents dominated by one large tent with flags on top snapping in the breeze. I remember thinking at the time that it looked like the English camp on the eve of the battle of Agincourt. This was my first introduction to corporate tents, and it has always amazed me that it was our British cousins of the staid and proper R and A that introduced heavy commerce to national golf championships.

The big tent turned out to be the Exhibition Hall, in which was displayed everything that had to do with golf and some things that did not. There were all kinds of golf equipment, golf clothes, golf destination travel booths, books, paintings, lawn mowers, and even baubles from the Royal Family's jeweler, Gerards. The tent was as crowded as a department store in Christmas week, and business was brisk. The Exhibition tent was and is great fun, and perhaps is as much a symbol of this championship as the memory of Vardon, Braid, and Taylor.

Nearby is a collection of concession tents laid out like a small village, with streets named after famous golfers. The air is filled with the smell of frying hamburgers and onions. It looks more like the midway of a carnival than the setting for a golf tournament. There is one tent that dispenses nothing but champagne; it is filled to overflowing. There are banks, airline offices, open bars, and clothing outlets. The entire scene would make an excellent setting for a P. D. James murder mystery.

That first British Open was a cultural shock, but in the years since, I have grown not only to accept the garish trappings but to sincerely enjoy the entire makeup of this championship. Despite all the distractions, the R and A manages to isolate the tournament, and for those that are interested in golf there is ample space to enjoy the competition.

The full force of the Old Course hits you as you make the turn at the twelfth hole and head back toward the town. In front of you rises the skyline of St. Andrews punctuated by the spires and towers of many churches, some of which are used to line up tee shots on the homeward holes. One of those towers is that of the Hope Park Church. In 1995, its tower was desperately in need of repairs; the Pastor wrote to the R and A saying that since the tower had served as a beacon for generations of St. Andrews' golfers, the R and A might want to help with the restoration. The R and A responded generously and enthusiastically, and the Hope Park Church Tower will remain as an aiming point for future generations of golfers trying to avoid the treacherous bunkers that are hidden from the tee just as their forefathers did a hundred years ago.

There is a comfortable feeling about St. Andrews. The town comes to you peacefully as you watch the scarlet-robed students moving through the streets, or visit the busy bookstores and tea shops. It would be paradise, if it weren't for the winters.

* * *

I have often had an ambivalent attitude toward the PGA, the last of the four Major Championships. It began life in 1916, about the time 700,000 soldiers were killed in the battle of the Somme and more than a million in the Battle of Verdun in what was called the Great War, or World War I, or the War to End All Wars. The championship was played at Siwanoy Country Club in Bronxville, New York, where James Barnes defeated Jock Hutchinson one up. For the next forty years, this championship would be the centerpiece of the PGA of America, a match-play championship that distinguished itself from other tournaments that were contested at stroke play. Match play is the essence of golf, the game most amateurs play. It is not as stringent as stroke play, where one triple bogey can ruin your day. Match play is a series of eighteen different contests, each hole a chance for a victory, each hole a chance to get even. Match play is exciting, as Tiger Woods demonstrated in winning his three Amateur titles, and it is more fun than stroke play. I remember Ed Seay telling me a story at the British Open in 1995. He had just come back from Ireland where he was checking on a golf course he had built for the Arnold Palmer Company.

"I was standing with the owner on this par-three hole," Ed said, "and the wind was blowing the rain sideways. I turned to the owner and said, 'I'll have to move this tee.' 'Why,' he asked. 'Well,' I said, 'on a day like this, you could score a twelve on this hole.' 'Ah,' said the owner, with a smile. "That beats a thirteen, doesn't it?' " And that is the joy of match play.

But match play and television do not get along. A match could last for eleven holes or twenty-seven holes and the strictures of network schedules could not permit that. The PGA decided to move with the TV times and, in 1958, they changed from match play to stroke play. The tournament lost its uniqueness but gained exposure. I still hope that one day the Championship will return to match play, especially now that the TV landscape is changing. In the meantime, I look fondly on the PGA because it was a milestone for me. The 1962 edition at Aronomink Golf Club was the first golf telecast I did, the beginning of a thirty-three-year run of tournaments. In 1965, ABC secured the rights for the PGA, and I did not meet up with it again until 1982 when I moved to that network from CBS. I covered nine PGA Championships for ABC until CBS took the tournament back in 1991.

In 1986, we saw the most dramatic ending of a major golf tournament in the decade when Bob Tway holed his sand shot on the final hole to beat Greg Norman at Inverness. It was a stunning moment and one that enriched this championship. Despite that and other remarkable moments, the PGA Championship of 1990 is the big one, and one of the most important tournaments in American golf. That championship was played at Shoal Creek near Birmingham, Alabama, and it changed the texture of golf in the United States.

Shoal Creek was the pet project of a successful Alabama businessman named Hall Thompson. He had built a handsome golf club around Shoal Creek in the rolling, pine tree countryside outside Birmingham. The PGA Championship was held there in 1984, as Lee Trevino won his second PGA title. Aside from the oppressive Alabama heat and thunderstorms that delayed play, the tournament went off without incident. The PGA returned to Shoal Creek six years later, and this time the thunder and lightning that struck had nothing to do with the weather.

Hall Thompson was asked during a newspaper interview prior to the tournament about the restrictions against African-Americans at Shoal Creek. Mr. Thompson replied that his club would not be pressured into accepting "the blacks." How wrong he was. The interview went national, and almost overnight changes that seemed unattainable were made. All of a sudden, some corporations did not want to be associated with a golf tournament held at a club with exclusionary rules. Led by IBM, several sponsors of the telecast pulled out, and both ESPN and ABC were the poorer for it. Now with the possibility that the PGA would move the tournament from Shoal Creek, an African-American businessman,

Louis Wille, was quickly accepted as a member, and the tournament went on as scheduled.

These restrictive measures at golf clubs have always been one of the vulnerable areas of how golf has been managed in this country. They go back to the formation of the first golf clubs in Scotland in the mid-eighteenth century. These clubs were made up mostly of Freemasons, members of the army, doctors, and the clergy. They had their secret rites, uniforms, and initiation ceremonies. When the game came to America, it came with those traditions and the trappings of wealth and privilege. Even the golf professional was looked upon as inferior.

The spirit that marked the refusal of Theodore Havermeyer of the USGA to expel John Shippen and Oscar Bunn from the 1896 U.S. Open was sadly lost somewhere in the beginning of the century when golf clubs began proliferating across America. No Jews or Blacks was the implicit and, sometimes, explicit rule. Often women were excluded. Jewish golfers were the first to respond to this discrimination; they went out and built their own clubs, usually bigger and better than the ones that would not admit them, all with great kitchens. And when they invited their goyim friends to play, they were the perfect hosts.

The African-Americans could not do the same thing because there wasn't a large enough middle class with the desire to play golf. One of the groups most hurt by these restrictions was the black golf professionals. Incredibly, until 1961 the PGA's constitution had a "Caucasians Only" clause. Until then, African-American professionals had to play on the lightly financed Black Tour, or become private professionals; for years Charley Sifford and Ted Rhodes labored as teacher-companions to Joe Louis and Billy Eckstine.

There was one African-American golfer whose dream to play on the regular tour burned so intensely it consumed him. Bill Spiller learned to play golf while working as a red cap at Union Station in Los Angeles. He became one of the stars on the black pro circuit. In 1948, he was shown the "Caucasian Only" rule in the PGA constitution by a PGA official and was disqualified from a tournament in California. Almost immediately, Spiller and Ted Rhodes sued the PGA for $250,000. The PGA said they would end their discriminatory tactics if Spiller would drop the lawsuit. He did, much to his chagrin. The PGA did not change the "Caucasian Only" membership clause; it merely changed the name of the tournaments to "Invitational," instead of "Open," and the discrimination continued. Not one of the PGA's best moments.

In 1952, there was a charity tournament in San Diego to which Spiller and four other African-Americans had been invited, including former heavyweight champion Joe Louis. At the last minute, the PGA disqualified them on the pretense that they did not have their player's cards. That atrocious act by the PGA inspired Spiller's finest hour: He broke into a PGA meeting from which he had been barred and told them what he thought of their actions. Then he stood on the first tee, an enraged Horatio, refusing to let the tournament begin.

The PGA relented somewhat. They wrote a clause allowing African-Americans to play in PGA events if invited by the sponsors. This was a breakthrough, small but significant. However, the "Caucasian Only" rule stayed on the books. It was ten years after San Diego before the clause was lifted from the PGA constitution, and again it was Bill Spiller and Charley Sifford who forced the issue.

By 1960, Spiller's eyesight had deteriorated to such an extent that he could no longer play golf. He became a caddie at the Hillcrest Country Club in Los Angeles. One day he told a member that he was banned from playing in PGA events because of the "Caucasian Only" clause. The member, Harvey Bravermann, told his friend, California's Attorney General Mosk, who had received a complaint from Charley Sifford at about the same time. Mosk threatened legal action against the PGA, who immediately moved the site of the 1962 PGA Championship from the Brentwood Country Club in California to the Aronomink Country Club outside Philadelphia.

In 1961, faced with growing legal challenges, the PGA finally eliminated the clause from its constitution. Bill Spiller was a man who wanted to play professional golf, and when he was denied that opportunity because of the color of his skin, he became an angry man. That anger drove him to break golf's color barrier, not with the heroic patience of Jackie Robinson, nor the elegant performances of Arthur Ashe, but with a scorching passion he could not and would not hide. He made more than a few enemies with his abrasive style, but he did make a difference. It would be the right thing if the PGA would memorialize Bill Spiller and his bittersweet victory.

When the "Caucasian Only" clause was eliminated from the PGA constitution, it was too late for Ted Rhodes, whom most considered to be the best African-American golfer. It was too late, too, for the cross-handed wizard Harold Wheeler of Philadelphia, and for Zeke Hartsfield of Atlanta. But it was not quite too late for Charley Sifford. Charley was able to achieve more than any of those early African-American golfers. Charley suffered the indignities a little more quietly than Bill Spiller, but no less painfully, and fought hard for the chance to play golf for a living. He earned the respect of most of the players on the tour because of his talent and his personality. Charley has never given up the fight.

Finally, in 1967, Charley won at Hartford. But he was still not invited to play in the Masters. In 1970, Pete Brown won at San Diego but he, too, was not invited to the Masters. In 1971, under growing pressure, the Masters declared that anyone who won a PGA Tour event in the fifty-one weeks from the end of one Masters to the beginning of the next would receive an invitation. A breakthrough, but too late for Charley and Pete and others. Lee Elder was the first African-American to play at Augusta, invited because he won the Monsanto Open in 1974.

But while things were improving slightly on the professional level, the membership at most American golf clubs was still restricted. Many of the leaders of the American golfing establishment, including members of the press and TV, belonged to these clubs. Many of us thought we could change these restrictive policies by working from within, but we were so thrilled to have been accepted into this elite world that when someone said, "Don't make waves; don't make trouble," we didn't make waves and we didn't make trouble. We were not completely silent, but our efforts to change the status quo were weak and ineffectual.

Then came Shoal Creek, and shortly the doors to these clubs were pushed ajar. The USGA and the PGA Tour and the PGA immediately issued statements saying they would play no tournament at a club that discriminated against race, religion, or gender. Almost all of our historic Open clubs and those on the PGA Tour and Augusta National immediately accepted at least one minority member. It would have been a happy story if these changes had been made because the hearts of men had changed. But it was corporate America, the main support of professional golf, that brought these changes about. Some of our large companies often bring about good things, especially if their bottom line is threatened. Shoal Creek was a textbook example of exerting pressure where it does the most good.

In the nine years since, more and more minorities have joined these once restricted clubs and those institutions have not crumbled. Indeed, they have flourished.

One of my most memorable moments in broadcasting the PGA Championship occurred at Riviera in 1983. Hal Sutton edged Jack Nicklaus by one stroke, and once again I stood behind an eighteenth green with Nicklaus. This time we watched Hal Sutton putt out for the win. I began the interview with Jack by saying, "We've got to stop meeting like this." It was the fourth time he had finished second in the PGA, and once again he masked whatever disappointment he felt at missing a record Sixth Championship and gave an insightful and pleasant interview. Those two Nicklaus interviews, at Pebble Beach at the U.S. Open and at Riviera at the PGA Championship, are my own personal bookends to the major championships.

The four major championships are becoming more vulnerable each year from two fronts. One is the tremendous increase in purses in the nonmajor tournaments which, to the dim-witted, will make winning any of the majors less attractive. The other threat is more vital. Golf is now a force around the world. A world tour is coming, and it seems a bit awkward that three of the four major tournaments are in the United States. I hope that the answer will be to add other majors rather than to diminish the present ones. For the last fifty years, the Masters, the U.S. and British Opens, and the PGA Championships have defined the game and its greatest players. Every sport needs these special competitions. They are what give these games the history and tradition without which they would be merely physical exercises.

Down, but not kaput, in
Germany in 1945—thanks
to Hymie Haas's clutch shot
at Omaha Beach.

Pushing paint in Philadelphia on my ten-minute sports show. Felton-
Sibley's hard, durable qualities nearly brought my career to a horrible
finish.

With Frank Chirkinian and Ken Venturi at the Firestone Country Club in Akron for the *CBS Golf Classic*. We've just finished for the day and are about to play and watch Venturi hit those knockdown eight irons that take two bounces and spin right.

Eight A.M. on the first tee at Firestone's south course. Next to Ken Venturi is Tommy Aaron and his partner Charles Coody, about to play Don January and Julius Boros. The pair that won the Finals would split $70,000—about what Greg Norman gets for a corporate outing today.

With "The Doc" on one of those sparkling California mornings. Cary Middlecoff made the job a pleasure, and his knowledge of the game, which he shared with me, helped me on my happy journey through the world of professional golf.

In the basement of the Butler Cabin at Augusta, describing the hole I was covering that year. It wasn't the eighteenth and there wasn't a mob scene in sight.

With my spotter and Jim Jensen at the eighteenth hole at Augusta National. As you can see, in the early afternoon, the crowd is the best behaved gallery in golf.

My first British Open at St. Andrews in 1970, inside the ropes with Dan Jenkins and Roone Arledge. Roone is explaining to us how all the bunkers on the Old Course got their names. Dan later put a cartoon balloon on Roone, which has him saying, "And now there's this interesting story about Mrs. Cheepe's Bosom."

Dan Jenkins accepting the Jerry Danford Award in Mike Manuche's Restaurant. *Left to right:* Jack Dolph, John McDonough, and Gene Peterson of CBS Sports; Dan; Bob Drum; Pat Summerall; and, with his C.C. Old Fashioned with a splash, Bill Brendle, the greatest ticket man in sports. Little did I know, but next year it would be my turn to accept the "coveted" award.

Canonero II's Preakness. *Left to right:* Juan Arias (white jacket), the trainer; Edgar Caibett, the owner; Gustavo Avila, the jockey; and, just about to wrest the microphone from me, the interpreter shouting fluent Spanish. Frank Wright's head can be seen over my left shoulder next to the camera-conscious policeman.

Secretariat, the greatest athlete I ever saw. He had it all: speed, power, stamina, an amazing heart, and, I think, a sense of how special he was. He was also the best-looking athlete I ever saw.

This picture explains Eddie Arcaro as well as anything can. We laughed a lot like we're doing here at the Kentucky Derby the year after a fire almost wiped out Churchill Downs.

With Willie Morris on his fiftieth birthday in Oxford, Mississippi. Aside from his considerable literary achievements, Willie was the best softball manager I ever played under, attributing his great success to "Jeffersonian Democracy and a strong double play."

One of my many great moments with Dave Marr. By the look on our two faces, I would think he has just saved me from another gaffe.

The ABC golf announcers at the seventeenth—the Road Hole—at St. Andrews on the morning of Nick Faldo's second British Open win. *Left to right:* Jerry Pate, Bob Rosburg, Roger Twibell, Dave Marr, Ed Sneed, Jim McKay, and Frank Hannigan (looking at me as if I had just been traded to the Fox Network).

Here I am tucked into the back of the Chevrolet Camaro Z-28 pace car at the 1982 Indy 500. Driver Jim Rathman and I are about to take a lonely ride around the Old Brickyard.

At the Sammy Davis, Jr., Greater Hartford Open at the Wethersfield Country Club. Sammy was funny and generous to a fault. We all miss the "Candy Man."

On the Cresta. Already I am out of control. Notice the splayed-out right foot, instead of being at a straight 90-degree angle. Bad form but, thankfully, not fatal.

With Justin Leonard and David Duval at a Winged Foot dinner honoring the All Americans. Even then, these two Walker Cup players had the look of champions about them.

Raymond Floyd and Jack Nicklaus at the party we threw the Tuesday before the 1986 Open at Shinnecock Hills. We invited twenty-five players, but only three attended: Floyd (who finished 1st), Lanny Wadkins (2nd), and Jack (8th).

Left to right: Don Dunphy, myself, Curt Gowdy, and the Great DiMaggio at the American Sportscasters Association dinner, April 23, 1998. The honor of being inducted into the Sportscasters Hall of Fame was enhanced by the presence of the Yankee Clipper.

Made for TV

"It was like touring Independence Hall with Thomas Jefferson."

At the far end of the spectrum from the major golf championships are the made-for-TV entertainments. They are a tradition that goes back to the primitive days of television of the 1950s, and reached prominence with *Shell's Wonderful World of Golf* and the *CBS Golf Classic* in the 1960s. When the PGA tour expanded, the TV shows faded away until the emergence of the Skins Game in 1983. That gave impetus to a new generation of made-for-TV golf shows. These have enabled players to earn extraordinary amounts of money in November and December after the Tour's official finale, the Tour Championship at the end of October.

Since I had been part of the *CBS Golf Classic* at the beginning of my golfing broadcast days, it was very pleasing, near the end of my career, to be part of the new *Shell's Wonderful World of Golf* series. The new edition has featured a happy combination of old, classic courses and new modern-day wonders that have been bull-dozed out of lava rock, wetlands, and deserts.

The first of the new series was a match between Raymond Floyd and Fred Couples at Pete Dye's Teeth of the Dog at Casa de Campo in the Dominican Republic. It is a marvelous golf course with dramatic holes along the shoreline and rather modest carries on some holes, from the tee to the fairway. I play a Pete Dye course in the California desert where the carries are 170 yards or more, an impossible task for me. But at Casa de Campo, the distances are more like 125 yards, a much friendlier environment. When I mentioned this to Pete, he said, "I built this course before graphite."

And so, fellow short hitters, we are being punished, not by golf-course designers, but by graphite.

The Shell series showed off places like the Teeth of the Dog and the Medalist Golf Club in Hobe Sound, Florida, and Jack Nicklaus's Manele Bay course on Lanai, along with Pebble Beach, Pinehurst No. 2, and the Old Course at St. Andrews. At Pebble Beach we had a rematch of the 1982 U.S. Open, Tom Watson against Jack Nicklaus. Tom didn't chip the ball into the hole at the seventeenth, but he did at the eighth hole. Nicklaus came within an inch of an ace at the twelfth hole. Watching these two old warriors clash again at this splendid golf course on a glorious, clear day was a treat beyond special.

The drowsy village of Pinehurst, North Carolina, is St. Andrews with warmer weather. Golf is the reason for its being, and the spirit of the game floats above the town like a friendly angel. Golf is everywhere in Pinehurst; it is in the streets, in the hotels, the restaurants, and the shops. It was the home of Donald Ross, golf professional and golf-course designer extraordinaire. He learned his trade from old Tom Morris at St. Andrews and at

Royal Dornoch in Scotland. There is a real bond between Pinehurst and St. Andrews as well as a spiritual one. Pinehurst No. 2 is considered the best of Ross's considerable output, and it was a natural venue for *Shell's Wonderful World of Golf*. On this particular day to this exceptional golf course in this remarkable village came the two icons of modern golf—Arnold Palmer and Jack Nicklaus.

Tee time for their match was 10:00 A.M. It was a gray, cool morning as director Jim Walton and I walked down to the course from the hotel at 8:00 A.M., but already the town was astir. The practice tee and putting green were surrounded by people. There were long lines in front of the coffee and Danish stations. By ten o'clock, six thousand people had come out to watch the match, and the town was deserted. I couldn't help but think how much like St. Andrews Pinehurst truly is. This was akin to the 1929 final of the British Women's Amateur between Joyce Wethered of England and Glenna Collett of the United States at the Old Course, when the whole town came out to watch. Or, in 1936, when Bob Jones played a friendly match at the Old Course and, again, all activity in St. Andrews ceased. The six thousand people that day at Pinehurst gave the affair a meaning far beyond the match itself. It was a thank-you note to these two players for what they have meant to the game.

The Old Course at St. Andrews was the site of a match between those two Ryder Cup rivals, Paul Azinger and Seve Ballesteros. It was a close competitive game until Seve hit his drive out of bounds at the sixteenth hole and Azinger claimed the prize. We taped the match on the Sunday before the Open Championship, which was being played at St. Andrews that year. We started late in the afternoon. The sun does not set until after ten o'clock at St. Andrews in July, and in that long summer evening, the Old Course and the town never looked better. The late sun deepened the green of the grass and cast an amber light over the old gray town. It is these long summer evenings that help the

147

Scots get through those long winter nights, and this particular one was worth a week in January. In addition, Ben Crenshaw, the historian and golfer, replaced Dave Marr on this show. Walking the Old Course with Crenshaw was like touring Independence Hall with Thomas Jefferson.

A few hours north of St. Andrews, up near the roof of Scotland, is the old summer home of Andrew Carnegie, Skibo Castle. It has been transformed into a luxurious private club known as the Carnegie Club at Skibo. It is a trip back to the turn of the century when Carnegie entertained the crowned heads of Europe and the leaders of nations. Carnegie's old golf course has been redone by David Steele and is a stiff test. On the day Greg Norman played Couples in a Shell match, the wind was blowing forty miles an hour and gusting even higher. The two players soldiered on, with Freddy providing the heroics with a pair of two-iron shots directly into the wind that ended up within eight feet of the hole. It was a Scottish memory to keep.

The Merrill Lynch Shootout Championship was another of those year-end golfing entertainments. There are ten shootouts held at different PGA tour events throughout the year, and the ten winners meet for the championship. Ten players begin on the first hole. The player with the highest score is eliminated until only one is left. If there is more than one high score on the hole, a shootout comes in the form of a pitch shot, bunker shot, chip, or a putt, with the player farthest from the hole eliminated.

Todd Lincoln managed the Shootout for Merrill Lynch, and he had great imagination in selecting the venues for the championships. It was held on Fisher Island off the shores of Miami, and at Coeur d'Alene, Idaho, where there is a par three with an island green reached by boat, and whose yardage can be changed, not by moving tee markers, but by moving the island green. The final three years of the Shootout, Todd brought the championship to the Mid Ocean Club in Bermuda. This Charles MacDonald gem was unknown to the younger generation of professional golfers, and it was delightful to see them react enthusiastically to this civilized island and this splendid, old-fashioned golf course.

The most memorable of the shootout championships was in 1987 at Ventana Canyon in Tucson, Arizona. It had nothing to do with the golf or the outstanding Tom Fazio course. That was the day the stock market plunged 508 points, and the rush from the hotel to the airport by the Merrill Lynch people and their clients was, well, awesome.

The most ambitious and daring of these postseason productions was called the *Chrysler 18 Holes of Championship Golf.* The logistics of the format demanded the timing of a perfect golf swing and the planning expertise of a military invasion. The eighteen holes were on eighteen different courses spread across the United States, and they had to be played in four days. Four golfers, Fuzzy Zoeller, John Daly, Tom Kite, and Davis Love, III, played the eighteen at stroke play. The first nine holes were taped on a Monday and Tuesday, the second nine holes on the following Monday and Tuesday. This was the schedule:

Day One: 7:30 A.M. Play sixteenth hole at Oakland Hills, Birmingham, Michigan. After last putt, vans take players and crew to Detroit Airport. Fly to Chicago's Midway Airport. Vans transport players and crew to the Olympia Fields Country Club to play the par-four fourteenth hole on the North Course. From there, a ride to Cog Hill Golf and Country Club for lunch. Golfers play the par-three sixth hole on the Dubsdread Course. Van to Medinah Country Club and the challenge of the par-four sixteenth hole on Course No. 3. To the airport and a flight to Jacksonville, Florida.

Day Two: 7:30 A.M. Play par-three seventeenth hole at Tournament Players Club at Sawgrass. Van to airport for flight to Hilton Head, South Carolina. Play eighteenth hole at Harbor Town Golf Links, van to Long Cove for the par-five third hole. Then, to airport for flight to Pinehurst, North Carolina, for the par-five eighteenth hole at the Country Club of North Carolina and the par-four fifth hole at Pinehurst No. 2. End of first nine holes.

One week later. Day Three: 7:30 A.M. Play par-five seventeenth hole at Baltusrol Golf Club's Lower Course. Van to Winged Foot Golf Club, Mamaroneck. Tenth hole on the West Course. Then, across the road to the Quaker Ridge Golf Club to play the par-four twelfth hole. A ride south to the Westchester Country Club for the 444-yard par-four second hole on the West Course. Then, to the Westchester Airport and a flight to Philadelphia. A van ride from the Philadelphia Airport to the Merion Golf Club and the par-four eleventh hole. Then, back to the airport and a flight to Los Angeles.

Day Four: 7:30 A.M. Play the par-four tenth hole at Riviera Country Club. Then, a flight to Palm Springs to play the par-three thirteenth hole at the Stadium Course at PGA West. Back to the airport and a flight to Monterey, California. Play the par-four fourth hole at Spyglass Hill, and, finally, end up at the eighteenth hole at Pebble Beach.

The eighteen holes played to a par 72 at 7,140 yards. The first day went off smoothly and on schedule, and our chartered plane deposited us at Jacksonville, Florida, at ten that evening. At 7:30 the next morning, our four golfers played the seventeenth at the TPC course, then we took the vans to the Jacksonville Airport. Now, the first dark cloud appeared in the form of a warning of a hurricane menacing the Atlantic Coast. The airport at Hilton Head Island could not accommodate our chartered plane so we had planned to take a smaller plane for the flight from Jacksonville to Hilton Head, and later from Hilton Head to Pinehurst. Because of the hurricane threat, it was decided to fly the bigger plane to Savannah and drive to Hilton Head.

We arrived safely on the island and went immediately to the eighteenth hole at Harbor Town Links. After the last putt was made, we took a twenty-minute van ride to Pete Dye's Long Cove Club and played the par-five third hole. Now, a decision had to be made: Our schedule called for us to fly to Pinehurst to play two more holes that day, but we had flown into Savannah because of the hurricane threat and that had added an hour and a half to our traveling time. We would not be able to get to Pinehurst with enough daylight to tape the two scheduled holes.

Fortunately, there is an abundance of excellent golf courses in the Hilton Head area, and the producers decided to cancel the Pinehurst trip and replace those two holes with two at other courses. One of the substitutions was the sixth hole at the Colleton River Plantation Course on the mainland, about fifteen minutes from Long Cove. Colleton River is one of Jack Nicklaus's best designs, and the sixteenth hole is a dramatic dogleg out toward the river. It is the heart and soul, the look and smell, of the Low Country.

We lost nothing of the esthetics of the show by playing at Colleton River, but we had lost valuable time. After two days, our golfers had played eight holes. We were one hole behind, and the next week we would have to play ten holes in two days, five on each coast.

The following Monday we all assembled at the seventeenth tee on the Lower Course of Baltusrol in Springfield, New Jersey. It was going to be a hot, humid, and very busy day. After the players putted out on this 630-yard terror, we piled into vans and made our way through the hazy, congested thoroughfares of northern New Jersey, across the George Washington Bridge, and up to the rocky green spaces of Westchester County in New York. Our first stop was in Mamaroneck, at the handsome A. W. Tillinghast-designed Winged Foot Golf Club where our foursome teed it up at the par-three tenth hole on the West Course, to the great delight of a group on an outing.

Then it was a short ride across the road from Winged Foot to another Tillinghast monument, the Quaker Ridge Golf Club. The par-four twelfth hole was the reason for our visit there and things were going along smoothly. We had lunch at the Westchester Country Club and, after the professionals had played the par-four second hole on the West Course, we were taken to the

Westchester Airport where our plane flew us to Philadelphia. So far, so good.

A slight problem arose when the van driver got lost on the way to the Merion Golf Club, and we were a little late in arriving. Fuzzy, John, Tom, and Davis played the marvelous par-four eleventh hole, The Baffling Brook, where Bob Jones ended his competitive golfing career, defeating Eugene Homans eight and seven in the 1930 U.S. Amateur Championship in the victory that finished off the Grand Slam. Those pleasant thoughts were on everyone's mind that late summer afternoon as the players retraced those historic steps.

Then reality intruded. Everyone was to fly to California that evening on a commercial airline. It was much cheaper than taking our comfortable chartered plane, but the five holes we taped that day had taken longer than planned, and it was not possible to get from Merion to the Philadelphia Airport in time for the last flight to Los Angeles. We had to play the last five holes the next day or we would have no show. Another command decision had to be made and this one hurt: We had no recourse but to charter a plane. The cost used up whatever profits the show would make. Despite this setback, and the pressure of playing five holes the next day or else, spirits remained high on the flight to Los Angeles, where we arrived early in the morning after a fuel stop in Kansas City.

At 7:30 the next morning, our four golfers played the short and wonderful tenth hole at Riviera. It is a 321-yard dogleg right with a long, narrow green. On occasion, it can be driven. That morning Davis Love drove over the green. John Daly tried, but came up short in the right rough. Both Tom and Fuzzy played short in the fairway. Fuzzy almost holed out for a two, and he and Tom birdied, Davis parred, and Daly took a double bogey six. The foursome had given us the full range of this tempting par four.

We played the two holes in the Palm Springs area in good time, including the par-five fifteenth hole at the Mountain Course of

the La Quinta Hotel. That made up for the hole at Pinehurst
No. 2. We arrived on the Monterey peninsula in the late afternoon. The competition took a big turn at the seventeenth hole,
which was the exceptional par-four fourth hole at Spyglass Hill,
with its long, narrow green set among the sand hills and ice
plants. Davis Love birdied the hole and needed only a par at the
eighteenth to win the $250,000 first prize.

We were losing the daylight when we arrived at the eighteenth
tee at Pebble Beach. We had to move quickly, since we would not
be able to get the four players together again. In addition, we had
moved in front of some fee-paying foursomes who were irritable
and impatient to play the final hole. Because of the light problem,
we decided to tape my closing piece on the eighteenth tee before
the players hit their tee shots. I had been scribbling some notes all
day and had a two-minute essay on our adventures, a sort of "I
hear America singing in the summer of 1993!"

I knew I had to shorten the piece as I was saying it, and in the
process I lost my concentration and we had to do another take.
Now the tension was palpable. Faces were tight, the sun was sinking, time was rushing by. The players were ready to hit. Everyone
was watching me. There would not be a another chance if I blew
it this time.

There was a surreal feeling about the moment. I was standing
on the eighteenth tee of Pebble Beach, one of the most enticing
places in all of golf. Off to the right was the seventeenth hole and
beyond it the seventeen-mile drive where the Monterey forest
rises majestically into a darkening sky. To the left, Carmel Bay
splashed gently against the rocks that edge the eighteenth fairway
that was now bathed in the last of the day's sun. It was an en
chanting sight, and yet I felt apart from it, suspended or trapped
in some dark place.

"Are you ready, Jack?"

I made it through this time and everyone breathed easily. The
players teed off. All of them hit the fairway—all of them except

153

John Daly. John hit a Lucullan hook into the bay. He turned and looked at Fuzzy.

"Here," said Fuzzy. "I'll do it."

And with that, he took the driver from John and threw it into the bay. The big club floated among the rocks and was rescued by two intrepid young men who held it aloft as if it were Excalibur. Davis Love, III, won the contest. It had been an exhilarating experience for everyone, an examination of the great depth and variety of America and golf.

The made-for-TV shows are great fun to do for one very simple reason: Everyone has a good time. Gone is the tension of a Tour event or major championship. Gone are the pinched faces of the players, the short tempers after a missed shot, the solemn pronouncements of announcers speaking in hushed tones. During the taping of these shows, golf once again becomes a sportive and lighthearted affair, even if the players are trying their best to win.

There are probably too many of these shows now, and there is some fallout from their success. Some players, after competing in November and December, don't show up for the West Coast tournaments in January and February. The problem will very likely cure itself, since these TV events will begin to diminish as the World Tour begins to flourish. In the meantime, I have been very fortunate to have had the best of them, from the *CBS Classic* to *Shell's Wonderful World of Golf*.

Sport of Kings

"This is not a business for people in short pants."

The most anticipatory sound in all of sports is the intense murmur that floats from the grandstand at Churchill Downs on Derby Day, and drifts across the track to the winner's circle. It is an incessant buzzing that builds in volume, getting louder and louder as the clock moves towards post time for the eighth race of the day, the Kentucky Derby. It is a sound that drowns out the raucous chatter from the infield where sixty thousand intrepid celebrants have crowded in since eight in the morning, many of them losing a battle with Harry M. Stevens mint juleps, a lethal dose of Bourbon that, when taken under a Kentucky sun, induces deep somnolence.

I was sitting on the porch of the pagoda that forms the winner's circle, listening to that drone from the grandstand on May 1, 1965. In a few hours, I would anchor the CBS broadcast of the Derby from that porch. I had never done a horse race previously; this was indeed high-level entry. And I was scared to death.

The Kentucky Derby had been a part of my generation's consciousness since childhood, aided and abetted by Hollywood's portrayal of the sport and by the radio broadcasts of the race by the wonderfully pebbly voice of Clem McCarthy. Even though few of us had been to a racetrack at that time, or even seen a live thoroughbred horse, we were caught up in the great idea promoted by Colonel Matt Winn that the Kentucky Derby was the greatest horse race in the world and that it was downright un-American not to be enthusiastic about it. The Colonel was one of America's great salesmen, right up there with P. T. Barnum and Michael Milken. He convinced the American people that his race at Churchill Downs in Louisville, Kentucky, on the first Saturday in May was a national observance. In truth, the race comes too early in the year for three-year-olds. It should be at a shorter distance or held later in the year. But Matt Winn overcame that reality and promoted the Derby into the race that most owners would like to win above all others. He also did wonders for Kentucky's other industry, Bourbon whiskey; the mint julep went national with the Derby. So persuasive was Matt Winn's campaign that the strains of "My Old Kentucky Home" could make youngsters from the streets of Philadelphia, who had never been further south than Wilmington, misty eyed.

The Kentucky Derby was one of the many plums that fell my way when Chris Schenkel departed CBS for ABC. He was a tough act to follow; Chris had been doing horse racing for years and was known and respected by the industry. In contrast, I knew few people. It was a daunting experience, but I had a lot of help.

My first source of aid was the producer of CBS's racing telecasts, Bill Creasy. William Neville Creasy is a graduate of St. Lawrence University. He is not the retiring, shy sort one associates with St. Lawrence men. He is a man who goes out looking for life's neon-lit streets. If there's a hurricane warning, Bill wants to walk on the beach. Two of his greatest loves are television and horse racing, both of which he pursued with great energy and talent. As a TV producer he possessed a quality too few have, good taste. And he was sensitive to the problems of the on-air people. He certainly was with me during the closing days of April, 1965. Bill literally held my hand all week. We watched tapes of previous derbies by the hour. No item was small enough to overlook.

I wasn't completely ignorant of racing, having gone to the track a couple of times a year as a small boy and always having enjoyed the writings of Red Smith and Joe Palmer about the sport. Like most of America, I was entranced by the wondrous appearance of Native Dancer in 1952 and '53, that gorgeous gray horse owned by Alfred Vanderbilt. He and television came along at the same time, and Native Dancer did for thoroughbred racing what Arnold Palmer would do for golf a few years later, making the sport more popular than it had ever been before. In that two-year period, this marvelous animal won twenty-one out of twenty-two starts, his only loss coming in the Kentucky Derby, when he finished second to Dark Star after being bumped on the first turn. Even that shocking setback contributed to the romance of this matinee idol and made us all more aware of the glories and heartbreak of the sport.

Racing, like all the very good things in life, is something you never master completely. There is always something new to learn, or relearn, and that week I was cramming my head with as much knowledge as I could. We attended every luncheon and dinner that Derby Week, with Bill making sure I met all the right people. He must have been very apprehensive about having a neophyte as his anchorman, but he never showed it; he was a constant positive influence who got me through a difficult time.

One of the first audiences I had that week was with the president of Churchill Downs, Walthen Kneblekampf. Bill and I were ushered into his office, where this tall white-haired gentleman rose and stretched out his hand.

"Welcome to Churchill Downs and the Derby," he said. His manner was friendly and he quickly put me at ease. There was another gentlemen in the room, and Mr. Kneblekampf introduced us. It was Bill Winfry, the trainer for Wheatly Stables. Bill Winfry had the favorite for the Derby that year, a horse named Bold Lad, by the stable's mighty sire, Bold Ruler.

"I'm glad to meet you, Jack," said Bill. "I'm a great fan of the *CBS Golf Classic*. That must be great fun to do, and you do a great job." For several minutes, Bill Winfry and I talked about golf, and I felt as if I had known him all my life. When Bill Creasy and I left Mr. Kneblekampf's office, I felt some of my apprehension slip away. Years later I realized what I had experienced in that office: Racing people, more than any other sporting group, will welcome you warmly and sincerely if you show just a little interest in their game. I have seen this happen many times over the years. If you like the horses, you have a whole world of friends.

Horse racing also offers the wondrous world of past-performance charts and a language that is both colorful and sparse. The past-performance chart is a companion piece to baseball's box score. Both are remarkable for their brevity and completeness. A box score tells you the entire story of a baseball game in that incredibly small space. A past-performance chart tells you the entire racing history of the horse in a similarly small space.

The language of the sport seems to evade the cliché. The well-used phrases like "can do" and "on the muscle" always seem fresh. The economy of words is a delight: "Wired foes by three under a hand ride" tells the story of a race won by a horse who led from beginning to end and won by three lengths without the jockey using the whip. All that in eight words.

Horse players are constantly using racing terms in conversation. A good person is known as a "stakes winner," a sure thing is "odds on." "To move up in class" means somebody or something has improved.

The language of racing is an excellent example of the advice I received from my first news editor, Alf Ringler at WCAU in Philadelphia. "Kid," Alfie said, "always keep the subject close to the predicate."

In the years that Mr. Kneblekampf was president of Churchill Downs I came to respect and delight in his company. He had a full and wonderful life, spending it in three different areas. He had run the Louisville baseball team, worked in the distillery business, and ended by being president of Churchill Downs. He was bright and resourceful. There are two men I have known in sports who were a cut above all the rest: One was Walthen Kneblekampf, and the other was Art Rooney of Pittsburgh. Both were good, tough operators, and both were gentlemen. That both of them loved horses may only be coincidental. To my mind, there is no one in sports today who can even come up to their shoulders.

Thanks to Bill Creasy, Bill Winfry, and Mr. Kneblekampf, I managed to hold together and on Saturday, May 1, I sat out at the anchor position listening to the crowd buzzing away and going over my notes for the hundredth time. The broadcast was scheduled from 4:00 to 5:00 P.M. with post time at 4:30. At about three-fifteen I heard that humming sound from the grandstand become louder until it was almost a roar. I looked up to see smoke curling up from the grandstand down to the left near the first turn. There was a fire, and for several awful moments, panic began to rise. The grandstands at Churchill Downs in those days were wooden and were as dry as tinder; a fire could easily sweep through the entire structure and become an inferno. On this day, of course, the stands were completely full. A full-fledged catastrophe seemed imminent.

It was averted because the wind that afternoon was blessedly blowing down the track in the opposite direction from the main part of the grandstand and the clubhouse. The situation was further eased by the response of the Louisville Fire Department, which quickly drenched the flames, and by the splendid behavior of the people who refused to panic. When the situation was well in hand, we all exhaled gratefully, realizing what a different day it could have been.

By now, four o'clock had arrived and we were on the air—but not as we had intended. The carefully crafted format of the one-hour show that had been developed by Bill Creasy and exhaustively gone over by Tony Verna, the director; Jack Drees, our race caller; and Gil Stratton who would help out with the postrace festivities, went right out the window. This is what confronted us as we came on the air at four o'clock: Fire engines and hoses were littered across the track. The seventh race, the one prior to the Derby, had not yet been run, and no one had any idea when post time for the Derby would be. Somehow, we ad-libbed our way through for an hour, using all the material I had crammed into my head all week. Finally, at 5:00 P.M., the horses were in the gate.

Now I was rooting strongly for the favorite, Bold Lad, to win, since I would feel very comfortable interviewing my newest close friend, Bill Winfry. But horse racing is often cruel, and Bold Lad, in contention to the top of the stretch, gave way badly and finished tenth. The winner was Lucky Debonair, a Kentucky-bred, California-raced colt owned by Mrs. Ada Rice, trained by Frank Catrone, and ridden beautifully this day by Bill Shoemaker. The presentation ceremony with the Governor of Kentucky and Mr. Kneblekampf went smoothly, and Bill Shoemaker gave us a wonderful interview, helped by the presence of Gil Stratton, who was a familiar face to Shoemaker and a good friend. Finally, we were off the air. A surge of exhilaration went through me. I felt free and giddy. The travail was over.

As we crossed the track heading back to the CBS remote trucks, both Gil and I thought we had gotten through the show in good style, despite the delay. When we reached the trucks, which were parked by the tulip garden behind the grandstand, we saw Bill McPhail, Bill Creasy, and Tony Verna. They were subdued, with faces longer than a 5:00 P.M. shadow.

"It wasn't your fault," said McPhail.

Gil and I looked at each other.

"What wasn't our fault?" I finally stammered.

"We lost our audio," said Tony Verna. "We had to use radio's audio. Nobody heard you or Gil."

Welcome to horse racing.

The next day we learned there had been another fire that day. This one was in a sewer near Baltimore, and it destroyed the cable that carried our audio lines from Louisville to New York. It also knocked out the telephone line between the White House and the Kremlin. Big stuff, that fire.

Two weeks later, we were in Baltimore for the Preakness. This looked to be much easier than the Derby. First of all, the show was only thirty minutes long, not an hour. Second, most of the field was made up of Derby horses and were already researched. For this race, CBS hired Eddie Arcaro as the color man, and thus began a great relationship with the Maestro, one of the most enjoyable athletes I have ever known.

There was no fire at Pimlico that day. But coming down the stretch, Dapper Dan, second in the Derby, cut across Tom Rolfe, third in the Derby, and there was an inquiry. It took the stewards twenty minutes to decide the race in favor of Tom Rolfe. Twenty minutes when we could not do the presentation or interview anyone. Eddie had wandered off somewhere and there I was again, tap dancing for all I was worth. It was another lesson in broadcasting horse races.

One of the nicest things about the Triple Crown Series in those days was the ride home from the Preakness. CBS chartered a railroad car, which was attached to the 7:30 train out of Baltimore to New York. Harry M. Stevens catered it, and all the racing writers and TV people would dine on fried chicken and crabcakes, mingling with Red Smith of the *Tribune* and Joe Nichols of *The New York Times* and the *Sports Illustrated* folks. There was great conversation and singing and most everyone ended up at Toots Shor's. Racing people know how to have a good time, possibly because it's a sport where you lose much more than you win. And I remember thinking that night in Shor's that my first two racing telecasts were a reflection of the sport and that the experience would be valuable training for the years ahead.

Each year, I became, if not more expert, at least more familiar with racing and very comfortable in the surroundings of the sport. In 1966, a Native Dancer colt named Kauai King won the Derby and the Preakness, and we arrived at the Belmont full of expectations. But Kauai King was rank that day, and finished out of the money. The unexpected continued to happen. In 1968, another Native Dancer colt won the Derby—but Dancer's Image became the first Derby winner in history to be taken down. The reason was that a medicine prohibited in Kentucky, Butazolidin, had been given to Dancer's Image, and though owner Peter Fuller appealed the ruling, it stood and Calumet Farms' Forward Pass was declared the winner. The ruling was handed down long after our broadcast was over. In cases like this, we would not know the final result of a horse race before we signed off the air. In 1969, Majestic Prince, a handsome chestnut from California, trained by Johnny Longdon and ridden by Bill Hartack, won the Derby and the Preakness, but finished second in the Belmont Stakes, and our chance of seeing a Triple Crown winner seemed more remote than ever.

Then, in 1971, in the first year of what was to become the Dominant Decade, a kind of magic touched the sport on both sides of the Atlantic Ocean, a magic that would last until 1979. It would be perhaps the greatest decade in racing since Charles the Second went down to Newmarket with Nell Gwynn. The first sprinkle of stardust came at the Kentucky Derby that year. A Kentucky-bred colt raced in Venezuela, and only a day or two out of quarantine, was in the mutual field with five other long shots. (The tote board only had room for twelve horses [since upgraded to fourteen], so when there were more in the race the longest-shots were grouped into the *field*, where a bet on one was a bet on all.) He was completely overlooked by most handicappers, writers, and broadcasters. There were twenty colts in the race and for the first three quarters of a mile, Canonero II dawdled along in eighteenth place while Calumet Farm's Bold and Able led the way. Leaving the backstretch, Canonero II was forced to come to the extreme outside and to circle the field. He took command in the stretch and held off a game Jim French to win by three lengths.

As Canonero II came thundering down the stretch, Eliot Burch, the esteemed trainer for Rokeby Farms who was our color man that day, turned to me and asked, "How's your Spanish?"

"Nonexistent," I replied.

"Well, just keeping saying, *'Felicidad, felicidad,'*" he said.

We knew very little about the animal or his connections, and as we watched them put the blanket of roses across the colt's withers, I asked Lynn Stone, who had succeeded Mr. Kneblekampf as president of Churchill Downs, which one was the owner, Edgar Caibett. Lynn shrugged his shoulders and rolled his eyes. He didn't know either. I don't know how we got through the postrace rerun and interviews. We could identify the jockey, Gustavo Avila, and the trainer, Juan Arias, but neither of them spoke English and Elliot and I were reduced to smiling and saying, "Felicidad, felicidad."

One night before the Preakness, at P. J. Clarke's in New York, I requested an interpreter for our telecast in case Canonero II repeated his Derby victory, and our producer, Chuck Milton, agreed. We hired the interpreter and we also hired a new color man.

Frank Wright was a graduate of Duke University, a man of wide interests, with a deep love of the English language and horses. He was a trainer of note and a first-rate student and teacher of horse racing. When Frank Wright came aboard, the editorial content of our racing telecasts improved dramatically. For the next ten years, with Frank Wright, Heywood Hale Broun, Charlsie Canty, and Chick Anderson, CBS produced racing telecasts that set high standards. Technically, we were advancing as our equipment became

was. His prance was almost a strut, and his body language suggested he was saying, "Hey, I'm something special." Something Special was one of the names considered by Meadow Stable for this colt. How fitting it would have been.

Secretariat began 1973 as he had finished in 1972. He won the Bay Shore stakes at Aqueduct by four-and-a-half lengths, the Gotham Stakes by three. His next race, the last prep before the Derby, was the Wood Memorial, on April twenty-first at Aqueduct. His trainer, the delightful Lucien Laurin, had another horse entered in the race, and to everyone's amazement and shock, it was that horse, Angle Light, who won, as Secretariat finished third.

You will find more rumors around the race track than in the PX at an Army base, and they now began to swarm around the handsome head of Secretariat. "Just a flash in the pan." "Overrated, never beat anything good." "If he can't beat Angle Light, he won't be on the board at the Derby." On and on it went as Secretariat, once the second coming of Man o' War, was now being written off as a flashy sprinter.

When we got to Louisville in Derby week, the rumors intensified. "Bold Ruler colts can't go a distance. The mile-and-a quarter race is too much for Secretariat." "I hear he is loaded with arthritis." "You know, I heard that too. I hear they may scratch him."

Derby day was clear, the track fast. Secretariat broke from the 10th post position and dropped back to last before beginning to move between horses entering the first turn. Then he moved to the outside and began moving on the leaders, Shecky Greene and Sham. At the top of the stretch he had only Sham to beat, and jockey Ron Turcotte flashed the whip at the big chestnut. Secretariat seemed to glide by Sham, his great stride carrying him home two-and-a-half lengths in front for a Kentucky Derby record time of 1:59 ⅖.

The reaction was overwhelming. Everyone knew they had witnessed a remarkable performance, even an historic one, and that this handsome colt, prancing in the winner's circle with the blanket of roses over his withers, might indeed be something special. On the winner's stand before the presentation, I said to owner Mrs. Penny Tweedy, "I guess we know now that Bold Rulers can go a distance." She smiled and said, with a touch of vindication, "You bet we do."

Later, when the broadcast was over, we learned that the winner had not only set a new record but that he had run each succeeding quarter of a mile faster than the one before, an unheard of accomplishment. Humans and horses usually are decelerating at the end of races.

Two weeks later, at the Preakness, Secretariat bounded out of the number-three post position, moved to the outside, and, at the clubhouse turn, made one of the most amazing moves ever seen. He accelerated like a racecar around the turn and passed everybody. He took the lead entering the back stretch and finished two and a half lengths in front of Sham once again. A controversy arose over the time of the race. The tote board showed 1:55, but the *Daily Racing Form* clocker had a new track record of 1:53 ⅗. Sandy Grossman, the director of our CBS broadcast, came up with an ingenious idea to prove the *Daily Racing Form's* figure: He split the TV screen in half, top to bottom. Canonero II at that time held the Preakness record at 1:54. In the upper part of the screen, Sandy had the Canonero II Preakness, and on the bottom, he had Secretariat's race. The videotapes started at the same time, and Secretariat crossed the finish line several lengths in front of Canonero II, which seemed to verify the *Daily Racing Form's* figure. The Maryland Jockey Club refused to accept the videotapes as evidence; they compromised and modified the official time to 1:54 ⅖.

None of this had any effect on Secretariat or the racing public — or on people who never went to the races. Secretariat had become the people's horse, and the three weeks leading up to the last race of the Triple Crown, the Belmont Stakes, were filled with stories and pictures of America's newest icon. It was not surprising. This was the year of the Watergate hearings, and we Americans were without heroes. Then, along came this handsome animal who won his races in dynamic fashion. This was a hero. Secretariat was on the cover of *Time, Newsweek,* and *Sports Illustrated.* Owner Penny Tweedy, trainer Lucien Laurin, Jockey Ron Turcotte, and groom Ed Sweat were swarmed upon to a terrifying extent.

Belmont day dawned clear, with the track fast. Sixty-two thousand fans turned out to see if we were to have the first Triple Crown winner in twenty-five years. What followed was the most dominating individual performance I have ever seen in any sport. Sham ran with Secretariat down the backstretch where he had to be pulled up, his gallant career ended by injury. From then on, Secretariat was on his own. His mighty stride ate up the ground as he moved further and further away from the field. Faster and faster he went until it seemed he would be airborne. Ten lengths in front, fifteen lengths, and still he was accelerating. Chick Anderson, calling the race for our TV broadcast, said, "Secretariat is moving like a great machine." Belmont Park was in an uproar as Secretariat thundered down the stretch, a lonely, heroic figure of perfection. He crossed the finish line thirty-one lengths in front of Twice a Prince in a new record time of 2:24, two-and-three-fifths seconds better than the record set by Gallant Man. Secretariat would have beaten Gallant Man by thirteen lengths.

People were in a state of disbelief. Most were cheering and laughing, some were crying, all aware that they had seen an historic performance. Jack Nicklaus told Heywood Hale Broun that he had sat alone in his living room watching on TV and cried as Secretariat came barreling down the stretch.

After his electrifying Belmont, Secretariat went to Chicago and won the Arlington Invitational by nine lengths. Then at Saratoga he was beaten by a length in the Whitney in a race Frank Wright said had been maneuvered by some of the jockeys to make sure Secretariat had no racing room. And the critics came back to life. "Never beat anybody in the Belmont," went the cry.

In September, the inaugural Marlboro Cup was held. (Since there was no tobacco advertising permitted on television, we at CBS had to call it "The Cup.") Secretariat faced a formidable field of older horses including Kennedy Road, Cougar II, and Onion, who had defeated him in the Whitney. As the field came swinging around the last turn and into the stretch, the blue and white blocks of Meadow Stable were leading the parade. Riva Ridge and Secretariat were one and two, and then the younger one proceeded to put away his older stablemate and won by three and a half lengths.

Two weeks later, Secretariat was beaten again, finishing second to Prove Out in the Woodward Stakes. The reasons are as unexplainable as quantum physics is to a child, but the critics of Secretariat were once again in full throat. And, once again, Secretariat silenced them. Trainer Lucien Laurin moved his charge onto the grass for the Man o' War Stakes at Belmont, and the big colt found the turf much to his liking, winning by five lengths over the talented Tentam. Then, for his farewell appearance, Secretariat's connections chose the one-and-five-eighths mile Canadian International Stakes on grass at Toronto's Woodbine Park. After the race, Secretariat would be retired to stud, syndicated for a then-record six million dollars.

It was very frustrating not to broadcast the farewell appearance after covering most of Secretariat's heroics, but CBS was not the network carrying the race, and I was in Los Angeles to do a football game. I watched the race on TV at the Beverly Wilshire Hotel. Secretariat's regular rider would miss the farewell race too; Ron Turcotte, forever linked with Secretariat, had been suspended for a short time and so Eddie Maple would be on Secretariat for the horse's last race.

The late October afternoon was damp and misty in Toronto and, at post time, the daylight was dying and visibility was at a minimum. Out of this Canadian gloaming, Secretariat moved past Kennedy Road, and by the time they turned for home he was ten lengths in front, running through the misty afternoon, once more alone and going ever faster. Suddenly through the fog the lights of the tote board hit rider and horse in the eyes. Secretariat shied a bit and then accelerated again. Halfway down the stretch, the light that defined the finish line was turned on, and once more Secretariat shied, and then again accelerated and flew over the finish line six and a half lengths to the good.

That was it. Secretariat's finale had been as theatrical and dynamic as his whole career, brilliant, incandescent, and wrapped in a foggy mist. And as he galloped off into that mist and into retirement and legend, there was a bittersweet feeling, a sadness that we would no longer see this ideal, this splendid thoroughbred race again. But, oh, it was an extraordinary experience to have been there in 1973.

After Secretariat, the procession of outstanding racehorses continued. In Europe, the decade produced champions like Nijinsky, Mill Reef, Brigadier Gerard, The Minstrel, Roberto, and many others. In the United States, three years after Secretariat's Triple Crown, we had another, and then another. Seattle Slew, a very talented and popular colt, won the three races in 1977, and a year later the handsome Affirmed, in an unforgettable rivalry with Alydar, repeated the feat. No Triple Crown winner was pressured as much as Affirmed; no colt ever gave chase as gladly as Alydar.

The distaff side produced its share of champions, with fillies like Susan's Girl and Optimistic Gal, and the greatest of them all, Ruffian. This big lady—and Ruffian was big, larger in the girth than even Secretariat—was never headed in winning ten straight races including the fillies' Triple Crown. On July 6, 1975, Ruffian met the Kentucky Derby winner of that year, Foolish Pleasure, in a match race at Belmont Park. If Secretariat's Belmont win was one of the most glorious days at this handsome track, this day was to be one of its most tragic.

The two thoroughbreds raced the first quarter of a mile in a searing :22 ⅗, with Ruffian about a head in front. Then, as they moved to the half-mile mark, it was suddenly all over. Ruffian's ankle snapped with a sound so loud that both jockeys heard it. The bone splintered as Ruffian kept trying to run on the shattered leg. Despite every attempt to save her, Ruffian had to be destroyed several hours later. Foolish Pleasure ran on and was declared the winner of the race as a stunned crowd of 55,000 looked on.

Our broadcast was in a frenetic mode as we tried to get a report on Ruffian. I interviewed Foolish Pleasure's trainer, Leroy Jolley. I began with something inane like, "Well, Leroy, I know you didn't want to win like this."

His reply was like a blast of cold air, sobering and realistic.

"This is not a business for people in short pants," he said.

Many people complained that was an insensitive remark, but Leroy was not being insensitive. He was not being sentimental, either; he was being realistic. Horse racing is a tough business. Horses break down quite often and it is always a blow, but when it is a very special animal like Ruffian, the loss is more profound and reaches beyond the racing community. Ruffian is universally considered the best filly ever to race. She is buried by the flagpole in the infield at Belmont Park.

At a distance of twenty-five years, it is still amazing to realize how many superb thoroughbreds there were in the 1970s in every division of each gender. Forego, who finished fourth in Secretariat's Derby, blossomed into a marvelous handicap horse in his fourth, fifth, sixth, and seventh years. This big gelding could carry weight and come from behind to just get his head in front. In the 1977 Marlboro Cup he carried 137 pounds, giving away eighteen pounds to Honest Pleasure. That was the highest weight given to a horse in ninety years in New York state. Forego was twelve lengths behind Honest Pleasure at the top of the stretch—then he started to run, moving like a runaway sixteen-wheeler down a mountain road. Honest Pleasure had the lead with ten feet to go, but Forego, with Bill Shoemaker hand-riding him, got his head in front to win one of the most exciting races of the decade. I shall never forget Shoemaker, struggling to the scale to weigh in, carrying his saddle with the lead weights in it. Shoe weighed about ninety-two pounds then, so the saddle and the lead weights weighed forty-five pounds. Bill was carrying half his own weight to that scale—but he was smiling, and later said in our interview that Forego was the best horse he had ever ridden.

It was a decade of great champions and thrilling races. There have been outstanding horses since then, including Sunday Silence, Easy Goer, and the remarkable Cigar, but there has never been the depth of quality that ran during the seventies. There are four measures of great thoroughbreds: They must dominate their year. They must defeat older horses. They must win on dirt and grass, and they must win giving away weight. Secretariat did the first three superbly. He never got a chance to carry weight, but I don't doubt for a minute he would have dominated the handicap division as he had as a three-year-old, but a small body of critics still persist.

A few years ago, on the Thursday evening of Derby week, I had dinner at the Seelbach Hotel in Louisville with Charlsie Canty, Frank Wright, and Leroy Jolley. I asked both Frank and Leroy why they said Secretariat was a very good horse but not a great one. I said look at his record.

"Didn't beat any good horses," said Leroy.

"Look at his times," I countered.

"Shaved the tracks for him," said Leroy.

I still don't know if they were having me on, and I don't care. Horse racing is based on opinion and, in my opinion, Secretariat was the best of the best decade in the sport. Eddie Maple, who rode Secretariat into the mists of retirement, had this reaction to the critics.

"I know he was the best," said Eddie, "and I'll say one more thing. Of those critics of Secretariat, not one of them ever rode him. They sure as hell never rode him."

Some Players

"This is what it's all about, isn't it?"

Most athletes are pleasant to be around. Even today, there remains in me that fragile flaw of sportswriters so unerringly defined by Stanley Woodward, that great sports editor of that great newspaper, the *New York Herald Tribune*. "Stop godding up those ballplayers," he wired Red Smith in spring training one year. We do have a way of letting our admiration of their athletic achievements carry us away, and the godding up of these young people, beginning in high school, is part of the reason some of them arrive in the professional ranks spoiled and arrogant.

There did not seem to be any danger of that thirty years ago, and one of the best features of being a sportscaster has been getting to know some of our top athletes. Professional golfers are particularly easy to god up, because they are so good at a game most of us play so poorly, and our appreciation of their gifts often makes us reckless with our praise. Most of them are like any other athlete; next to the heading, "Special Interests," most golfers list fishing, hunting, and other sports. But when you find the ones with broader taste, you've met a marvelous companion.

Mike Souchak has made himself into one of the world's foremost wine experts. When he first came on the Tour, Ken Venturi said Mike couldn't tell the difference between a bottle of Thunderbird wine or a Château Lafite. Today, Mike has a splendid collection and can converse for hours on the different grapes, soils, and the amount of sun each vineyard gets. When you go to Mike's house for dinner, he doesn't tell you what you're going to eat, he tells you what bottle he is opening.

Gene Littler is an expert on antique cars and used to have a collection of bygone models as elegant as his golf swing. Some of today's players have interests other than sports: Andrew Magee lists "whistling and traveling" as his special interests, befitting a man born in Paris. Jeff Sluman likes old cars and can talk to you about the stock market, and more and more players are beginning to list golf-course design as an interest. It is the fashionable avocation of the moment.

It has been my experience that all of the great golfers have been extremely interesting people, and I have treasured the moments I have spent in their company. Bernard Darwin once described Gene Sarazen as being like the Cheshire Cat in *Alice in Wonderland*; the cat would disappear beginning with his tail and ending with his head, but his grin would linger long after he had faded away. So, too, said Mr. Darwin, does Gene Sarazen's grin remain long after he has gone. The only time I saw the Squire play was at Baltusrol in the U.S. Open in 1967. He was paired with Johnny Farrell, and it was a delight to watch these two dapper gentlemen from another era. I first met Mr. Sarazen at the Tony Lema Memorial Pro-Am on

Marco Island a few years later. Ken Venturi was working there and invited all the CBS golf team to play. Gene was a marvelous host, and every time I have been in his company I am refreshed, for he is the American Dream—a man who came from the caddy yard at Apawamis Country Club to mingle with presidents and kings. His old friend, Freddy Corcoran, one of golf's noblemen, put that rags-to-riches story in the archives one day when Gene and Sam Snead were playing an exhibition match just outside Paris. In the gallery was the former King of Belgium and the Duke of Windsor. Freddy rounded up the photographers and writers with the cry, "Come watch two ex-kings watching two ex-caddies."

It was Gene Sarazen who planted the seed that became the Senior Tour. He was sitting with Freddy Raphael at the Masters one day when he excused himself to find out who his playing partner was going to be in the first round. He returned and told Freddy that his partner would be Arnold Palmer—the Old Legend playing with the New Legend. That sparked the idea in Freddy's mind to develop the Legends Tournament, which in turn led to the Senior Tour.

In 1987, a chain letter made the rounds, not promising three dozen golf balls or a dozen golfing shirts, but only that something good would happen to you if you did not break the chain. This was the letter:

Do you know who, in 1923, was:

1. President of the largest steel company?
2. President of the largest gas company?
3. President of the New York Stock Exchange?
4. The greatest wheat speculator?
5. President of the Bank of International Settlement?
6. The great bear of Wall Street?

These men should be considered among the world's richest men. Now, more than fifty-five years later, do you know what became of these men?

1. The president of the largest steel company, Charles Schwab, died a pauper.
2. The president of the largest gas company, Howard Hopson, is insane.
3. The president of the New York Stock Exchange, Richard Whitney, was released from prison to die at home.
4. The greatest wheat speculator, Arthur Cooger, died insolvent.
5. The president of the Bank of International Settlement shot himself.
6. The greatest bear of Wall Street, Costbar Rivermore, died by suicide.

That same year, 1923, the winner of the most important golf championships, the U.S. Open and the P.G.A. Championship, was Gene Sarazen. Today he is still playing golf and is solvent.

Conclusion: Stop worrying about business and play golf.

My most recent encounter with Gene Sarazen was in April 1998. I presented him with the first Dave Marr Memorial Award at the Shell Houston Open. Despite a rotator cuff problem, he was still swinging a golf club and still grinning.

Byron Nelson was another of those legends I met after his playing days were over, but not his influence on the game. Over the years, Byron has been a confidant and teacher to many players— Ken Venturi and Tom Watson, to name just two. He has remained an active positive influence in the game. He is a disarming man, polite and unassuming, but you sense there is a competitive force beneath the gentle demeanor. His record of eleven straight victories in 1945 remains one of the most outstanding streaks in any sport at any time. His scores during that year would stand up today, and he accomplished these feats on golf courses that were hardly in good condition, due to wartime restrictions, and with equipment that would seem primitive today. I have asked him what those conditions were like during this time of gasoline shortages and no golf-ball production; he has always demurred as if it would be not quite proper to make his achievements more exceptional. They were exceptional, and Byron Nelson is exceptional.

I first met Sam Snead during the year the CBS *Golf Classic* was at La Costa. I lost a contest on the putting green to him, and since that day I have found him to be friendly, pleasant, and every bit a legend. There is a twinkle in his eye as he begins one of his jokes, usually scatological, and the Snead grin gets wider as the stories get longer. The West Virginia twang is still there, but I find little trace of the hillbilly or put-the-money-in-the-tomato-cans mentality.

My knowledge of Sam began with a story George Fazio told me. On a hot, humid day in 1936, George and a fellow Philadelphia professional, Bud Lewis, were on the first tee at the Hershey Country Club about to begin a practice round prior to the Hershey Open. Up the road that winds around the first tee came a Model A Ford. The driver stopped and yelled over, "Hey, can you wait for me?" "Sure," said Fazio, "hurry up."

Ten minutes later the stranger arrived at the first tee.

"He wore," said Fazio, "shoes that had holes in them and were turned up at the toes."

The stranger's first ball was sliced out of bounds into the chocolate factory. The second he topped down the hill, and the third he hooked into the bushes. While George and Bud exchanged painful glances, the young man hit his fourth shot seven feet from the pin, 324 yards away. The Snead legend had begun.

One of the best golf lessons I ever received was just watching Sam warm up one day. It was on the range at Inverrary. Sam began with the wedge, hitting it with that beautiful swing that is the most graceful in golf. He went through most of the clubs in the bag, hitting each of them with the same easy motion until, twenty-five minutes after he began, he was booming 280-yard drives with the same tempo and action that he had used with the wedge.

I did a profile on Sam for the CBS *Sports Illustrated Show* at the time of his sixty-second birthday. I called him at the Greenbrier and caught him just as he came off the golf course. He had shot sixty-three that day.

"I almost shot my age today," he said. "I got to do it this year. Next year it'll be too easy."

Sam comes from Ashwood, Virginia. You go north from Covington, Virginia, up Route 122, past the Cascades Golf Club where the young Snead had his first golfing job, to a town called Healing Springs.

"Don't go too fast through Healing Springs," said Sam, "or you'll miss Ashwood. The roads get smaller and smaller until they just run up a tree."

We found Ashwood all right and the school Sam had attended, now replaced by a newer structure up on a hillside. It was recess time, and in the back of the new school, youngsters were hitting golf balls into primitive cups dug in the ground. The Snead heritage is strong.

The first time I played with Sam was at Jupiter Hills in Florida. It was a pro-am in which the amateurs played with a different pro each day. The second day, our team drew Sam, who had shot an eighty the first day. I was riding with him, and after a birdie at the eighth hole, he said, "Look at that. I'm ten shots better now than I was yesterday at this point," and he went on, determined to wipe out the eighty with the best score he could shoot, as charged up as if he were fighting Hogan for the Masters thirty years before. The last time I played with Sam, he was eighty-two years old, and had just recovered from a separated shoulder. He hit the ball 230 yards down the middle of the fairway with that same easy swing he had used more than seven decades before. Sam is the most graceful athlete and probably the greatest all-around athlete we have produced in this century.

* * *

In 1953, Ben Hogan was the colossus of the sport. He won all three of the major tournaments he entered that year, including his record-tying fourth U.S. Open. This handsome Texan owned the game. A man of imperial presence, he inspired a generation of golfers with his heroic comeback from a near-fatal automobile wreck, his disciplined approach to the game, and his dedication to winning. The golfing boom was due in great part to the man in the white cap.

It is important for today's golfer, from the professional to the twenty-four-handicapper, to know how much of an influence Ben Hogan has had on the game. He was the man who first began hitting balls to a caddy with a shag bag. The endless hours he spent on practicing led him to that almost flawless swing, which did not break down under pressure. He was meticulous in his preparation for a major tournament, often hitting three balls on each hole to find the best route to the green.

He was an impeccable dresser in well-tailored blues, grays, and tans, and had his golf shoes custom made in London. They had an extra cleat to help keep him down through his swing. His concentration on the golf course was laserlike. Once, playing with George Fazio at Riviera in Los Angeles, George holed out an eight iron on a par-four hole for an eagle. When they finished the round, Ben refused to sign the scorecard.

"You've put a two down, that's a par-four hole," he said.

"Yes, I know," said George. "I holed my second shot."

Ben was so lost in his own thoughts he never saw the shot or heard the reaction to it.

All of this contributed to his reputation as a cool, calculating customer who never smiled. "The Wee Iceman," the Scots called him. "The Hawk" was his nickname on the tour. But, off the course, he could be a very affable and amusing companion. He was a great raconteur. One year at the Colonial Invitational in Fort Worth, a tournament Hogan had won five times, I was the guest speaker at the dinner they hold for former champions. To

179

my great delight, they seated me on the dais between Valerie Hogan and Ben, and the Hawk was in a talkative mood.

"Is there anything you'd like to know about any of those old golfers?" he asked me. "I've had a lot of great times with them."

He pointed down to a table filled with golfers who had led the way on the professional tour in the years just before and after World War II.

"See that fellow?" he said, pointing to Johnny Bulla. "Right after the war, he had gotten ahold of a secondhand airplane. We were playing in Florida, and about ten of us decided to chip in and fly to our next tournament, which was in Arizona. I was the copilot. When we got to Arizona, I had to make an emergency landing and I damn near crashed the plane. It would have wiped out half the golf tour. That was the end of Golf Tour Airlines." And on and on he went, regaling me with stories of the old days on the tour, as delightful a dinner companion as I have ever had.

The last time I saw him was at *Golf Magazine's* incredible dinner at the Waldorf Astoria in New York on the evening of the day that Curtis Strange defeated Nick Faldo for the U.S. Open title at The Country Club in Brookline. It was a celebration of one hundred years of golf in America, and in that ballroom in Manhattan that evening was the greatest gathering of golfers in one room the world has ever seen. Standing at the podium, I looked to my right and saw Sam Snead, Patty Berg, Byron Nelson, and sitting next to the lectern, Ben Hogan. Looking to my left were Jack Nicklaus, Tom Watson, Nancy Lopez, and Lee Trevino. In the rows behind were Cary Middlecoff, Ken Venturi, Ben Crenshaw and a hundred other champions, past and present.

Ben was often very shy; I was told he didn't want to speak that evening. But, when I asked him if he wanted to say a few words, he bounded to his feet and from the lectern gave a golf lesson on the grip and hand action that riveted the audience on an evening of unforgettable history.

Ben was forever studying the game and the odds. At the Carling

World Championship at Pleasant Valley in 1965, I sat with Henry Longhurst and Ben in the Grill Room after our television rehearsal. The two were old acquaintances and had a warm relationship.

"Henry, I heard the rehearsal and you sound as good as ever."

"Thank you, Ben," mumbled Henry, almost embarrassed by the compliment.

"Just one thing, though," said Ben. "When one of those putts comes up short you said 'never up, never in.' . . . That's not true. It's a myth.

"I lost two U.S. Opens because I putted past the hole and missed coming back. If you're short, your second putt is on the same line. It's easier."

As we walked back to our television towers, I said to Henry, "I've always heard that 'Never up, never in' is one of golf's truisms."

"Ah, yes, Jack," said Henry, in that deep, almost catatonic way of his. "But, remember, that's Ben Hogan."

I do remember Ben Hogan, and I wish I had known him better and hope his memory lasts beyond the next hundred years.

Ben Hogan continued to be a factor in major championships until 1960, but the years and the accident were making it difficult to walk seventy-two holes. It seemed that his successor would be one of a handful of bright young Californians. Ken Venturi, Billy Casper, and Gene Littler were winning tournaments and making people take notice. However, sometime during the 1958 Masters Tournament, a young player from Western Pennsylvania on his way to victory looked into the TV camera and golf had a new leader. Arnold Palmer took the sport into the television age and on to the large purses and commercial affiliations that young stars take for granted. Today's players owe Arnold a great debt.

Although Arnold's game was superseded by those of Jack Nicklaus and Tom Watson, he has never lost his role as golf's leader. Even today he attracts old and young fans by his presence and personality. I share two things with Arnold. We've both had prostate cancer. Arnold's reaction to the harrowing news was a measure of the man's character and was exactly in the style he exhibited on the golf course: He took immediate and aggressive action and had the operation, and today he has become an effective speaker for the Cancer Society, bringing hope and encouragement to thousands.

The other infirmity we share is of a much lower profile. Several years ago at Greg Norman's Shootout, I was talking with Arnold on the practice range. When I went back up to the clubhouse area, a young friend, eyes ablaze with excitement, asked, "What were you and Arnie talking about?"

I hated to dampen his ardor.

"Hearing aids," I said.

A journalist's life is a happier one if the people he writes and talks about are the great ones, whether they are politicians, statesmen, entertainers, or sports figures. My generation was fortunate to have great subjects, and golf provided many of them. The expansion of the game led by Arnold Palmer gave us many heroes, from Arnold himself, swaggering up the fairway, to the world traveler Gary Player, the irrepressible Lee Trevino, the stoic Tom Watson. Finally, standing just above them all, was Jack Nicklaus.

He did not have the vital personality that made Arnold the most popular player, nor the quiet, icy mystique of Ben Hogan, but he fashioned his persona by changing from an overweight, crewcut *infant terrible* to a slimmed-down mature statesman of the game. And he played the best golf more times than anyone else. Unlike Ben Hogan, Jack came from a loving and stable middle-class home. His best friend was his father. Charles Nicklaus was a great admirer of Bob Jones. He had watched Jones win the U.S. Open Championship at Scioto Country Club in 1924, and he instilled in Jack the qualities that the Georgian displayed so winningly: sportsmanship and a gentlemanly approach to the game. There are a lot of similarities between Jones and Nicklaus. Both had close relationships with their fathers. Both grew up in a country-club surrounding with great teachers: East Lake and Stewart Maiden for Jones; Scioto and Jack Grout for Nicklaus. Both had a tendency to eat too much, both in their early years had marvelously warm tempers, and both loved the game for what it is—an opportunity for friendship and competition.

Jack shared two things with Ben Hogan. The first was a work ethic that was astounding. Hogan's practice sessions are legendary; Nicklaus's are less known, but one of my favorite Nicklaus stories is told by a Scioto neighbor, John Bishop, who lived on the second hole of the golf course. One winter afternoon in a heavy snowstorm he looked out his window and thought he saw someone swinging a golf club.

"When I walked outside to get a closer look, I found Nicklaus hitting one iron shots in the bitter cold. He was about nineteen then. He had shoveled out an area in the snow to hit from. He had a caddie down by the green who shoveled out a target area. Nicklaus was hitting shot after shot into the clearing, and the caddie didn't have to move. It was unbelievable!" Ben Hogan said he dug his golf swing out of the dirt; Nicklaus dug his out of the grass and snow.

Another thing Nicklaus shares with Hogan is the ability to manage the golf course. They always put the ball where it sets up the next shot perfectly. They seldom beat themselves. I have always thought that if Jack could have struck the ball as well as Ben, and if Ben could have putted like Jack, they would have won every tournament they entered. In one of golf's great symmetries, Hogan and Nicklaus were paired together in the final two rounds of the 1960 Open. It would be Ben's last serious run at the championship, and it was Jack's first appearance in our national championship. Ben said, "The kid should have won by eleven shots." Well, the kid would go on to win as many opens as Ben did and would become what Hogan had been—the best of his time.

Here are three examples of the Nicklaus mystique from 1978, an average year in the Nicklaus era.

At Inverrary that year, there was no immediate reaction to Jack's birdie at the fourteenth hole. He was still several shots off the pace in that final round. And, when he missed the green at the fifteenth, we started to look for another story to follow. Then he chipped it in the hole for his second straight birdie, and you could sense a change, catch a whiff of something special about to happen. When he rolled in the putt at sixteen for a two, few doubted the Nicklaus legend was being polished.

This was the Bear in full stride, completely focused on the task at hand, the competitive fires warming the glorious putting stroke. His opponent, Grier Jones, and the rest of us could only watch with awe. A birdie at seventeen from fifteen feet. Then an approach to five feet at eighteen for his fifth straight birdie and the championship. We saw one hour of almost perfect golf that, through the hundreds of tournaments played in all the years since, remains a vivid memory.

That was in February. In November of that year, the usual suspects were in Australia for the country's national championship. Through the intercession of Ben Wright, I was invited to be one of the broadcasters on Australian TV's Channel 7. The network was owned by Kerry Packer, who at the time was the Ted Turner of Australia. Packer was a media mogul, a prodigious gambler, and an entrepreneur. In 1978, he was establishing a professional cricket league and was building up the Australian Open Golf Championship. Packer had hired Jack Nicklaus to redo the Australian Country Club in Sydney. He had increased the purse from $25,000 to $250,000 and had induced or seduced some Americans to travel down under to enrich the field. One of the inducements for the Americans was a fishing expedition by the Great Barrier Reef, the world's largest coral reef, off the coast of Queensland. Jerry Pate, Bruce Lietzke, Ben Crenshaw, and Jack Nicklaus fished those famous waters with good results. Especially Nicklaus. He landed a 1,352 pound sailfish. It was out of the water eleven hours before it was weighed or it might have been a record.

Before he teed off for the first round, I asked him how long it had taken him to land the big fish.

"Six hours and twenty-five minutes."

"You must be exhausted," I said.

"No," he said with a shrug. "I had trouble walking for about ten minutes, but that was all."

Privately, we all thought that because of the exertion of catching the fish, Jack would not be among the top ten in the tournament. He shot a one over par seventy-three that day, and was six strokes off the pace set by Australian Graham Marsh.

That night we were all invited to a dinner party at Kerry Packers' house where Nicklaus, Crenshaw, Pate, and Lietzke were houseguests. It was a big rambling house filled with antiques from Asia. Oriental statues and Chinese boxes were everywhere. We were shown into a room with a bar, a long narrow room with an enormous snooker table at the far end. On the wall were pictures of the senior Packer, founder of the empire, who, among other things, had competed for the America's Cup with a boat named after Kerry's mother. A model of the Gretel's hull stood against the wall next to a picture of Kerry's father with President Kennedy and a framed letter from Mrs. Kennedy saying that she was sending a yachting flag of the president's to the Packers.

There were about fifteen people in the room. Lou Graham and his wife, the Graham Marshes, Kristy and Tom Kite were there, but there was no sign of our host or his illustrious houseguests. It felt like the opening scene of Agatha Christie's *Ten Little Indians*. There was the snooker table, no host, and we wondered if there would be a tape recording telling us we were prisoners.

Finally, as dinner was announced, the host and houseguests arrived. They had been playing tennis out in the back of the house, and not too many of us noticed that Jack Nicklaus was wearing an ice pack on his shoulder. The dinner was first rate with acres of Sydney rock oysters, succulent and sweet, bright red-shelled lobsters, all accompanied by a marvelously dry wine from the Hunter Valley.

After dinner, there was Waylon Jennings on the cassette deck, and while we were preparing to leave, Nicklaus came out into the hallway with a driver in his hand. He tried to swing, but he could not lift the club as high as his shoulder. This very brilliant man had played tennis in his street shoes and, in trying for a backhand, had slipped something in his shoulder.

The next morning, I stood on the practice tee with Jerry McGee, who was playing with Nicklaus in the first two rounds. Jerry had been on the practice tee for half an hour and there was no sign of Nicklaus.

"Do you think he'll play?" I asked.

"I don't think so," said Jerry. "That shoulder must be very bad."

Just then we looked up to see a large crowd moving across the first fairway toward the practice tee, and we knew that Nicklaus was on his way. He was dressed in navy-blue slacks and a brightly striped shirt. He smiled and was in good spirits.

"How's the shoulder?"

"Feels fine," he answered.

"When we left you last night," I said, "you couldn't lift your arm as high as your shoulder."

"I know it," he said. "I took a Butazolidin pill right before dinner and one before I went to bed. I couldn't get comfortable in bed, couldn't move without hurting. But this morning I feel fine. I'll tell you in a minute."

He began to hit some short irons, a wedge or a nine iron. The shots were beautifully struck, the swing smooth.

"Feels okay," he said. "Feels fine."

And off went Jack Nicklaus, Jerry McGee, and young Michael Clayton, the Australian amateur champion, for the 9:45 tee time.

By 10:30, Jack had three birdies. On the opening of the television show, Ben Wright and I discussed the fact that Nicklaus had sustained a shoulder injury the night before while playing tennis. At 10:30, reporting the fact that Jack was three under par, I said he was a walking advertisement for Butazolodin and tennis. At 10:40, word came that Kerry Packer had called saying if we mentioned Nicklaus and that tennis game again we could just get off his network. We didn't do either, and we didn't have to because now the story was of the incredible round Jack was having. When it was over, his card showed a six-under sixty-six, a course record and good enough to give him the tournament lead, four shots ahead of Ben Crenshaw and Bob Byman. It was that second round that won the tournament for Jack's fifth Australian Open.

That week in Australia, like the closing round at Inverrary, symbolized the competitive makeup of this man: The almost-record sailfish, the tennis injury, and the winning of the championship were all clues to what makes Nicklaus, Nicklaus.

Probably my most cherished memory of Nicklaus occurred in the middle of 1978 at the British Open at St. Andrews. There he received the most dramatic and moving ovation I have ever seen. It happened late on a gray afternoon at the Old Course. The laughter of children playing on the beach was drowned out by the rolls of applause that spilled out over the ancient links as Jack walked up the eighteenth fairway to claim his third British Open. People on the roof of the Russacks Hotel and the other buildings that line Links Road endangered their lives by joining in the applause. Thousands rose to their feet in the grandstand across the way.

Ben Crenshaw, on the terrace of the clubhouse, joined in the applause as it rose over the old gray town, across the buildings of the University and into all the nooks and crannies of the churchyard where Young Tom Morris is buried. The applause that swelled into the late afternoon was intense, stately, and dignified. There was no yelling or cheering. Just this steady, deep applause that seemed to go back to the beginning of the game. It was the Scots' highest tribute to the man they knew was one of the best ever, and certainly the best of his time.

These things happened in 1978 when Jack was thirty-eight years old. There were still great moments ahead. In 1980, after a winless 1979, Jack responded to those who thought age had nibbled at his talents by winning two more major championships. His record-tying fourth U.S. Open (his second at Baltusrol) and his record-tying fifth PGA championship at Oak Hill in Rochester silenced the critics. Both wins were laced with irony. It was at Baltusrol that Jack was treated rudely when some of Arnold's more rabid fans in 1967 actually booed him and cheered when he mishit the rare shot; but in 1980, when he won again, the crowd was completely on his side, chanting, "Jack is back, Jack is back." He had finally become the gallery's favorite. And, in winning his fifth PGA Championship, Jack tied the record held by the great Walter Hagen, and he accomplished the feat in Walter's hometown. Jack appreciates those little tucks of history.

He also knows that you can't win every time, and that you must accept that which you cannot control with good grace. Golfers are particularly adept at this demonstration of civility that gives ample proof that good manners do not detract from the determination to win. You do not have to be an angry boor dealing in tantrums when you lose to protect your competitive nature. "Show me a good loser and I'll show you a loser" was a funny line for Joe E. Lewis, but its application in sports is a disservice perpetrated by hormonal imbalances in many team sports. More to the truth is, "Show me a sore loser and I'll show you a person who needs therapy."

Since Jack finished second in major championships nineteen times he has often been the one congratulating, and he does it as well as anyone. One of the more memorable of Jack's nineteen second-place finishes occurred at the British Open in 1977. The championship was played that year for the first time at Turnberry on the west coast of Scotland. It was the same Turnberry I had seen from the deck of the *Ile de France* in 1944 on that cold, misty morning when the course had been used as an R.A.F. training base. Even today, the remnants of the old runways can be seen; some of them are used for parking when Turnberry hosts a championship. In 1977, the place was festive. The big White Hotel with the red roof perched on the bluff overlooking the golf course gleamed in the bright sunlight that glinted off the Firth of Clyde. Scotland was in the midst of a heat wave. It was not quite as bad as the year before at Royal Birkdale where things were so dry that part of the golf course caught fire. But it was still hot and dusty at Turnberry in 1977, the antithesis of British Open weather.

After thirty-six holes, Jack Nicklaus and Tom Watson were tied, both shooting 68–70, 138. In the third round, both players turned in impeccable sixty-fives to be coleaders at seven under par. They were paired together for the final round. At that time, Tom Watson was the premier challenger to Jack Nicklaus' dominance. He had beaten Jack at the Masters that year and was beginning a five-year stretch in which he would win seven major championships. He was ten years younger than Jack and, like Jack, loved the fight of a major championship. On the first tee that Sunday, it was as if they looked at each other and said, "Let's step outside and settle this thing between us." And that's exactly what they did, making the rest of the championship virtually match play and leaving the rest of the field hopelessly behind. The ground of the Ailsa course trembled from the powerful woods and irons, and the putts that plopped in from near and far. The summer afternoon was aroar with the shouts and cheers that greeted one great shot after another. The gallery looked like a medieval migration as they hurried from one hole to the next. Watson birdie; Nicklaus birdie; back and forth they went. Up past the lighthouse. Down past the R.A.F. Memorial. The two players making a masterpiece.

At the par-three fifteenth, Nicklaus had a one-stroke advantage. There he, and all of us, watched as Tom Watson sank a treacherous, impossible putt of sixty feet to pull even. As they walked to the next tee, Watson turned to Nicklaus and said, "This is what it's all about, isn't it?"

"Yes," said Jack. "This is what it's all about."

Tom took a one-stroke lead at the par-five seventeenth with a birdie to Jack's par. At eighteen, Watson hit a two-iron right in the middle of the fairway. Jack, trying to make something happen, took a driver. He almost put it out of bounds to the right, but it stayed in play, and from there he somehow put his second shot on the green twenty-five feet from the pin. Watson struck a seven-iron three feet from the hole. Then Nicklaus, squeezing one more moment out of this glorious day, holed his putt for a birdie. Tom now had to make his three-footer for the win, which he did. Watson, 65–Jack, 66. The nearest player was Hubert Green in third place—eleven shots behind. Since that summer day in 1977, Nicklaus and Watson are as much a part of Turnberry as Robert Bruce and those R.A.F. pilots commemorated there. After Watson sunk the winning putt, Nicklaus embraced him and said, "I did my best. You did better."

On the evening after the British Open at Muirfield in 1992, Jack, Terry Jastrow, and I drove up to St. Andrews. On the way, I mentioned that I talked with Greg Norman about the house he was building at Lost Tree Village in Florida where Jack lives.

"How far are you from Jack?" I asked.

"Oh, about a drive and a wedge," Greg replied.

He paused for a moment and then with a wide white grin said, "Jack's a drive and a three wood from me."

Jack smiled at the story and then said, "You know, Greg's got ten thousand square feet in that house." Then he paused a moment and said, "If I count my maintenance shed, I'd have eleven thousand square feet."

The competitive juices are never still.

The reason we were going to St. Andrews was to begin taping a video entitled *The Greatest Eighteen Holes in Major Championship Golf.* Jack Nicklaus had selected what he considered to be the best eighteen holes on courses that had hosted major golf championships. Our anchor position for the show was the bridge over the Swilcan Burn that golfers cross from the eighteenth tee to the fairway. This stone footbridge was built in the middle of the twelfth century and is as old as golf. The first time Roone Arledge played the Old Course he remarked to his caddy as they crossed the bridge, "Just think, the spikes of every great golfer in history have gone over this bridge."

"Except one," said the caddy immediately. "Ben Hogan."

He was right. Ben never played St. Andrews. That disappointment still hangs about this town, which would have loved to have given Ben the affection they bestowed on Bob Jones, Jack Nicklaus, and Arnold Palmer.

When you cross that bridge, you look up the eighteenth fairway at one of the most familiar sights in golf. The R and A clubhouse sits imposingly behind the first tee. The war monument beside it and the town stretches out to the right off of Links Road. That morning, the view from the bridge was as familiar as my backyard. Still, without the grandstands and other paraphernalia of the open championship to distort the scene, it was as if I was seeing it with my own eyes for the first time. And to be there on the King William IV Bridge with Jack Nicklaus was like being born rich and handsome with a scratch handicap.

From our position at the bridge, Jack and I would lead into each of the eighteen holes Jack had selected. The par threes were the seventh at Pebble Beach, the twelfth at Augusta, number four at Baltusrol and the twelfth at Royal Lytham. Jack broke the par fours into two categories—four short ones and six long ones. The short ones were the twelfth at the Old Course, the seventh at Augusta, the tenth at Riviera, and the eleventh at Merion. The long par fours were the eighth at Pebble Beach, the tenth at Augusta, the eighteenth at Muirfield, the eighteenth at Riviera, the eighteenth at Oakmont and the Road Hole, the seventeenth at St. Andrews. The four par fives were the thirteenth at Augusta, fourteenth at St. Andrews, seventeenth at Baltusrol, and the eighteenth at Pebble Beach. Par seventy-two—6,958 yards.

After we finished at the King William IV Bridge, we went out to tape Jack playing the twelfth hole. When he had finished, we had some time before the crew could set up at the fourteenth hole, and Jack said to me, "Let's play down to fourteen."

"I don't have any clubs," I said.

"You can use mine."

And so I played the thirteenth, fourteenth, and, later, the fifteenth and sixteenth holes at the Old Course at St. Andrews with Jack Nicklaus, using his clubs. I didn't play very well, but it was one of the most unforgettable days I ever spent on a golf course.

A few weeks later we were taping at the eighteenth hole at Baltusrol, and Jack was re-enacting his third shot to that par five in the 1967 U.S. Open. In that championship, Jack and Arnold were tied after three rounds, a shot behind the leader Marty Fleckman. That final round turned out to be a battle between Nicklaus and Palmer. Birdies at six and seven for Jack while Arnold went par-bogey put Jack in the lead for good. But there was a little drama at the final hole. Jack hit a poor drive and had to get back to the fairway with an eight iron. That left him with 223 yards to the green for his third shot to this par-five hole. He hit a beautiful two iron to the green, and he sank the putt for a birdie and a new Open record of 272.

Now here we were, twenty-five years later, on a summer morning on the eighteenth fairway at Baltusrol, asking Nicklaus to duplicate that two iron.

"I don't know whether I can do it," Jack said.

"Sure you can," said Terry Jastrow. "Where was the ball?"

"Well, I had 223 yards," said Jack. He looked up to the green and then walked a few steps and dropped the ball. "Right about here," he said.

His first shot went a little to the right, but he nailed the second try, right onto the green. Everyone went up to tape Jack putting out. When he had finished, Terry decided he would like Jack to hit one more shot. Back down to the fairway they came. Jack was measuring as he walked, and as he reached the spot where he had just hit from, he announced, "224 yards."

After twenty-five years, he had measured the distance to the green with his eye and had been just one yard off. Although Jack, along with Deane Beman, were the ones that brought the yardage book to the tour, Jack Nicklaus could have played just as well without one.

It has been a pleasure to be in his time.

New York New York

"It'll be ten minutes, Arthur."

In the days before astounding amounts of money came into professional sports, athletes were often seen around town. There was an easy relationship between the players and the print and television people who covered them; it was a far more pleasant situation than exists today, when that relationship is as abrasive as the one between politicians and the media. In New York in the sixties and into the eighties, athletes and media all mingled together in a group of wonderful watering holes, many of which are now only fond memoires. The center of these gathering places was to be found on historic West Fifty-second Street, once known as "Swing Street." The block between Fifth and Sixth Avenues was home to at least a dozen jazz clubs, places like Leon and Eddie's, Club 18, The Famous Door, and Jimmy Ryan's. And right in the middle of it all was the doyen of speakeasies, the 21 Club.

The street was one of New York's brightest attractions, even though, by the time I arrived in the early sixties, much of this cultural landmark was already gone. The handsome CBS building had taken over the entire northwest corner of West Fifty-second and Sixth Avenue. Across the street, the other new buildings wiped out all the old haunts. The music that had driven the street was gone, except for the Hickory House between Sixth and Seventh Avenues, where Billy Taylor and Marion McPartland would make the place sparkle with their pianos. But the Hickory House was also nearing the end. A great New York institution was dying, done in by the fortunes of real estate, and the street was taking on a new character.

The sporting gentry and the communications community would be the last occupants of this urban valley. The gentry moved from west to east on the street, beginning at Mike Manuche's Restaurant on the south side near Seventh Avenue. The circular bar was packed at lunchtime with people from ABC and CBS sports, Time-Life people, advertising executives and CEOs. Every Monday, Claude Harmon, the golf professional at Winged Foot, would hold court at the corner banquette in the bar, eating his steak charred rare and telling stories, many of which contained some delightful golfing tips. Vince Lombardi was a regular at Manuche's when he was in town. Howard Cosell would mesmerize the bar with his routines. Manuche's was a cozy, comfortable place with good food and good company.

If we were not at Manuche's, we would be up the block on West Fifty-second Street between Fifth and Sixth Avenues. There were three places of note on this historic stretch of New York pavement. The first was Rose's Restaurant, owned by Buzzy Buzzallino. Rose's catered mostly to TV time salesmen, but it embraced all who entered. One of Buzzy's friends was actor William

Gargan, who was raising money for the American Cancer Society. Bill Gargan had lost his vocal chords to cancer and he was tireless in getting money to fight the disease. One of his fund-raisers was a golf tournament that Buzzy helped him put together; every restaurant on the street and beyond sponsored a team of four players. It was a one-day outing at the North Shore Country Club on Long Island. We called it the Restaurant Open.

Bill Brendle, the sports publicist for CBS, was a regular at Rose's. He was a man of many parts who worked and played with the energy of a two-year-old. He was one of the last Runyonesque characters in New York. If he had been around in Damon's time, he would have been known as Billy Ticket; no one was better at getting tickets to a big event than Bill Brendle. You need two Super Bowl tickets the night before the game? If you were a friend of Billy Brendle, you'd get them.

He had an extraordinary memory. If you asked him for something at the end of a long evening, he'd call you the next morning and complete the deal. The only time he almost forgot something was one night before a Super Bowl in New Orleans. A group of us were in Al Hirt's club about eleven o'clock when Bill suddenly slapped his forehead with the heel of his hand.

"Oh, damn," he cried. "I forgot to call the White House."

As we all looked at each other in amazement, Bill went to a pay phone and called the White House to arrange a telephone hookup for the next day between the president and the winning coach. From then on, whenever we could, we'd say, "Hey, Bill, don't forget to call the White House."

"C.C. Old Fashioned with a splash" was his drink and he could go the distance at the evening games. He died in his sleep at home the Monday after a Super Bowl, peacefully, but too young. He wrote his own epitaph one day in Rose's; he paid his bill by check with the request, "Would you mind dating that tomorrow, because I spent today's last night."

Right next to Rose's was the last great sports bar, Toots Shor's.

Actually, Toots was a restaurant filled with people from all segments of the community who loved sports. Nobody loved them more than the proprietor, a Philadelphian who started his New York career as a bouncer at Leon and Eddie's, one of the leading spots on West Fifty-second Street. The first Shor's was on West Fifty-first Street. It was torn down to make room for another building. There was a closing dinner party attended by 250 of Toots's closest friends, all of whom were headline names from the sports, politics, entertainment and business communities.

A year later, Toots opened on West Fifty-second Street, not far from where Leon and Eddie's had been. The new Shor's was not as intimate as the old place. It had an enormous round bar with dark paneled walls. The dining room was barn-like and the food slightly suspect. The steaks and the roast-beef hash were great, but everything after that was an adventure. When Frank Gifford came back from his trip to Vietnam he was remarking one day how bad the food had been. "How did you get by?" someone asked. "I trained at Shor's," said Frank. No one laughed harder than Toots. If the food got only two stars in the *Times*, the drinks were off the chart. They were olympian: large bucket glasses filled to the top. The lightest, golden scotch turned the color of burnt sienna.

Shor's was a must stop for lunch or cocktails and occasionally dinner. All of the top sportswriters and broadcasters were regulars: Red Smith, Jimmy Cannon, Bob Considine, all made it part of their beat. Athletes abounded, not just from the local teams, but from all over the country. TV and the entertainment world crowded against each other in glorious congress, usually between five and seven o'clock.

On Mondays, a group from ABC, CBS, and *Sports Illustrated* would meet at the big round bar. All of us had worked on a sporting event over the weekend and so Mondays were our Fridays. Dan Jenkins, always disdaining the cliche, one day said, "I'll see you at Shor's at 5:42 on Monday", and thus was born the 5:42 club, a loosely structured group who discussed where we had been, where we were going, who was doing the best writing, which were the best movies, the urban riots, the war in Vietnam, and all the things that were part of our world in the sixties and seventies.

Toots was the perfect overseer for the "joint," as he called it, celebrating as much or more than his best customers. But he could be very solicitous. One day, just before noon, Bill Corum, sportswriter and later president of Churchill Downs, was at the bar drinking martinis.

"Bill," said a concerned Toots, "you shouldn't be drinking those things. They'll kill you."

"You're right, Toots," said Corum. Then he turned to the bartender and said, "Ziggy, make me a Gibson."

The happening that gave the last great Toots Shor's its personality was a hundred dollar wager between Toots and Jackie Gleason. Toots was a big man, well over six feet and weighing over 260 pounds. Jackie at the time was in one of his fat modes. They were arguing about who was in the better physical state. Toots said, "I know I'm in better shape than you. I'll bet you a hundred dollars I can beat you running around the block."

"Done," said Gleason. They went outside. "You go that way," said Gleason, pointing toward Fifth Avenue. "I'll go the other way. First one back here wins."

Toots went huffing up Fifty-second Street toward Fifth Avenue and Gleason went towards Sixth Avenue. At the corner, Gleason stopped and took a cab back to the restaurant. He was sitting at the bar fifteen minutes later when Toots came puffing in, red in the face and exhausted.

"Jimminy Crickets," said the crestfallen Shor. "How the hell did you beat me? Here's your $100."

"Thanks, pal," said Gleason, pocketing the money. They sat at the bar drinking for about fifteen minutes when the realization broke over Toots' face like the rising sun. He turned to Gleason and said, "Wait a minute, you creepy bum, I never passed you."

We called it the longest take in show business.

Next to Shor's in those days stood the 21 Brands building and, next to that, the 21 Club, the former speakeasy, then and now an elegant restaurant with one of the great bars in the world. It was the last stop on Fifty-second Street. You could live a lifetime between Manuche's and 21.

In those years the place of choice for late-night dining and drinking was located in a modest looking building on the northeast corner of East Fifty-fifth and Third Avenue. P. J. Clarke's was one of many Irish saloons that grew under the Third Avenue El. It had gained notoriety when it was used in Ray Milland's movie, *The Lost Weekend*.

When Danny Lavezzo bought the place from the Clarke family, he added a room onto the back of the saloon that changed the nature of the place. Now it was possible to get a great hamburger, a cup of chili, and other tasty dishes. Danny also added a decent wine list, and Clarke's, while still maintaining its Irish saloon ambiance in the front, had become something more. Ed Trysinski, co-author of *Stalag 17*, liked to call it a "café," claiming it had many of the attributes of the Parisian invention. For others, it resembled the coffeehouses of sixteenth century London. Irish saloon, café or coffeehouse, you could find it all at Clarke's, which became the Mermaid Tavern of our prime years in New York.

The back room is a long, narrow affair with a large service bar on the left wall and a tiny, open kitchen on the right at the front. You enter the back room through a short hallway that leads from the front bar. Between the front bar and that entrance was a small area, the middle room, with a large mirror on the wall, nine or ten tables, and an entrance door from Fifty-fifth Street. On the walls of the middle room are Irish memorabilia—pictures of Michael Collins, old boxers, and the like. In the front, the bar runs down the left side of the room and is splendidly stained with the spillage of the years. Across from it at the front end is a small grill that once was used to cook hamburgers, and across from the bar at the other end is the men's room. The men's room in Clarke's is like no other. It is not a separate room. It is a dark paneled cabinet that sits on the bar room floor. Inside are two of the grandest porcelain urinals in the plumbing universe. Each is about five feet high and four feet wide, large enough to contain a small family. Their blood lines must go back to the Baths of Caracalla. A juke box sits next to the door to the men's room, from which Streisand's "Secondhand Rose" and Sinatra's "Witchcraft" played so often they became part of the place. Clarke's was the spot that everyone came to sooner or later in the sixties and seventies in New York. It attracted an even more eclectic group that Manuche's or Shor's.

One of that eclectic group was Ed Wilcox, who sat every night at a table in the middle room next to the mirror. Ed was a writer whose wit could cut diamonds. Once he was sent a notice that his bill at Clarke's was overdue. He answered with a bristling "How dare you" letter, saying he would pay when he was ready. He added this postscript, "This is your first notice." One Sunday night after a Giants home game, Ed was at his usual table when Frank Gifford and Kyle Rote came into the bar to use the men's room. Immediately Ed signaled the bartenders:

"See what the backs in the boy's room will have."

If it wasn't Ed singing out his *bon mots*, it was the ritual greeting of Phil Collins, one of the bartender/waiters. Phil was an ex-boxer with an Irish ex-boxer's face that held a wondrous smile. "Ah," he would say as you entered through the Fifty-fifth Street door, "The smaht after-theater crowd." To which you were obligated to reply, "Good evening, Phil, where are the girls?"

"They're upstairs shaving," Phil would say. "They'll be down in a minute."

It was like a password code that granted you immediate entry.

Clarke's patrons could be divided roughly into two groups: the regulars, those who would come in four or five nights a week, and the out-of-town regulars who would come in every time they were in New York. In that latter category was Edward Bennett

Williams, the noted defense lawyer and then-owner of the Washington Redskins. One night someone asked him how in the hell he could have defended Jimmy Hoffa. Mr. Williams gave an impassioned, angry argument on the right to a fair trial and defense. It was very exciting. Arguments were rare but exquisite in Clarke's. When Hugh Carey was governor of New York, he made a trip to Ireland. On his return he held a press conference at Kennedy Airport. At that time he made a plea to Americans of Irish descent to stop funding the Irish Republican Army. That evening he came to Clarke's and was waited on by Paddy Baker, one of the regular bartender-waiters. He immediately challenged the governor on his IRA stance. Soon the governor and the waiter were in a scalding debate over the issue. Finally, the governor said, "Ah, what am I arguing with you for. You didn't vote for me. You're from Queens."

"I'm from Brooklyn, Governor," said Paddy, walking away.

On another evening Danny Lavezzo was sitting with the British actor Trevor Howard when Lawrence Harvey walked in. Howard immediately jumped to his feet and the two actors shouted, hugged and kissed. As Trevor sat down, he said to Danny, "In England we would have merely nodded."

The regulars were a group made up of newspapermen, actors, policemen, airline stewards, many types of athletes and Wall Street warriors. Most of them loved the race track and the language was often spiced with racing terms. Freddy Finklehoff, who made two fortunes in Hollywood and lost both at the track, was telling a story about Harry Cohn, the less than saintly head of Columbia Pictures. "Jack," Freddy said, "this guy may be dead, but it doesn't move him up any."

Billy Mack was a steward with TWA. Billy was as big as a jockey and looked like a leprechaun. He had a quick mind, Irish humor, and a gambler's head for figures. One day at the racetrack, Billy was sitting in the stands handicapping the next race when Danny Lavezzo came along with Walter Matthau. Danny introduced them and Walter Matthau asked Billy how he was doing. Billy looked up and said in fluent New Yorkese, "Disastrous." At the time, Matthau was preparing for Neil Simon's play, *The Odd Couple*. There is a little bit of Billy Mack in Matthau's Oscar Madison.

Clarke's was a great place to get the latest news. Norm Miller, sportswriter on the *Daily News*, was a regular. Leonard Lyons would stop in every night to get an item for his column. Jack O'Brien would come in from an opening night and give his critique. There was Pat Doyle, who was on the police beat on the *Daily News*; he was called "Front Page" because he looked like every newspaper man you saw in the movies. One night he came in all excited and pleased: "We had a great murder tonight. It'll go five days, at least."

Charley Burke was a policeman in the Bedford-Stuyvesant section of Brooklyn. He once had the beat on the Upper East Side where his duties included walking Bernard Baruch to his office every day, but now Charley was in a beleaguered precinct and pulling the swing shift.

"You'll never guess what happened this evening," he said one night. "Two guys broke into a gas station near the precinct. The cash register was empty, but they found the keys to the pumps. So they turned on the lights and started selling gas. When the third car pulled in, two guys got out with guns and said, 'This is a holdup.'"

The place was so popular in those days that Danny rotated two maître d's to handle the seating in the back room. Jimmy Ennis was a very pleasant man who never intruded and went about the business of seating people quietly. Frankie Robundo made the job an event. He became one of the powerful elite on the East Side. Clarke's seldom took reservations; some regulars would occasionally call ahead and ask for a table, but mostly it was first come, first served. Frankie Robundo was the man who made the calls. One especially busy night, with the hallway jammed with hungry people, Frankie looked up to see Supreme Court Justice Arthur Goldberg waiting in line. With a nonchalant wave Frankie called out:

"It'll be ten minutes, Arthur."

Actor/producer Martin Gabel; John McMartin of Broadway; Walt Frazier of the then-champion New York Knicks; Jimmy Martin, a contractor from Yonkers; all were Clarke's regulars, sitting each night in the back room or gathering around the end of the bar by an old safe on top of which they stacked the dirty dishes. "The Garbage" was the in place for several years.

One snowy, cold evening, Ari Onassis called and said he and his wife were coming in and they would like to have the table by the window in the middle room. Danny asked some of the regulars if we could sit at the next table and act as a buffer for the famous couple. Several of us, including Jimmy Martin and Billy Mack, were happy to oblige. In due time the shipping magnate and his wife arrived. A few minutes later, Mrs. Onassis left the table for the ladies' room. When she had gone, Billy Mack turned to Mr. Onassis and like an old acquaintance over a cup of coffee inquired, "Is it still snowing, Ari?"

These lines perhaps do not have a Churchillian ring to them, but "It will be ten minutes, Arthur," and "Is it still snowing, Ari?" describe the essence of Clarke's as well as any.

There were other stops we made in those years. Early on, Pete Peskey managed Eddie Condon's in the Sutton Hotel where Eddie, Bobby Hackett, and other great musicians made great sounds. Occasionally we would drop in at the Carlyle when Bobby Short was in residence. Elaine's had scored an immediate success and was the literary saloon of the seventies and eighties. But it was Clarke's, with its egalitarian atmosphere firmly managed by Dan Lavezzo, that was the center of our Manhattan merry-go-round. Danny is a remarkable man. He is the product of the best schools, but is so shy and self-effacing that you would never know it. He is a wonderful conversationalist with a variety of interests. His passions include horse-racing, tennis, and the New York Giants. Most patrons of Clarke's don't know who Danny Lavezzo is, but the regulars do; without Danny, Clarke's would have been just another Irish saloon.

Today there is very little left of that New York, of that world where the shakers and the makers met in public houses. Elaine's still keeps the lamp lit, and 21 still looks the same. They have maintained the marvelous flavor of the twenties and thirties and the feeling of sophistication that is so lacking today. Clarke's is still at Fifty-fifth and Third Avenue, and on occasion, when Danny Lavezzo is there, it resembles the old days. But not very often. The old crowd has died or retired to Florida, and the young makers and shakers go elsewhere. Today there is nothing like the joints on Fifty-second Street or the old Clarke's. Today's sports bars are glitzy stores jammed with television monitors all flicking constantly. The noise level approaches uproar, conversation is impossible. The professional athlete is seldom seen around town, unless it's for a paid appearance. They have become as modern-day Garbos, reclusive behind the walls of their suburban estates. Change is inevitable, I know, and I also know that what I mourn are the years of my long-gone youth, but every great civilization has had a P. J. Clarke's, a place to talk, argue, laugh, and exchange ideas. And my generation was fortunate to have had some great ones.

International Events

"You went too fast."

One of the first results of television's voracious appetite was the expansion of the subject matter in sports. The basic games were joined by some very esoteric pastimes, such as auto-thrill shows, college circuses, and dog-sled races. The expansion included a lot of international events, which required an ever-ready passport. If you worked on the *CBS Sports Spectacular* or on *ABC's Wide World of Sports*, you literally saw the world.

When I joined CBS Sports full-time in 1965, they had lost the Olympic Games to ABC, so they acquired the rights to as many other international events as they could. The Marv Sugarman track series was one example, and so were the Pan-American

Games. This sports carnival is a competition of Olympic events between the countries of the Western hemisphere from Canada to Patagonia, held the year before the Olympics.

In 1975, the host country was Colombia, but some economic and political problems forced them to withdraw at the last moment. Mexico City saved the games by offering their facilities from the 1968 Olympic Games. This Pan-American meeting was the one in which the Cubans unveiled their world-class athletes and training program. Sprinter Silvio Leonard and middle-distance runner Alberto Juantorena joined boxer Teofilo Stevenson as the early stars of this remarkable program that produced a percentage of champions far in excess of the country's population.

The Cubans were very proud of their accomplishments, and they invited CBS to come to Havana to see how the program was set up. Good propaganda for the Castro regime. I was selected as the correspondent and Ed Goren was the producer. After an almost endless bureaucratic dance to acquire visas from the Cuban consulate, we flew to Havana with a group of Cuban athletes whose events had been completed. On the flight came the news that Cuba had defeated the United States in baseball, and the cheers rocked the plane.

Our host was the director of the sports program, an engaging, bright man named Mario Escolino. His brother was a doctor who had fled to Miami after Castro came to power. Mario had chosen to remain and become part of the new government. The Cubans were courteous and hospitable, and let us film everywhere. We thoroughly enjoyed Mario's company and had many frank political discussions without rancor, even on the day the Rockefeller Commission Report was published, revealing that there had been a U.S. plot to assassinate Fidel Castro. Things were a little awkward at dinner that evening, but Mario never lost his composure.

When we had completed filming, Mario gave us a grand lunch in a lovely building in the plaza by the cathedral. There were Cuban cigars and cordials after the meal and more talk. Someone asked Mario why so many people left Cuba if the revolution was such a success. Mario responded with spirit.

"Do you know who left? Five groups," he said, ticking them off on his fingers. "One, the gamblers. Two, the pimps. Three, the prostitutes; four, the criminals; five, the very rich. Where are they now? In Las Vegas and Miami. There is an old Spanish proverb," Mario continued, " 'If the enemy you have defeated wants to leave, build him a silver bridge.' "

I liked Mario. The next time I was in Havana was about eight years later. I asked our interpreter about Mario. "Oh," he said, "he's a colonel in the army, training troops in Latin America." I hope they didn't build him a silver bridge.

The opening and closing ceremonies of those 1975 Pan-American games were held in Aztec Stadium, which then was an old, gray concrete structure. It had barbed wire on top of the partitions that separated the lower-priced seats from the higher-priced ones. On opening day, Pat Summerall and I were in our announcing location, high up in the stadium on a rickety platform that teetered dangerously over the seats below. Pat was interviewing Pele, the great international soccer star, and zealous Mexican fans were trying to climb over the barbed-wire partitions, pushing and screaming, all trying to touch Pele. The platform was rocking and it seemed only a question of time before we would all go crashing to our deaths. I could see the headline:

PELE AND TWO OTHERS KILLED IN STADIUM COLLAPSE.

Somehow, order was restored, and Pele was escorted out. Now I had to get down to the field to open the show. The field was ringed with soldiers and, as I stepped out on the grass, one of them turned and barred my way with a rifle at high point, bayonet fixed. I showed him my credentials, but he was not impressed. He kept motioning me back with the point of the bayonet. My Spanish was insufficient for the task, and finally, near panic, I was rescued by a Pan-Am official and got to my position just in time. The theme song for these games was "Cielito Lindo," sung beautifully by a chorus of school children from Pueblo. Now, when I hear that haunting melody, all I see is barbed wire and bayonets.

The last Pan-American games I covered were in 1991. ABC had acquired the rights and Havana was the host city. The State Department was not very happy with ABC for televising these games, because it gave Castro some desperately needed cash, but ABC went ahead. Havana and the entire country were feeling the effects of the U.S.'s economic sanctions. There was a serious shortage of gasoline, and Castro had imported thousands of bicycles from China to help with the transportation crisis. On the other hand, there were signs of an increase in the tourist business. Several beach resorts were filled with Scandinavians and other Europeans, but the overall appearance of the capital city was shabby. Still, the government honored American credit cards in most places, and several old Havana haunts had reopened. The Floridita, one of Ernest Hemingway's favorite stops, was always busy. The Hemingway Daiquiri, made with fresh grapefruit juice, was a runaway best seller. A small bodega, which Hemingway also frequented, was doing a booming trade. It was a narrow two-story building. The walls of the bar were plastered with photos from the thirties and forties. The Hemingway drink there was the *mojito*, another seductive rum concoction. The black bean soup was outstanding.

When I had returned to Havana for a boxing show in the eighties, I had gone out to the Hemingway *finca*, or country home, at San Francisco de Paula. It was in fragile condition then, because the government had no money to maintain the place. Tourists were not allowed inside the main house; instead, they walked around the veranda and looked into the open windows. In the living room by an easy chair was a table that served as the bar, and the bottles were there, the bright yellow of the Gordon's gin label standing out. In the writer's bedroom there was a copy of *Collier's* magazine on the bed, along with a pair of reading glasses and an old fisherman's hat.

The best Hemingway experience I had in Cuba happened at the games in 1991. One of our technicians, Finbar Collins, asked me one day if I would like to meet the Old Man of *The Old Man and the Sea.*

"How can I do that?" I asked.

"Just be at the Terrace in Cojimar at noon and we'll have lunch with him."

I had paid my respects to Cojimar and the Terrace earlier. Cojimar, just east of Havana, is the small fishing village from which Hemingway sailed on his boat, the *Pilar.* It was also the setting for the Nobel Prize–winning novel, *The Old Man and the Sea.*

The Terrace is a fairly large restaurant/bar overlooking the Cojimar harbor. It has a wide outdoor patio, but this day Finbar motioned me inside to one of the tables in the dining room just as our guest was arriving. There were seven or eight people at the table, three of us from ABC Sports. The others were newspapermen from South America. One of them, as eager as we were to talk with our guest, acted as the interpreter.

Gregorio Fuentes was a spry and alert man with lively eyes set in a gnarled, walnut-colored face. He was more than willing to talk, and enjoyed being the center of attention. We asked him to tell us all he could about Ernest Hemingway and their adventures aboard the *Pilar.* Gregorio said that Hemingway was an excellent fisherman, not just a recreational one, but a man who could have made his living from the sea. He liked a drink and was a good man on a boat. The best times, Gregorio said, were during World War II, when the *Pilar* patrolled the north coast of Cuba looking for German U-boat activity. He said the story of a man catching a large fish only to have the sharks eat it was an old one, and had happened more than once in the waters off Cojimar. No, it had never happened to him.

Señor Fuentes answered our questions with animation, obviously enjoying his celebrity status and the *cerveza,* and as he talked, it didn't matter that he was perhaps being used as an attraction for the restaurant. He was an old man enjoying his memories. And it didn't matter either that at the time Hemingway wrote *The Old Man and the Sea* in 1950, Gregorio had been a young man in his late thirties. In that dining room, brightly lit by the Cuban sun, an extraordinary moment was occurring, that moment when the line between fact and fiction blurs. Gregorio had *become* Santiago. This man sitting with us and answering our questions, this man with the merry eyes in the worn face, was *the* man who admired the great DiMaggio, who was befriended by the boy Manolin, the man who fought the *galanos*, and dreamed of lions on the golden beaches of Africa. That afternoon Gregorio and Santiago were the same man. He was the Old Man.

That year we stayed in the hotel that Meyer Lansky had built in the fifties when gambling was a major Havana attraction. The lobby still has a faint trace of early Vegas. The hotel is right on the ocean, across the street from the Malecon, the promenade that defines much of Havana's waterfront and where every evening the young Habañeros gather. In front of the hotel by the taxi kiosk was a mongrel dog. He was a tan, smooth-haired little thing, and he had one hind leg missing. From early morning to late at night he would be by the entrance steps, moving about on his three legs among the cars or sleeping by the kiosk. Our technicians named him "Tripod."

The official mascot of the Games was a cuddly bear, but it occurred to me that Tripod was the perfect symbol for those Pan American games in Havana. He was hopping about and coping despite his shabby appearance and handicap, much in the way the Cuban people were coping. The closing piece I did for the last show was the story of Tripod and how all of us had become attached to him and how he, and not the little bear mascot, should have been the symbol of the Games. The Cuban officials, thinking we were disturbed by Tripod, took him away to be destroyed—but quick work by the Americans rescued Tripod, and Jack Arute of ABC was given permission to take him to the

United States where, the last I heard, he had found a happy home in Florida.

Television sports requires programming twelve months a year, so many of our international events occurred in the winter months and centered around winter sports. We did ski races in Austria, ski jumping in Germany, and ski flying, which is jumping from a bigger hill, in the mountains of Bohemia in the Czech Republic. My first assignment with ABC Sports was an amateur boxing tournament between the United States and the then-Soviet Union. The matches were held in Moscow during a bitter-cold week in January 1982, in which a state funeral was held for Andrei Susalov, a major force in the Communist Party.

It was somewhat alarming on the morning of the funeral to open the doors of our hotel rooms and find the corridor filled with plainclothes KGB men all staring at us unsmilingly. It was a long six days in Moscow, but relief was on the way: From Moscow, I flew to Switzerland for two weeks in St. Moritz. I don't believe it is possible to move further, culturally or economically, in one day than to go from the Intourist Hotel in Moscow to the Kulm Hotel in St. Moritz.

The Kulm Hotel was the first luxury hotel in the world's first famous winter resort. It is elegant, comfortable, large, and expensive. It overlooks a lake that freezes so thickly that they hold horse races on it. The Kulm Hotel was first owned by Johannes Badrutt, who began a long line of eminent Swiss hoteliers. One evening in the autumn of 1864, Badrutt made a wager with four of his English guests that if they came back to St. Moritz in the winter and did not find the weather better than in London, he would pay all their expenses. The offer was taken, and the following December, on a sunny, clear day, the English, perspiring and nearly blind from the glare of the sun, were greeted by Badrutt in his shirtsleeves. And, thus, the winter resort was born.

The Kulm Hotel—and later the Palace, owned by Johannes's son Casper—became the social center for "Those of blue blood, of scarlet women and black sheep." They invented apres-ski before skiing was popular. Tobogganing was the sport in St. Moritz in the early days, and in 1885, a group of English staying at the Kulm invented the Cresta in response to an international toboggan race in Davos. Then in 1887, a very brave man named Cornish rode the Cresta lying on his stomach instead of sitting up, and, with that, the Cresta became a special and enduring part of St. Moritz.

The *Cresta* is an ice run, three-quarters of a mile long, with a 514-foot drop from start to finish. It has ten very demanding turns, or corners, as it snakes its way down from St. Moritz, past the village of Cresta, and ends in the tiny town of Celerina. Thanks to Mr. Cornish, the rider makes the journey on his stomach on a steel-runnered sled called a *skeleton* or *wagon*. You steer it with your body and brake with the spikes on the toes of your special shoes. The sled will be going seventy miles an hour when you hit the last corner. It is the ultimate bellyflop.

I first read about the Cresta in high school in a wondrous story by Paul Gallico. Years later, as a panelist on a TV game show, I identified Paul Gallico as the mystery guest from a single clue: "The mystery guest's most thrilling feat was riding the Cresta." This from Paul Gallico who had stepped into the ring with Jack Dempsey.

I was eager to finally see this unique challenge that has developed into a worldwide fraternity of enthusiasts. One of the passionate believers was our producer, Doug Wilson, one of the best and most delightful with whom I have worked. Doug was a veteran of the Cresta, earning a dislocated shoulder when he went off the course at Shuttlecock, the most severe of the turns, a wide, highly banked affair that is difficult to complete if you are going too fast.

I thoroughly enjoyed my first exposure to the St. Moritz Tobogganing Club, the organization that runs the Cresta. They are a charming and boisterous group, mostly English and Swiss, but also a sprinkling of international daredevils. The Cresta run is opened at seven and closes around noon before the sun can soften the ice. At nine o'clock in the morning, the bar in the clubhouse is going full speed. After the last race, everyone walks up to the Kulm Hotel for lunch on the terrace overlooking the lake.

I kept my distance on that first visit to the Cresta, turning down all suggestions of taking a ride. My devout cowardice was strong and unyielding, seeing the dangers that lurked on every run down that icy trail. But, when we returned in 1985 to televise the 100th anniversary of the Cresta's International Race, I was not so fortunate. That year, the St. Moritz Tobogganing Club gave a dinner for the American television people. Doug Wilson and the club's president, Sir Roger Gibbs, made several toasts, and in the height of our gaiety it was decided that I would ride the Cresta in the morning.

I awoke the next day remembering that it was my oldest son's thirtieth birthday and that I was almost sixty-one years old, and since I had come this far in life, why did I want to ride the Cresta? The phone rang at 7:30. It was Doug Wilson, who was more excited than I was. "Remember," he said, "8:30 at Junction." How could I forget? I was apprehensive, but not overly so. I suppose I had blocked out the evil thoughts of what might happen, telling myself I would go so slowly that it would take me five minutes to get to the bottom.

At Junction, which is across from the clubhouse, and where all novices start, I was saluted on the loudspeaker by the distinguished Secretary of the St. Moritz Tobogganing Club, Lt. Col. Digby J. Willoughby. He requested all those riding for the first time to come up to his very private office at the top of the clubhouse. There were four of us, and we were asked to sign a paper relieving the club of any responsibility in case of an injury or worse. Then Digby began his lecture.

Lt. Col. Digby J. Willoughby is a retired officer of the famous Gurkha Rifles, a group of Nepalese who served England heroically in both World Wars. He has the good looks of a Trevor

Howard. His cigarette is held in a holder and he speaks in the staccato rhythm of the English public-school graduate.

"First of all," he began in the tones of a schoolmaster, "you are not going for speed. Is that clear?"

We all nodded.

"Now the first thing to remember is your feet are your brakes. Dig those spikes into the ice, and to do that you must keep your feet straight at a ninety-degree angle. Don't let them splay outward. Keep your elbows close to your sides. Now, in case you leave the course at Shuttlecock or elsewhere, remember to push the sled away from you to the left. It weighs eighty pounds and can hurt you if it gets in the way. Now, any questions?" We shook our heads in unison.

"I have one more thing to say to you."

We looked up expectantly.

"Never, I repeat, never, set foot in this room again. Good luck!"

Giggling, we marched down the stairs and across the track to where our wagons awaited us. Doug Wilson was there to repeat the instructions.

"The feet are the brakes. Dig in with your toes."

Finally, Digby announced my name. I felt strangely calm. The one thought I had was that I would inevitably go out at Shuttlecock and I must remember to thrust the sled to the left. The shoes I had borrowed were old and the spikes not very sharp. That, combined with my thin ankles, left me with little or no braking ability, and by the time I hit the first two turns, Rise and Battledore, I was out of control, going faster than I thought possible. Fear rushed over me, mixed with exhilaration.

As I approached Shuttlecock, I got ready to push the sled away to the left. Up, up the banked turn I sped and I pushed the sled to the left as hard as I could. At the very rim of the turn the force of the push carried me back down the bank, and instead of flying out I was now locked in the icy embrace of the Cresta, thundering down the course and holding on for dear life.

When I passed under the bridge at Bulpetts, I relaxed a bit, sensing I would make it safely down. But the next moment my heart was leaping upward as the last two turns, Scylla and Charybdis, flashed by so quickly I had no time to think. The sled was on its own, going faster with every foot. Finally, I crossed the finish line, and came to rest on the upward slope that is the end of this awesome sleighride. A Swiss carrying a long stick with a hook on the end of it retrieved the sled. I was in a state of absolute euphoria. I said to him, "Is this where I'm supposed to be?" The man didn't even grunt. He was completely indifferent and oblivious to the fact that I had almost killed myself. I began to shake and run at the mouth. My right knee was sore, but only bruised, and then a feeling of well-being and accomplishment came over me.

My time was seventy-two seconds, 20.25 seconds slower than the record. At the bar in the clubhouse they plied me with congratulatory drinks. I was one of them. In the midst of the celebration, Digby walked in and fixed me with those ice-blue Gurkha Rifle eyes.

"You went too fast."

There is another thing that endears St. Moritz to me: It isn't far from Klosters, and Klosters is where Irwin Shaw used to spend the winter months in a cozy, bright apartment on the main street of the village across from the Chesa Grischuna Hotel. I had been an Irwin Shaw fan since I read the first chapter of *The Young Lions,* and it was a great delight to meet and get to know him when I moved to eastern Long Island in the mid-seventies.

In those days, the community center of Bridgehampton was Bobby Van's, an unpretentious restaurant/bar on Rte. 27. Bobby was a Juilliard-trained musician, and the piano bar was a popular spot when the owner was performing.

The man who made Van's a Hampton's institution was Willie Morris, the writer/editor from Yazoo City, Mississippi, the University of Texas, and Oxford University. Among Willie's many talents was the capacity to bring together the townspeople who had been born and raised in the community and those of us who had moved there later in life. The unofficial mayor of Bridgehampton was Willie's black labrador, who was easy to spot as he made his rounds checking on his constituents. Willie was also the playing manager of the softball team that played each Sunday in the field behind Bridgehampton High School, where Carl Yastrzemski had starred before ascending to the Red Sox. The team was called the Golden Nematodes. The nematode is a virus that attacks the potato, and the team's mascot was a jar of dirt that sat on the bench next to the manager.

Willie had written a lovely essay about the village and Bobby Van's that appeared on the *New York Times* op-ed page, and from then on, Van's was a smashing success. The regulars included Truman Capote, James Jones, John Knowles, Irwin, Joseph Heller, and a glittering list that rivaled Elaine's and P. J. Clarke's in Manhattan.

Irwin was full of energy and interested in everything, and along with Willie Morris, the most avid sports fan of the group. One evening I gave a dinner party for Lindsey Nelson, then broadcasting the Mets games, and Frank Wright, my horse-racing guru. Irwin and his wife Marian, Gloria Jones, and Willie all crowded into my small kitchen. Irwin was delighted to talk horses with Frank, especially about the great Ribot, the Italian thoroughbred who had raced in Europe in the sixties. Then Lindsey told an eyewitness story that happened on the eve of the liberation of Paris in 1945.

Lindsey had been the public relations officer for the 9th Infantry Division in Europe. In that position, he got to know every Pulitzer-Prize-winning newspaperman of the war. In August 1944, the Allies broke the back of the German army in France and were closing in on Paris. The Allied command, diplomatically and with a fine sense of propriety, held up the American, British, and Canadian forces so that the French Second Armoured Division could have the honor of being the first unit to enter the city.

On the night of August 24, the night before General Le Clerc led his division down the Champs-Elysees, some American units were billeted in the town of Rambouillet, southwest of the capital. In a cafe there that night, Ernest Hemingway, a correspondent for an American magazine at the time, was giving the public-relations officer of the 1st Infantry Division a hard time. "Bullying him," was the way Lindsey put it. A photographer for the Associated Press, Harry Harris, who would later cover the Mets with Lindsey, kept telling Hemingway to stop bothering the officer, whom everybody liked. But Hemingway persisted. Finally, Harry, not a very big man, turned Hemingway around and hit him right on the jaw, knocking him down and out for the count, to the cheers of the assembled crowd. When Lindsey finished the story, Irwin cried, "My god, I came into that cafe about fifteen minutes later, and when they told me what happened I didn't believe them."

I went to visit Irwin in Klosters during that two-week sojourn in St. Moritz. The train ride from St. Moritz to Klosters in winter is a trip through the pages of childhood storybooks. The tracks lead through dark-green forests and wide, white meadows where chalets and farmhouses wear three feet of snow on their roofs. Swiss trains are among the best in the world; they start smoothly and quietly, and their whistle is one of the most delightful sounds I know, soft as a baby's giggle as they pipe away at the ski-run crossings. I stayed at the Hotel Chesa Chrischuna in Klosters and had a great time. The Shaws were wonderful hosts.

In 1984, I was assigned to cross-country skiing and the biathlon for the Winter Olympic Games in Sarajevo. The good news about the assignment was that the teams would be training in Davos for a week before the games began. Davos is just down the road from Klosters, and that's where we stayed that week, in the Viren Hotel at the foot of the main street, a block from Irwin's apartment.

Marian and Irwin invited me to dinner several times. Feeling embarrassed that I couldn't return their hospitality, I said goodbye to them one night, only to have Irwin call me the next morning and insist that I come to dinner that night. There would be someone there he wanted me to meet. That someone was Alfred Del Negro, an old friend of the Shaws'. He had a story Irwin wanted me to hear.

Alfred Del Negro was a Greek who had been educated in Switzerland. There, he had become an accomplished skier, so much so that he decided to enter the 1936 Winter Olympic Games at Garmisch-Partenkirchen, Germany. He was the only Greek in the games, a one-man team. He was billeted in a private home owned, he said, by a big, kindly *Grossmutter*-type woman. The day before the opening ceremonies there was no snow in Garmisch and a disaster seemed imminent. When Mr. Del Negro mentioned this to his landlady, this kindly grandmotherly woman said:

"In der Morgan Der Fuhrer kompt, in der Morgan the Schnee kompt."

The next morning, Adolph Hitler arrived in the middle of a heavy snowstorm.

It is traditional Olympic practice that the first nation in the opening parade is Greece, the founding country of the Olympics. Mr. Del Negro, as a one-man Greek team, was looking forward to carrying his country's flag and leading all the athletes into the stadium. However, when the Greek ambassador to Germany heard about Mr. Del Negro's participation in the games, the ambassador decided he wanted to carry the flag. Mr. Del Negro objected strenuously and a fearsome quarrel erupted. A compromise was struck: If you look closely at the film of the opening parade of the 1936 Games, you will see the Greek flag being carried by a young boy, the son of the butcher of Garmisch, an arrangement made through the intercession of Mr. Del Negro's landlady. It is one of my favorite Olympic stories, and I am indebted to Irwin for insisting I come to dinner that evening.

Irwin had requested that his ashes be scattered over his favorite ski run in Klosters. It is against Swiss law to do this, but Marian and their son Adam dispersed half of them over the Gotschnagrat, and kept the other half for America. Marian gave these remains to their great friend Bob Parrish for safekeeping. Bob put them on a shelf in his garage in North Haven. I read about this in Michael Schnayerson's biography of Irwin while on an airplane. When I got home, I telephoned Bob and said I'd like to come over and toast Irwin in his garage.

"You're too late," said Bob. "Marian came by last week and took the ashes with her."

It really didn't matter. If you knew Irwin, you didn't need an urn to toast him.

We left the comfortable confines of Klosters and the Viren Hotel for Sarajevo and my first Olympic experience. It was overwhelming. There is nothing in the annals of network television to compare with broadcasting the Olympic Games in the days before cable TV. Nineteen eighty-four was the last year a single network would broadcast both the summer and winter games, and one of the last before cable networks would relieve some of the programming load. Even today, with cable help and other advances, broadcasting the Olympic Games is the most daunting, complex, and satisfying accomplishment in television.

In Sarajevo, we were burdened by the eight-hour time difference with New York, which required that all of our coverage would be taped and broadcast later. The difficulty in this is not so much that the results are known before we go on the air in the United States, but that taping requires an enormous amount of post-production work. When we broadcast live, there is no post-production; when the event is finished, you are finished. That's why most of us prefer live television.

Most of the ABC team stayed at the Hotel Bosnia on the edge of town out past the airport. It was the same hotel in which the ill-fated Archduke Franz Ferdinand and his wife Sofia stayed the night before they were murdered. The organizing committee had fixed it up with new mattresses and new reading lamps, and it was as comfortable as a turn-of-the-century hotel could be. We would leave the hotel at six in the morning in an ancient van and go up to the top of Mount Igman, the venue for the cross-country skiing and biathlon events. It was here that Tito and his partisans had fought successfully against the Germans and now, forty years later, the mountain top was peaceful and quiet. The cross-country trails meandered through an evergreen forest, and the silence was broken only by the rifle shots of the biathletes and the cheering of the crowds at the finish line. The thin, clear air of the mountain was far different from the smog that hung over Sarajevo on the floor of the valley.

The races would be over around noon, and I would go back to the hotel while the producer, Amy Saks, and director Larry Kamm went to the television center to edit the shows to the allotted time. At six o'clock I would go to the center and wait until we could get a recording studio booth to put the voice on the edited version of the competition. Then we would wait until either Chuck Howard or Roone Arledge okayed the finished product. Often that didn't happen until one or two the next morning.

They were long days but exciting ones and, although some of the work was drudgery, at the end there was a tremendous feeling of accomplishment and a trunkful of memories.

The weather on Mount Igman was mostly good, but over on Mount Bjelasnica where the alpine ski races were held, a series of violent snowstorms postponed the events for several days. As a result, cross-country skiing got a lot of air time. Amy Saks, our peerless producer, kept Diana Nyad, Bill Koch, and me loose while working those long and sometimes frustrating hours. She had a marvelous aura of calm and a sense of direction that never wavered. She got more out of us than we knew we had in us. Dear Amy died of lupus before her thirty-fifth birthday, a tragedy for her young family and a great loss for television.

The rigor of the cross-country schedule left little time for sightseeing, but I did manage to get into downtown Sarajevo a few times. This ancient city is known to most of the world as the place where World War I started. It was here that Archduke Franz Ferdinand, heir to the Austro-Hungarian Empire, and his wife were assassinated in a plot to gain independence for Bosnia. The royal couple were to have been killed on the morning of June 28 as they were riding in an open car to City Hall for a reception, but the bomb that was thrown into the car was immediately picked up by the Archduke and thrown out, wounding a few people but leaving the royal couple unscathed.

After that abortive attempt, the plotters broke up, crestfallen and ashamed. One of them, Gavrillo Princip, decided to drown his sorrows and had a few slivovitzes in a corner cafe. He was very surprised when he left the cafe to see the car carrying the Archduke and his wife make a wrong turn into the street where Princip was standing. Only a few feet separated the assassin and the Hapsburgs. Gavrillo fired pointblank, and history took a sharp turn. The cafe where Gavrillo consoled himself that June afternoon became a museum dedicated to him in 1984. Outside, on the sidewalk where he pulled the trigger they have embedded his footprints, in the manner of movie stars at Grauman's theater in Hollywood.

Golfers and baseball fans might be interested to know that Princip shot from an open stance, like Lee Trevino and the pupils of the late Charley Lau.

The reason for one of my trips downtown was to do a piece on the three religions of Sarajevo. The city was founded in the twelfth century and was a crossroads for trade between Europe and the Orient. It was the dwelling place of many peoples of many religions. We were going to show the mosques, synagogues, and Christian churches standing side by side in apparent peace. The essay never aired and, in view of later events, it was probably a good thing.

My last visit downtown was to the arena for the closing ceremonies. I did a wrap-up piece on the games, and stayed to watch Torville and Dean skate a program as Robert Preston sang "I never send roses" from the musical *Mack and Mabel*. It is the best thing I have ever seen on ice skates.

The people we dealt with in Sarajevo, Muslim, Christian, and Jew, were some of the nicest, most cheerful people we've ever met. Our interpreters, drivers, TV people all went out of their way to be pleasant and helpful. Every request was answered with a *nemo problemo*. We became very fond of them. When the war broke out, we were more than saddened and dismayed at the killings and destruction that descended on Sarajevo. The shelling of the Hotel Bosnia, the bombardment of the broadcast center where we had spent so many hours, and the twisted steel of the Olympic Stadium hit home very hard. We wonder, even now, what happened to those happy people we knew in 1984. Those were the games of Scott Hamilton, Bill Johnson, and Torville and Dean, but our lasting memories will be of the kind and cheerful people we knew in the days before ethnic cleansing.

Nineteen eighty-four was a busy year. After Sarajevo, we had the usual annual events: The Kentucky Derby, Preakness and Belmont; the U.S. Open at Winged Foot; and then, in one eight-week period, we broadcast the Women's U.S. Open at Salem Country Club in Massachusetts, then flew to St. Andrews for the British Open, then to Los Angeles for the summer Olympic Games, from there to Alabama for the PGA Championship, back to California for the National Diving Championships, and then to Oklahoma for the U.S. Amateur Championship. Eight straight weeks of quality events, the centerpiece, of course, being the Olympic games.

Those games were a turning point in the Olympic movement. Early on, before the Russians announced they were not coming in response to the United States boycott of the 1980 games in Moscow, the organizing committee got little help from the local, state or federal governments. Under the leadership of Peter Ueberroth and Harry Usher, the committee introduced corporate financing in a big way and changed forever the way Olympic games are marketed. These were the games of Carl Lewis, Greg Louganis, and Mary Lou Retton—but these were also the games that earned a $250 million profit.

They were also the most comfortable games in terms of traffic, the availability of restaurant reservations, and access to the venues. Many Angelenos left the city for the duration of the games and the freeways were moving very well. My assignments put me in the presence of two of the biggest personalities of the games.

Gymnastics felt the absence of the Russians as much as did any sport, but the boycott did not detract from the glorious performances of the United States men's and women's teams. The men defeated the world-champion Chinese team and the women had to compete against the formidable Romanians led by Ecatarina Szabo, who looked like a girl in a Fragonard painting.

The men's team of Mitch Gaylord, Bart Connors, Tim Daggett, Peter Vidmar, Jim Hartung, and Scott Johnson set a new standard for American gymnasts. The Americans had a slight lead over the Chinese as the United States came to the last event, the high bar. Pauley Pavillion was aquiver with excitement as Tim Daggett began his routine. He performed magnificently, and then ended with a double back lay-out somersault with a full-twist dismount, which he nailed perfectly. He received a perfect ten from the judges and earned the first Olympic medal for the United States team, and a gold one at that.

The women's team won the silver medal behind the Romanians, but it was a little package of dynamite from Fairmount, West Virginia who lit up Pauley Pavillion with a dazzling display of athleticism and an incandescent smile. Mary Lou Retton came to her last event, the vault, in the all-around competition needing a 9.95 score to tie Szabo of Romania for the gold medal. When the green light flashed on for Mary Lou's turn, a hush descended on the arena, a silence so deep you could hear nothing but the breathing of the contestant as she measured the runway. Then she was off and running, the pounding of her feet as loud as hoofbeats. Then, onto the springboard and off, pushing up from the vault incredibly high, twisting and turning and then landing so perfectly not a hair on her lovely head moved. Everybody in the Pavillion, coaches, judges, contestants and casual onlookers knew it was a perfect vault, a ten and a gold medal for Mary Lou. She ran over and embraced her coach and then waved to the crowd who were cheering and laughing and crying and feeling wonderful.

After the excitement of the gymnastic competition, I moved over to the diving events, where a completely different story unfolded. Greg Louganis was so far ahead of everyone else that the sense of competition in the men's division was replaced by an eagerness to see just how good this young man could be. And he didn't disappoint; he went further than anyone thought possible in this sport. He was far out by himself, jumping higher than anyone else, doing his twists and turns and somersaults seemingly in slow motion before entering the water without a ripple. His dives were perfection.

Years later, when the news came that he was HIV-positive, it was a double blow, for the young Louganis had a body of perfect proportions, as beautiful as the human form can be. He was strong and supple with superb musculature, and to have it exposed to the ravages of this terrifying disease was incomprehensible. My memory of him will forever be that of his final dive from the platform, that body stretched out against the summer sky in one shimmering silhouette before slipping silently into the water. He was the best there has ever been. And in that display of power, beauty, and grace, he displayed the best of what these world sports—those not bound by team or time or the bounce of a ball—have to offer.

Places in the Heart

"I sit in my chair and play a different course every day."

My work, which has been a labor of love, has given me the opportunity to play golf in many delightful and historic places around the world. The experience has buttressed my belief that there is no such thing as a bad golf course; some are just better than others. I have never had more enjoyment than when I was beginning the lifelong, elusive search for the perfect swing at the Main Line Golf Club forty years ago. Since then, I have had the opportunity to play some of the storied courses in the world. I will not attempt to name all of them nor to rank them in order of excellence. What follows are some of those courses that have given me many pleasant moments.

The list begins in my hometown of Philadelphia. All of our large cities have an abundance of good golf clubs, but Merion and Pine Valley stand apart. Architect Hugh Wilson folded the eighteen holes of Merion into the Pennsylvania countryside so artfully that they seem to have been there forever. Merion is also adrip with history. It was here that Bob Jones began and ended his brilliant career, and where Ben Hogan made his magnificent comeback from a near-fatal accident, winning the 1950 U.S. Open in a playoff against George Fazio and Lloyd Mangrum. Jones and Hogan are a presence at Merion, but it is the golf course that makes the impression, an impression as strong now as it was eighty years ago when it was the Merion Cricket Club. At first glance, Merion appears to be a short, easy layout, but it is not long before one realizes that our forefathers knew that length was not the only way to challenge the hapless golfer.

Bob Jones's record at Merion lends the place an aura that only Jones could produce—an aura that perhaps only Augusta National and Merion have. It was at Merion that the fourteen-year-old Georgian first came to national prominence by becoming the medalist in the 1916 U.S. Amateur Championship. And it was at Merion, fourteen years later, that he ended his stunning playing career.

In 1930, after winning the British Amateur and Open Championships and the U.S. Open, Jones came to Merion in September for the U.S. Amateur Championship. He won it when he defeated Eugene Homans eight and seven, thus achieving the Grand Slam. The thirty-six hole match ended at the marvelous short par-four eleventh hole. Every year the members of Merion mark the anniversary of Jones's victory by assembling in the early evening at the eleventh tee in black tie to raise a glass to Robert Tyre Jones, Jr.

Dan Jenkins has named the first tee at Merion the best first tee in golf. I would wholeheartedly second the motion. The tee is right up against the clubhouse terrace and the intimacy is quite appealing. All of Merion is appealing, for Merion is a trip back to the 1920s with today's comforts.

Just across the Delaware River, on the edge of Clementon, New Jersey, is the closest thing there is to the number one golf course in the world. Pine Valley was the inspiration of a Philadelphia hotel man named George Crump. He wanted to build the finest and most difficult golf course in the world. And he did, with some advice from H. C. Colt, A. W. Tillinghast, George C. Thomas, and William Flynn. When you cross the railroad tracks and go through the main gate of the club you enter a place of sand and scrub, of pine trees and grass. Pine Valley lies deep in the Pine Barrens of New Jersey, as isolated from the world as an island in the Arctic Ocean.

It is a very difficult golf course, but so stunning in its appearance that fear flies away the moment you step onto the first tee. Pine Valley is the epitome of target golf. You must hit over the scrub and sand to the fairway, and then over more sand and scrub to the green. The wayward shot is severely penalized, but if you hit the fairways and greens it becomes a walk in the park. The first time I played Pine Valley, George Fazio was in our foursome. He missed the first green and took a double-bogey six. George then proceeded to hit every fairway and green, had three putts lip out on him, and shot sixty-five. The course is probably too difficult for most of us, but the difficulty does not diminish the thrill of trying to score a few pars among the triple bogeys. Pine Valley can lure you into complacency. A couple of pars and you're sure you're going to break ninety. And, then, a drive just misses the fairway or an approach shot takes a bad bounce, and suddenly you are struggling to keep from making a ten. Pine Valley's individuality is revealed in one of the Club's historic performances.

Woody Platt was an outstanding amateur golfer from Philadelphia. He played golf in a long-sleeved shirt with a necktie and had a powerful and graceful swing. On this memorable day at Pine Valley, Woody birdied the first hole; then he eagled the second, ıg a six-iron. At the par-three third, he scored a hole in one, and then he birdied the fourth hole. He was six under par for four holes. The fourth hole at Pine Valley is right by the clubhouse.

"Can't do any better than that," he muttered, and left the course for the bar where he stayed for the rest of the day. Woody knew Pine Valley would never let him get away with such an outrageous start. You must never fight Pine Valley; you must let it come to you—and with a couple of pars and a bowl of the club's famous snapper soup, you will have had one of golf's greatest experiences.

Pebble Beach and Cypress Point are even closer to each other than Merion and Pine Valley and, although they share the same renowned peninsula, they are quite different. Pebble Beach is a big, broad golf course with some of the most difficult and beautiful holes in the world. Holes six through ten would be enough to place Pebble at the top. But there is a lot more. The fourth hole, for instance—a short par four, uphill to an intriguing green; the par five fourteenth with its green that can shatter the confidence of the most intrepid player. Then, of course, there is the eighteenth—the all-time postcard champion. Pebble Beach is the product of designers Jack Neville and Douglas Grant, and had the foresight of the founding father, S. F. B. Morse. It was Mr. Morse who insisted the land along Carmel Bay be used to build the golf course, and not for real-estate development. That's why Pebble Beach is the majestic place it is today.

Cypress Point is quite different. Where Pebble Beach is a big, burly golf course, Cypress is smaller, more quiet. It wanders through the Monterey Forest with a series of elegantly designed holes. The fourth hole, with its generous bunkering, could be the most handsome par four in the world. At the eighth and ninth holes, the golfer is presented with two short par fours that exact dire results from a careless shot. The course then explodes dramatically as it skirts the ocean's edge at fifteen, sixteen, and seventeen. These are not the calm waters of Pebble Beach's Carmel

Bay; these are the waters of the great misnamed western ocean, whose surf crashes against the headlands and sends spray and spume flying amid the barks of sea lions and the cries of seagulls.

The sixteenth hole is the landmark hole at Cypress Point. It is a par three that requires a long carry over the rolling surf, usually into a brisk wind. It is a marvelous hole, but its notoriety has over-shadowed the par-three fifteenth hole. This is my favorite par three in the world. It is not as fearsome looking as the sixteenth. In fact, it is a benign-looking hole of exceptional beauty. The grandeur of the site is overwhelming. The hole measures 125 yards from an elevated tee across a chasm of the Pacific to a shelflike green. The fifteenth tee at Cypress is one of the loveliest spots on earth, a place where one would like to build a home, or be buried, or spend as much time as possible. It is easy to see how Bob Jones was impressed with Alastair MacKenzie's work at Cypress, and why he engaged him to work on Augusta National.

The entire Monterey Peninsula is a fascinating place. The great green pine forests run down to a rocky sea coast producing great moments of sunshine, fog, wind and rain. It looks as if it was created exclusively for man to build golf courses on it. Spanish Bay, Spyglass Hill, the Monterey Peninsula Golf Club, all are marvelous examples of creative design, and they all capture completely the spirit of the place. Even the public course at Pacific Grove has a certain panache that makes a round of golf there a special event. But it is Pebble Beach and Cypress Point that are the chief seducers in this most seductive place.

The east coast of the United States has nothing that looks like the Monterey Peninsula. Its ocean, north of the thirty-fifth parallel, is far different from the California ocean, changing color and temperature with the four seasons. On eastern Long Island, it rushes to land on great sandy beaches, not against rocky headlands. Along this happy stretch of seaside are several historic and outstanding golf courses. The present Shinnecock Hills dates from 1930, when William Flynn redesigned some of the old holes and created new ones on land generously given to the club by its president, Lucian H. Pyng. Flynn's design is so good the course looks as if it was built a hundred years ago. It has a par of seventy and is filled with subtleties that change as the ever-present wind changes. The old white clubhouse sits on a hilltop, and from its porch you can look out at eight holes and the deep blue waters of Peconic Bay. It is a place of tranquility, even on a blustery day, because everything is where it should be. Every tee, every green, every bunker is in the right place. It is a course you never tire of and one you are reluctant to leave.

There are other outstanding and enjoyable clubs in the area. Maidstone is right on the ocean, winding its way among the sand hills and ponds of East Hampton. Right next to Shinnecock is an American golf heirloom, the National Golf Links, designed and built by the Father of American Golf, Charles Blair MacDonald. It is a splendid example of his work, an excellent golf course, and should be studied by every serious student of the game.

There has been a fourth course incorporated into the area. Architect Rees Jones designed the Atlantic Club and set it among the potato fields of Bridgehampton. It is a stern test on a treeless tract of rolling farmland, and we are going to hear a lot more about it in the years to come. Eastern Long Island, like the Monterey Peninsula, has several eminent golfing treats, but it is Shinnecock that sets the tone. Venerable, rich in history, internationally famous; it remains unpretentious, a place where the observance of the game is a simple and rewarding undertaking.

My experience in the New York metropolitan area revolved around Winged Foot and made me an enthusiastic fan of A. W. Tillinghast, whose work stretches from coast to coast. At Winged Foot, Tilly put down thirty-six superb golf holes. The four Open Championships it has hosted were played on the West Course, so it has received most of the publicity. But the East Course is just as challenging and just as beautiful. Tillinghast's signature is in his bunkering and contoured greens, and they are displayed thoroughly at Winged Foot. Both layouts are textbook examples of parkland golf. The original tree plantings by the designer were meticulous throughout and included grand English lindens, elms, and oaks. A symmetrically perfect elm to the right of the tenth green East was heroically kept alive for years before succumbing to the Dutch Elm disease in 1993. The day they cut it down was a milestone in the history of the club. As a rule, I don't like trees on a golf course, but Winged Foot is a most welcome exception.

The Terrace off the grill room at Winged Foot is one of the top ten outdoor rooms in golf. The ninth and eighteenth greens of the West Course and the eleventh and eighteenth greens of the East Course spread out before you, decorated by a line of trees across the four holes. Stress is hard to come by as you sit under the large blue-and-white striped awning on an early autumn afternoon looking out at the handiwork of A. W. Tillinghast

Since its founding in 1923, Winged Foot has had four golf professionals: Mike Brady, 1923 to 1937; Craig Wood, 1938 to 1945; Claude Harmon, 1946 to 1977; and the present resident, Tom Nieporte, who has been there since 1978. Winged Foot obviously is as fine a place to work as it is to play.

There are enough golf courses in the British Isles to keep you busy and enchanted for a lifetime, courses that beguile and challenge the low handicapper and hacker alike. My favorite golf course outside the United States wanders among the sand hills of western Ireland where the Shannon meets the sea.

The late playwright Marc Connolly used to tell a story of his first visit to the west of Ireland. He attended a Saturday night dance and overheard the following conversation between a Kerry couple.

He said to her, "Are ye dancin'?"
She said to him, "Are ye askin'?"
He said, "I'm askin'."
She said, "No, I'm sweatin'."

231

The speech and rhythms of the West country are far different from the melodic lilt of Dublin, where English is spoken perhaps more beautifully than anywhere on earth. The speech of western Ireland reflects the nature of the land, a harsh and terrible land that gives off a beauty more memorable than that of tropical islands and sleepy lagoons. Nowhere is that beauty more evident than at Ballybunion. Tom Watson has defined it as sharply as one of his iron shots: "Ballybunion looks as if it was laid out on land as it was in the tenth century."

You will know that Ballybunion is different from the very first tee. A disturbing sight greets you there: A graveyard on the right side just down off the tee, perhaps not so safe a resting place for the faithful departed who have often been annoyed by slices, pushes, and draws that didn't quite make it. The eleventh hole at Ballybunion is the most dramatic, most awesome, most memorable par four in golf. The small tee clings to the top of a sand dune with a fifty-foot drop to the beach, and the Atlantic Ocean below. The view is breathtaking. Off to the right the coastline curves away, and right before you are 449 yards of roller-coaster fairway, bordered on the right by the sea and rough, and on the left by a sandhill. You must skirt the cliff on the right to find a small piece of fairway between the sandhill and the sea. The approach shot is over a deep valley of a fairway through a narrow gap between two more sandhills to a green the size of an Irish penny. Not a single bunker was necessary to protect it. Tom Watson calls the eleventh hole one of the toughest in the world; it is that, but it is also one of the most enjoyable and memorable, a symbol of the land on which it lies, difficult, beautiful, wild, and exciting. There are a second eighteen holes now at Ballybunion, the work of Robert Trent Jones Jr., and, in time, they will take their place alongside the original ones. In the meantime, the old course is an Irish monument. If you want perfect fairways, no rough, flat greens, and calm, balmy days where the wind does not howl like a banshee, Ballybunion is not for you, nor you for Ballybunion. But if you are one of life's seekers, a Ulysses with three pitching wedges seeking what lies beyond the western stars, go at once to Ballybunion.

Ballybunion is the most remarkable of a superior group of golf courses in Ireland. Lahinch, to the north of Ballybunion, is another place that time has forgotten, misplaced or ignored. It is on the Atlantic Ocean just south of the Cliffs of Moher, where a Norman keep molders away above the links. For years, the barometer on the clubhouse wall has been broken and a sign directed you to observe the goats. If the famous goats of Lahinch were huddled against the clubhouse wall, bad weather was here or on its way. If the goats were out on the golf course, fair skies would be above you, or so the legend went. There was a summer heat wave the first time I played Lahinch. When I had finished my round, those goats of Lahinch were huddled against the wall of the clubhouse. When I remarked to the barmaid of this seeming contradiction, she replied with withering Irish common sense, "Oh, you dear thing, they're just for getting out of the sun and into the shade."

Across the country on the edge of Dublin is the regal Portmarnock Club, a handsome layout by the Irish Sea. It is the home course and birthplace of Ireland's great amateur, Joe Carr, who was born on the second floor of the clubhouse. Portmarnock's peninsula was once the property of the Jameson whiskey family and it has a much different look than the courses of western Ireland. Portmarnock is flatter and browner; it looks more civilized on the surface, but it can be as demanding as any course in the world.

North of the border, in Newcastle, is Royal County Down. I was invited to play there on a Saturday, a day set aside for fiercely fought interclub team competition. My host waved aside my worries of intruding, put me on his team, gave me a five-course lunch and invited me back anytime, even though I had let the side down disgracefully. At Royal County Down you will need your camera as much as your putter to record these holes that are laid out where the mountains of Mourne go down to the sea. These Irish courses have a beauty and challenge you will carry with you the rest of your days.

Scotland and England, beyond St. Andrews and the other courses on the Open rota, also offer exceptional golfing experiences. Royal Dornoch, north of Inverness, up near the top of Scotland, is a truly special place. When you look out over the course from the third tee, you are at once aware that this piece of land was meant to be a golf course and only a golf course. Old Tom Morris laid out the first nine holes in 1877 and Donald Ross, a native of Dornoch, was the professional. It was here he began his study of golf course design that resulted in so many wonderful courses in the United States. Royal Dornoch is a grandparent of American golf course design and one of the most satisfying places in golf. On a summer evening you can begin to play at 7:00 P.M. and know you have plenty of time to finish your round in the delightful quiet of a long Highland twilight.

One of the pleasures of attending the British Open at Muirfield is its proximity to so many wonderful places to visit and play. The East Lothian coast of Scotland, spreading out from Edinburgh along the Firth of Forth to the North Sea, is a bonny piece of real estate of lovely homes and golf courses. Out where the Forth flows into the North Sea is the attractive town of North Berwick. Among its many charms is the North Berwick Golf Club, thirty-six holes that lie along the water and haven't changed in a hundred years. The fifteenth on the west course is the original Redan hole; the green slopes from front to back, a feature that has been copied on golf courses around the world. It is a course that requires you to hit over stone walls and into greens hidden by sand hills. Adjacent to the sixteenth fairway is the Marine Hotel, one of whose features is a nine-hole course for children only. Adults are not only not welcomed, they are not allowed.

There are other authentic examples of pure Scottish golf within ten miles of North Berwick. Down on the coast of the North Sea is

Dunbar, a perfect example of a late nineteenth-century golf course, unpretentious, natural, and great fun to play. Beyond Muirfield toward Edinburgh, you will find Gullane with its four courses. Number two will do quite well if you can't make up your mind. Just up the road from there is the Royal Musselburgh Golf Club, leaking history all over its sandy soil. Royal Musselburgh was where the Gentlemen Golfers of Edinburgh, later the Honorable Company of Edinburgh Golfers, moved from their original site on the common ground at Leith. In 1872 it was decided that the open championship would rotate between these three clubs, St. Andrews, Prestwick and Musselburgh. The nine holes at Musselburgh hosted the championship six times until the Honorable Company moved again, this time to Muirfield, taking the Championship with them.

But Musselburgh had more than the Open to establish it as a monument. It was the site of many a big money match in the last part of the nineteenth century. It was the home of the golfing Park family, Mungo, Old Willie and young Willie, and there was little love lost between Musselburgh and St. Andrews, the home of the Morrises and Kirkcaldys. In a big money match at Musselburgh in 1882, Old Willie Park was two up with six to play against Old Tom Morris. The partisan crowd was at fever pitch and the referee, a former amateur champion named Chambers, stopped play because spectators were interfering with the balls. Old Tom was really teed off, and he and Chambers retired to Mrs. Foreman's pub and refused to come out. Willie Park went on alone and claimed the prize. The last time I was there it cost about three dollars to play these nine holes of history, surely a bargain for the serious student of the game.

All of these golfing opportunities and history far outweigh the occasional outbursts of bad manners from the secretaries of the Honorable Company of Edinburgh golfers, and that's why Muirfield is just behind St. Andrews and St. George's as my favorite venue for the Open.

West of London, in the wooden valleys of Berkshire, lie the

thirty-six holes of Sunningdale, as perfect a golf club as it is possible to attain. The membership is eclectic, eccentric, and quite exceptional. They are at once cordial and formidable. One day I was playing the Old Course with Clive Clarke, a British Ryder Cup player and former director of golf at Sunningdale. He had given me a shot a hole except on the par threes. I had won the twelfth hole, using my stroke, and as I stood on the tee of the par-three thirteenth, Clive said, "No stroke here. You'll have to do it yourself." Whereupon I hit my tee shot onto the green and into the cup for a hole in one. We decided that was enough excitement for one day. We walked back to the pro shop where Clive bought me a lovely watercolor of the thirteenth hole and inscribed it with the story of my ace. I had used a seven wood for the shot, which was a lot of club for a downhill hole. Clive cautioned me, "When they ask you what you hit, merely say, 'a seven'."

One Sunday, years before, I had wandered over to Sunningdale to look around. As I stood on the putting green looking at the old clubhouse with the big clock facing the course, it began to rain, and several of us took cover in the starter's shack that stands next to the pro shop and looks out at the large, perfectly shaped oak tree that stands by the 18th green.

Inside were the caddy master and, sitting in a chair behind the counter, a little man of about sixty-five, hair still dark, a face that looked like a pair of leather shoes that had been left out in the rain. A cigarette, which he never removed when he spoke, hung down from the left side of his mouth; his face had more lines than a range ball; and he was holding court.

"Come in, come in, it's only a shower. We'll be playing soon."

As soon as he found out that a couple of us were Americans, he launched into a spirited commentary.

"I caddied for Joe Kennedy, you know. Here and at Royal Berkshire. He and Jack and young Joe would come out at four o'clock and each would hit a couple of balls on each hole. Royal Berkshire was thought to be the place where the Germans would land, so it was all land-mined. If the Kennedys hit a ball into the rough they'd say, 'Never mind.' When the round was over, we'd go back and find the balls and sell 'em back to 'em. When he was leaving to go back to the States, the old man said he wouldn't be back and offered me his wardrobe. But I was a week late in picking it up and someone else had got it."

"Was Sunningdale opened during the war?" I asked.

"Oh, yes," the old fellow answered. "Those two bunkers there to the right of the eighteenth green were made by German bombs. They just filled them with sand. Makes the hole, don't it?" And, indeed, the two bunkers to the left of the eighteenth green do make a difference.

"Had two of your jockeys out last week," the old boy continued. "Cauthen and the little feller, what's his name?"

"Shoemaker," I said.

"That's it. Shoemaker. He's a little one, that Shoemaker."

The rain kept coming down and the little man kept talking as fast as the raindrops.

"You ought to play the new course. It's three shots harder. It was built in 1921. Where you from in the States?"

"Philadelphia," I said.

"Philadelphia, eh? You know Billy Hyndman?"

"Yes, I do," I replied.

"Well, you know, I caddied for Bonnalack that year. I knew he was going to win the British Amateur because he was sinking every putt. Had Billy Hyndman in the finals, and Bonnalack was in bed forty minutes before tee-off time. Hyndman shot seventy-two that day and lost by eleven shots. Bonnlack shot sixty-one.

"Doesn't Gerald Micklem live around here?" someone asked.

"Right over there," said our commentator, pointing. "Used to caddy for him, too. Smart man. Once gave him a five wood on a par three where the tee was a hundred feet above the ground. 'No,' he said, 'give me the four wood. Look at how small that fellow is on the green. He was six feet when he left here.'"

With that the rain stopped and the sun came out and we all left that little shack. From that moment, I knew Sunningdale was a different place, and so will you.

Once, when I was doing the track-and-field shows in Europe, Ralph Boston and I played in Stockholm where the course, like many over there, is measured in meters instead of yards.

"This par three is one hundred meters," I said, looking at the tee marker.

"Just like the hurdles, Jack," said Ralph. "That's 110 yards. Still a nine iron for me."

I have played in Nairobi at the Muthaiya Golf Club using a pair of rented clubs with hickory shafts. The old English pro, rotund and knickered, called them "a bit ropey." Two barefooted Kikuyu boys caddied for us. The rough was thick and wiry and we were not too disposed to look for a ball that missed the fairway. We had gin and tonics in the grill room of the clubhouse afterward, a room bathed in golden sunset light and filled with English Army officers. Time had stopped.

The wonderful places of golf are endless. We can enjoy the game in the Atlantic gales of Ireland, in the dry sunshine of the California desert, in the mountains of Switzerland and North Carolina, and on islands in the Pacific. There are many of these places I have not seen and never will, and many I have not mentioned here that have given me great pleasure. Golf offers such lasting memories—memories to enjoy in the cold of winter or to buttress us in the darkness of difficult times. Reg Murphy, former president of the USGA and renowned newspaper publisher, was once kidnapped and placed in the trunk of an automobile for forty-eight hours. He kept his sanity in that black, claustrophobic place by playing, hole by hole, every golf course he could remember.

When George Knudson, the Canadian golfer, was dying of cancer, Ken Venturi called him. In the course of their conversation, Ken said, "George, it must be so difficult. What do you do all day long?"

"Kenny," replied George, "I sit in my chair and play a different course every day. Today I played Cypress. It was a cool day with the mist coming in off the sea. I shot seventy-one."

The expansion of the game continues, spurred on now by the phenomenon that is Tiger Woods and his performances in 1996 and 1997. A World Tour is imminent and whatever form it takes will cause disruptions and controversy, but this is inevitable as long as corporations are the bankrollers of professional golf. It is the future. If it brings more nations and people into golf, it will be a good thing.

No one admires or is in awe of the touring professionals more than I. I have enjoyed their company, and reporting on them has been a delight. Many of them have become friends. I admire them because the overwhelming majority remain almost alone in the assembly of professional athletes who call rule infractions on themselves. But the professionals are only a part of the game. They are the public relations department. We are the game of golf. We amateurs who slice with abandon and three putt promiscuously. Dogged victims of inexorable fate, Bob Jones called us. We who slog fearlessly around the course in carts or carrying our own bag or with a caddy, or pulling our trollies behind us in America, Great Britain, South Africa, in the countries of the Pacific Rim, on municipal layouts or private courses, we are the ones who make up the great body of the game.

Golf has an infinite variety of places, but no matter where we play, competition, friendship, and self-knowledge are the end results. My happy golf travels have taught me that the difference between a Pebble Beach and a Main Line Golf Club is truly incidental. One has an ocean and breathtaking views, the other was split by U.S. Highway 30 and had hard, bumpy greens. But the thrill of the well-hit shot, or the frustration of a poorly hit one was exactly the same. Golf accommodates itself anywhere. It travels better than beaujolais. Golf is the most moveable feast of all.

Other Times, Other Sports

"Players are accused of lacking personality,
when it is education they lack."

Baseball

Baseball was the sport of my childhood and my first love. I was fortunate to grow up in a city with two major league teams, even though for most of my life, the A's and the Phillies were seldom World Series bound. Shibe Park was an important part of my youth and early adult years. I was too young to have seen the great Connie Mack teams of 1929 and '30, so I suffered all through grammar school, high school and college with the struggling A's. My heroes were Bob Johnson, Ferris Fain, Frankie Hayes, and, later, Bobby Shantz. When the team was sold and moved to

241

Kansas City, I felt I had lost something; even today when I watch the Oakland A's, I feel a flicker of anger and I completely understand the heartbreak and ire of Brooklyn over the loss of the Dodgers. Baseball teams were part of the substance of their cities in those years. Today, with unrestrained free agency and the lobbying for new stadiums, they have become just another corporation on the tax rolls.

My first professional experience with baseball came in 1951, the year after the Phillies won the National League pennant. I had started at the CBS affiliate WCAU on Labor Day, 1950. I was writing and delivering a five-minute newscast, and watched from afar as the Phillies won the pennant on the last day of the season in a thriller against the Dodgers. By November, I had moved over to the sports side and subsequently, covering the Phillies, got to know most of that "Whiz Kids" team. They were the first professional athletes I got to know personally.

The only play-by-play baseball I did was in connection with one of the best assignments that ever came my way. CBS did a major league *Game of the Week*. The announcers were Buddy Blattner and Dizzy Dean, the eminent linguist who introduced *slud* as the past tense of *slide* into the baseball vernacular. The network needed some protection in case of a rainout. The cost of an insurance policy was prohibitive, so they scheduled a standby game with a full standby crew. I was the play-by-play announcer and Frankie Frisch was the color man on that standby crew. The show ran for three years and, in that time, we got on the air for about six innings—but we were paid every week.

That period was my postgraduate education in baseball. Sitting by the Fordham Flash on those summer afternoons was a remarkable experience. This Hall-of-Fame second baseman knew every facet of the game. He was a marvelous psychologist; he had to be to manage that St. Louis Cardinals team of the thirties. The Gashouse Gang had Pepper Martin, Joe Medwick, Dizzy and Daffy Dean, plus Leo Durocher. Those five players gave new

meaning to the word *flamboyant* and would make today's oddly acting players look normal. Frisch got them to play together and win.

Frank had utter disdain for the player who did not hustle all the
time, the player who didn't run out every ground ball, or chase
every foul fly. He didn't like a player who didn't love baseball with
the same intensity he did. Most of the players in the early sixties
didn't like to hear Frisch talk about hustling and how it was back
in the 1930s, but Frank was a hero to many others. I often arrived
at the ball park, whether it was Yankee Stadium, Shibe Park, or
Memorial Stadium in Baltimore, to find the Flash holding court
in the stands behind home plate for the ushers and the vendors.
He would regale them with his stories and opinions and they
loved him.

Frank had a variety of interests outside baseball. He was a firm
believer in good food and was a great fan of the violinist Fritz
Kreisler. He was also a good handicapper at the racetrack. He
picked the three horses that finished in the famous triple dead-
heat in the Carter Handicap at Aqueduct in 1944. He went to the
track that day with sports columnists Frank Graham and Red
Smith. In those days, baseball players and managers were prohibited from going to the races under pain of suspension and fines, so
neither Frank Graham nor Red Smith wrote the story of Frisch's
handicapping feat, giving up a wonderful column to protect
Frank. Just like today.

In the 1960s, games were taking two-and-a-half hours to play
and that infuriated Frank.

"Look at that," he'd fume. "Three and two on every batter. The
ball is so lively the pitchers work the corners on the .180 hitters.
Why, we played a 6–5 game against the Phillies in old Baker Bowl
once in fifty-eight minutes. Let the batter hit the ball."

His theory made sense to me thirty years ago, and it makes
sense to me today. Games in 1997 were averaging two hours and
fifty minutes to play, with more three-and-two counts as the pitchers flinch from giving the batter anything to hit. If they took the

rabbit out of the ball so that only the legitimate sluggers could hit it out of the park, and returned the strike zone to the shoulders and knees and the width of the plate, games would be faster, more interesting, and pitchers would last longer. I know giving this advice is like whispering in a hurricane. Today's superstars have reduced this beautiful game to strikeouts and home runs. The nuances that make it such a fascinating pastime are disappearing. Few players today know how to slide, bunt, or hit the cutoff man. It's headline news if a pitcher goes nine innings. These changes would have appalled Frank Frisch.

The last game we were assigned to in the *Game of the Week* standby series was in Baltimore, the Orioles against the California Angels. We were standing behind the batting cage watching batting practice when Albie Pearson, the Angels' leadoff hitter, walked by. Frank called him over.

"Albie, did you never notice how deep Brooks Robinson plays at third base? I used to get ten or twelve extra hits a year bunting on deep-playing third basemen."

"Thank you, Mr. Frisch," Albie said.

Albie came to the plate to start the game and laid a perfect bunt down the third-base line. He could have walked to first base. Brooks never made a throw. The smile that lit Frank's face was beatific.

Those standby games made for marvelous weekends, and they came to an end only when CBS bought the New York Yankees. In those innocent days, since the network was an owner, it could no longer broadcast the games. I didn't see too much of Frank after that; he sold his house in New Rochelle and moved up to Rhode Island, near Westerly. Occasionally he would come into town for an old timers' game and we'd do an interview. One night, the two of us were sitting alone at a table at Toots Shor's. There was some baseball happening, perhaps an all-star game. Soon, we were joined by Red Schoendienst and then Stan Musial, and then everyone was coming over to say hello and the Flash was in his element.

One St. Patrick's Day weekend, my wife, Bert, and I were in Boston visiting our daughter Ann and looking at a college for our son Jack. On the way back as we were passing through Westerly, I said, "That's where Frankie Frisch is living."

"Well, why don't you stop and see him?" said Bert. "You never call him or write to him. He might be glad to see you."

So I stopped and called him, and he said come right over. He was glad to see us. His wife, Ada, had just died a month or so before, and one of the dogs had also gone, but after a slight tearing up when he told me the news, he was merry-eyed and combative once again. "What's a slow slider, Jack?" he asked in the familiarly squeaking voice dripping with derision. "God, we used to call that the nickel curve."

He was in good spirits, and insisted we stay for drinks and dinner. He was having some friends in and he wanted us to meet them. We did, and then went down the road to a seafood place and had lobster for dinner and white wine and marvelously good conversation. I made a date with him for the following spring to film him at his home, just about the time when his petunias would be coming up.

Next spring never came. The Old Flash was killed in an automobile accident in Maryland driving back from a speaking engagement. What the Gas House Gang couldn't do, nor generations of umpires and thousands of chicken lobsters, an interstate highway and an automobile did, and the Flash was gone. You can still see parts of him around, whenever you see an athlete hustle, whenever you see someone using all of his talents. There is a bit of Frank Frisch in Pete Rose, some in Fred Patek, and there will be parts of him in youngsters still to come who play children's games with grown-up skills. That's what Frank Frisch knew, that they were games but it was important to play them well and to enjoy them. Otherwise, you were a ribbon clerk.

Tennis

Tennis and I were first introduced at the Waterview playground at the corner of McMahon Avenue and Price Street in East Germantown in Philadelphia in the 1930s. Germantown had a rich tennis history; it was the home of Bill Tilden and the Germantown Cricket Club. Most of my gang were aware of the happenings at Wimbledon and Forest Hills through the radio and the Fox Movietone news. We knew all about Fred Perry and Ellsworth Vines and Don Budge and Helen Wills Moody and Alice Marble, all of whom were romantic figures to us in those depression days, the men in their white flannels, the women in their white skirts and visors.

My first professional brush with the sport occurred in the fifties, when the Australian Davis Cup team came to the Philadelphia Cricket Club. Over the years, my tennis assignments have been more sparse than I would have liked: a handful of tournaments, some made-for-TV extravaganzas and seven U.S. Opens, but they were enough to experience some extraordinary moments and to know some extraordinary people.

In the sixties, Jack Kramer and I did a CBS Tennis Classic, a round-robin affair that was won by Pancho Gonzales. Then, in the seventies, the network moved into a series they called *Winner Take All*. This was during the tennis boom that had been abetted by the Bobby Riggs–Billie Jean King television match. The series was set up by Bill Riorden, then Jimmy Connors's manager, and CBS. The format was simply this: The winner got $100,000, and the loser got nothing. The first of the matches was played at Caesar's Palace in Las Vegas, far from the traditional homes of tennis. Jimmy Connors beat Rod Laver in a splendid match that was a successful afternoon for tennis and television. The second match, still at Las Vegas, was between Connors and John Newcombe; again Connors won, but the TV ratings were not quite as good.

The third match took place in Puerto Rico at the Dorado

Beach Hotel. This time Connors's opponent was Ilie Nastase. Jimmy was in a feisty mood and Nastase was preoccupied; there had been an earthquake in Romania that day and Ilie had relatives there. Then, halfway through the match, it all fell apart. Pat Summerall and Tony Trabert were doing the play-by-play, and, at one point, Pat mentioned the winner-take-all component of the match, $100,000 to the winner, nothing for the loser. Shortly after, the phone rang in the TV truck. It was Barry Frank, the head of CBS Sports who had replaced Bob Wussler, the man who had made the deal for these matches with Bill Riorden. Frank told producer Frank Chirkinian to relay the information to Pat that "winner take all" was a misnomer. "Appearance money" was given to the loser. This correction was made on the air.

We all felt a little bit used. For over a year we had been going on the air with the winner-take-all promotion and believing it, and now we learned our leaders had misled us. No one was more incensed than Pat, who almost got physical with Bill Riorden while giving him a piece of the Summerall mind. After that, the *Winner Take All* series lost its charm and died a natural death.

The United States Open, of course, is another thing altogether. It is one of the premier sporting events, and during the years I covered it, this tournament suffered a personality change rivaling Dr. Jekyll's. Those years began with the championship matches being played at the West Side Tennis Club in Forest Hills. This club was the repository of American tennis history and the home of our national championship since 1924. This is where Bill Tilden and Rene Lacoste won, where Bobby Riggs and Jack Kramer played, where Helen Wills Moody and Helen Jacobs dueled, where Maureen Connolly and Chris Evert roamed the baselines, where Arthur Ashe and Jimmy Connors prevailed. Forest Hills was the look and tradition of American tennis.

The West Side Tennis Club, however, was not prepared to respond to the popularity that tennis was enjoying in the 1970s, a popularity that was straining the resources of the club. So, Slew

Hester, then president of the USTA, picked up the tournament from the grounds of the venerable club and put it down in the middle of bustling Flushing Meadow. Where in the twenties only a lonely country road with the gas station and optometrist's sign from *The Great Gatsby* had stood, now LaGuardia Airport, Shea Stadium, and the Long Island Railroad clattered away. Into this clamorous setting came the USTA Tennis Center and the United States Open Tennis Championship. Overnight the tournament became very American—big, loud, and brassy. The white-flannel world was left behind on the terrace of the West Side Tennis Club as the new generation of players, led by Connors, Borg, McEnroe, Gerulaitis, Evert, Navratilova, and Austin had their time on center court. Billie Jean King and her contemporaries fought long and hard to improve the prize money for women, and tennis was on a roll.

Then, as quickly as the game's popularity had expanded, the boom stopped. Interest in the game didn't diminish as much as it ceased growing. The end of the tennis expansion is one of the perplexities of modern sport. It is especially puzzling when compared to golf. Golf continues to grow, yet it is far more expensive, time-consuming, and not nearly as available as tennis.

Today professional tennis reflects the world in which we live. The money has become almost disgracefully abundant. Ion Tiriac, the former Romanian Davis Cup player, leveled a broadside at today's players during the Wimbledon championships in 1994. "Money," said Tiriac, who also managed Boris Becker, "is the root of most of tennis's evils. Having ten million dollars in the bank by the age of sixteen, and parents who are only bookkeepers, means you create a superstar who can't cope with the demands of life."

Tiriac went on to admonish today's stars to give something back to the game, and stated that in addition to spending six hours a day on tennis, they should give two hours to improving their English and French, read a book a week and the newspapers every day. "The players are accused of lacking personality, when it is education they really lack."

These criticisms have validity in almost every sport today, but I fear Mr. Tiriac's words mostly fell on pierced but deaf ears.

There are exceptions, of course. When Jim Courier won the French Open, he made his acceptance speech in French. The few times I have been around Andre Agassi he has been a very pleasant young man with a demeanor that belies his appearance in those abominable tennis clothes his sponsor drapes on him. Vitas Gerulaitis flew all night from Seattle to give a free clinic for the Long Island Cancer Society on the Saturday morning before his tragic death.

Tennis has produced some outstanding people. Arthur Ashe was one of the most influential figures in American sport over the last fifty years, and the game continues to attract interesting and bright people. It has been a wonderful experience for me to know some of them. Tony Trabert has become a solid friend over the years and I have enjoyed many fine times with his mentor, Bill Talbert. When they all get together at Wimbledon or the U.S. Open, it is one of the best groups in sports.

One lesson I learned from covering tennis occurred at the 1975 U.S. Open. The winners that year were Manuel Orantes and Chris Evert, but the big story spun around a nineteen-year-old Czech girl, Martina Navratilova. On that Labor Day weekend she sought political asylum in the United States. This was in the frigid days of the Cold War, and Martina was leaving behind in Czechoslovakia a family who could possibly be punished for her desire to live and play tennis in the United States. Martina held a press conference to announce her defection. Producer Frank Chirkinian sent me there to bring Martina down to our studio for an interview.

The scene at the press conference was near bedlam. The press of the world were hurling questions at this young woman in half a dozen languages, their strident voices disturbing the peace at Forest Hills. Still cameras flashed away. Through it all, Martina sat and quietly answered every question patiently, mostly in English, her second language. Her poise would have made Cary Grant look like Jim Carrey.

She was the same in her interview on CBS. She very patiently explained to me that she wanted to be the number one tennis player in the world, and to do that she felt she had to live in the United States. Throughout the interview she was completely in control of her emotions. I marveled at her composure, and ever since that day, I have tried to give all young athletes a little breathing room. At nineteen, I could not have handled myself the way Martina did that day, facing a noisy press and answering questions in a second language. It made me realize how much we expect of our young people, and how much we forget what it was like to be nineteen years old.

Ali

The heavyweight champion of the world has always been a major celebrity who transcended sports, and no one ever played the role more avidly than Muhammad Ali. From the time he flashed his wonderful smile at the 1960 Olympics until his supple body was muffled by Parkinson's syndrome, he was the biggest personality in sports. He was the quintessential ambassador for boxing. He took the title of World Champion seriously, fighting for that trophy around the world.

His refusal to be drafted during the Vietnam war forced us all to look again at our society. Despite the fact that his refusal to go into the army alienated a lot of people, his innate dignity and personality overcame much of that animus, and when he returned to boxing after a three-year suspension, he was warmly accepted in most quarters.

The first telecast of an Ali fight that I was involved with occurred on February 20, 1976 in San Juan, Puerto Rico. At that time, CBS, which had been so dominant in prime time, was beginning to feel the competition from ABC and NBC. Consequently, Bob Wussler, the head of CBS Sports, was able to secure three hours of prime time from the network in the hope that Ali would defeat the situation comedies and police dramas on the other networks, as well as his opponent, who in this case was the less than well-known Belgian stonecutter and heavyweight, Jean-Pierre Coopman.

The fight was held in the El San Juan Hotel, marking a departure from the traditional venues of arenas and ballparks. Furthermore, the two fighters worked out in the hotel. With the change in venue came a change in the crowd; those who paid five dollars to watch the workouts were not the cigar-smoking, slouched-hat, hard-core boxing fans, but were mostly tourists, flower-shirted, sunburnt visitors from the north, bathingsuited matrons, more than a few youngsters who looked in awe at the champion, and babies whose mothers wanted Ali to hold them while they took a picture. Ali was wonderful with the children, and the atmosphere was far different from heavyweight fights of the past, when the two antagonists would be secluded in remote training camps until the morning of the fight. For Coopman, it was his fifteen minutes of fame. He was guaranteed $100,000, had picked up a retainer fee from a bicycle firm, and for the moment was bigger than waffles in Belgium. He was known as the Lion of Flanders.

The festivities took place in the ballroom of the hotel on a Friday night. The Lion of Flanders proved to be the gentlest lion since Bert Lahr. Ali carried him for five rounds before Jean-Pierre faded away. It was an awful fight and a bad show, but such was the power of Ali that CBS won the ratings by such a great margin that they came in first for the entire month thanks to those five forgettable rounds of boxing.

The second Ali fight I worked was the Ken Norton affair in Yankee Stadium, September 28, 1978. This was more like the old days: a big heavyweight fight in Yankee Stadium. It was the first heavyweight championship fight held over second base in seventeen years. There had been fifteen fights held there, and Joe Louis had been in eight of them. The second Louis–Schmeling and the second Louis–Conn fights there had been million-dollar gates and had solidified the stadium as *the* place for a championship fight. Furthermore, Ken Norton was no Lion of Flanders. This would be the third meeting between the two fighters; Norton had beaten Ali in San Diego on March 31, 1973, and then, in September of that year, Ali beat Norton in Los Angeles. This was their rubber match at the big ballpark and everyone was anticipating a great time, unlike that bland evening in Puerto Rico.

When we arrived at the stadium we all wished we were back at the El San Juan Hotel in Puerto Rico. The New York police force was on strike and was holding a demonstration outside the ballpark. In addition to a massive traffic jam, there was no crowd control, and the crush of people trying to get inside the stadium was dangerous and frightening. Once inside, we were told to hold onto our wallets because every pickpocket and mugger in New York was roaming untroubled through the crowd. It was an evening tinged with terror.

The fight was a good one, with Norton dominating the first part. Then, Ali put on a flurry in the final two rounds and the judges, in a close vote, gave the nod to the champion. It was a controversial decision; many, including myself, thought Norton had won. I tried to avoid the alarming crowd that was swarming around the main entrance to the stadium, so I walked to the corridor under the stands to find another exit. The corridor was empty, but as I walked quickly along, I suddenly heard footsteps and voices. I turned around to see Ken Norton and his handlers hurrying to their dressing room. The fighter was sobbing loudly; he, too, thought he had won.

My final Ali assignment came on February 15, 1978, as CBS once again used Ali to beat up on the sitcoms of ABC and NBC.

His opponent was Leon Spinks and the fight was held at the Hilton Pavilion in Las Vegas. Since the Norton fight, Ali had defended his title twice. He defeated Alfredo Evangelista in fifteen rounds and Earnie Shavers, also in fifteen rounds. Now he was putting the title on the line once more, this time against the 1976 Olympic light heavyweight gold medalist. Leon Spinks had just seven professional fights. He had won six of them, five by knockouts, and had one draw. On the basis of this sparse record, he was now taking on the champion of the world. The press was calling it a terrible mismatch; with more truth than jealousy, they wrote, it was another made-for-TV affair that was not good for boxing.

Rehearsal for the show was at noon, and air time was five o'clock, Las Vegas time. I went up to my announce position at the end of the pavilion and there was Ferdinand Pacheco, the fight doctor. He was the boxing commentator for the show.

"Well," I said after exchanging greetings, "another bum of the month for Ali."

"What do you mean?"

"Everyone thinks this is a terrible mismatch. Spinks doesn't belong in the same ring with the champion.

"Do you know how old Muhammad is?" asked the doctor.

"Yes," I said. "He is thirty-six."

"Yes, thirty-six, and he has been fighting for sixteen years, and he has absorbed a lot of punishment. Especially in the three Frazier fights and the bout in Zaire with George Foreman. That rope-a-dope experience was terribly hard on his cardiovascular system. Ali's body is older than thirty-six. This is no pushover."

Age, of course, is every athlete's final undefeated adversary and we were all aware of Ali's maturity, but to hear that his beautiful body could be suffering and perhaps disintegrating was a new and shocking bit of information. It was then not quite as surprising as it might have been when Spinks won the fight. It was a dramatic evening and another ratings winner for CBS. Spinks may have won the fight, but Ali nailed *Starsky and Hutch* and *Police Woman.*

Ali defeated Spinks seven months later, and regained the title once more, but the end was near. Larry Holmes knocked Ali out in 1980 to take the title, and then Trevor Berbick beat him in ten rounds and sent him off to retirement. The age of Ali was over.

That age lasted twenty-one years, a generation when Muhammad Ali dominated the sports world and places beyond. I think Joe Louis was the best heavyweight in my lifetime, Marciano was second, and Ali, with his fast hands and feet and graceful moves, third. He had Joe Frazier to bring out the best in him; their three fights are a legacy for both men. Ali was much more than a heavyweight champion. He went far beyond his sport, stinging American society like a bumblebee and floating among us like an avenging butterfly. He lost and regained the heavyweight title, bruised our minds about Vietnam and racial matters, lost three years at the height of his powers, and was the best promoter boxing has ever known. And he did it all with a twinkle in his eye.

The Two Strangest Days

Horseracing has given me great moments spent with many great friends. It gave me a distinction of sorts and a place in the tournaments of trivia. In 1979, I broadcast the Woodward Stakes which was won by Spectacular Bid. No one finished second.

In racing, if only one horse goes to the starting gate, there is no race and no betting, but the horse must run the distance in order to be declared the winner, and for the owner to collect the purse. This is called a *walkover*. In 1979, none of the other three-year-olds wanted to test Spectacular Bid again, and the trainers of the older horses were not overjoyed to give away weight to the Kentucky Derby and Preakness winner. One by one, the field defected. About an hour before post time, the last horse scratched, leaving Spectacular Bid alone and setting up, as far as I know, the only walkover on national television.

We tried to make the best of it, wiring jockey Bill Shoemaker so he could talk to us as he steered Spectacular Bid around Belmont Park. But even that didn't work: As Shoe was leading the colt into the starting gate, his earpiece fell out and we never had communication with him. All we had was a solitary horse and rider galloping around the track in silence. Morning works are a lot more exciting.

In my pantheon of odd events, the companion piece to the 1979 Woodward Stakes was the 1993 Grand National at Aintree, England. This granddaddy of all steeplechases has been run since 1839, deterred only by two World Wars. The Grand National bears little resemblance to the affair in the movie *National Velvet*. This race is not for the faint of heart. The large field of horses must circle the course twice, running four and one half miles and clearing thirty barriers that test the courage of horse and rider alike. After the last jump there are 494 yards to the finish line, where the last measure of stamina and heart are taken. It was in this testing stretch that the legendary Red Rum won his first of three Grand Nationals, making up twenty-five lengths on Crisp in one of the most remarkable performances in all of equine history.

The racing fans of Great Britain are far more daring than their American cousins. Most American horse bettors stay away from steeplechases because they're difficult to handicap, but the crowds at Aintree bet more than three times the amount we bet on the Kentucky Derby. The Grand National has the faint aroma of Victorian England about it; a time when the gentry viewed the world from horseback. It has had its critics, too, ever since that first race in 1839. Some people think it is criminal to force horses into such dangerous situations where pileups occur and where the horse can be hurt or killed. Cruelty to animals is their cry, and each year they appear at Aintree with banners and slogans in protest of the race. They were there in 1993, and the protests that year became more vocal and a few protesters came onto the racecourse. This caused a false start of the race, and the field of forty horses was called back to the starting line. Forty horses is a large field, and the starting gate has yet to be built that can accommodate that many. The Grand National is started the old-fashioned way, with a tape across the track; the tape is held until all the horses are lined up as fairly as possible, then the tape is dropped and the race is on. When the start is not a good one, a steward down at the first jump holds up a red flag and the horses return to start again.

That is what happened in 1993. The horses were recalled for a second start. The tape was dropped again, and off went the field hell-bent for the first jump. But the protesters were once again coming onto the course, and the steward once again raised his red flag declaring another false start. However, this time many riders did not see the flag and off they went, merrily jumping and galloping around the course. It was not until they had completed the first circuit that they realized what had happened as they saw the rest of the field still at the starting post. What to do now?

Some of the field had run half the race already, and some had not run at all. The decision, greeted by the betting public with clamorous outrage, was to cancel the 1993 Grand National. It had never happened before, never in 154 years. Our half-hour show was reduced to a ninety-second report of this embarrassing historic event that they will talk about for another 150 years. The Woodward Stakes walkover in 1979 and the Grand National of 1993 were unforgettable lessons in the uncertainties that make horseracing such a fascinating and bewitching pastime.

Another Track, Another Time

My very first play-by-play experience occurred on a lovely summer evening in eastern Pennsylvania in 1948. I was working at a 250-watt radio station in Pottsville and, on that evening, I was sent to cover the midget automobile races on a quarter-mile dirt track just outside of town. The combination of my inexperience and the dirt track turned the broadcast into a fiasco. The midget cars sent up a cloud of dust after the first lap that became like a sandstorm in the Gobi desert; visibility was zero as the heavy dust rose in the summer evening, turning the blue-green world into a dirty brown and blocking out the sun. The broadcast was a shambles and I returned to the studio shaken and alarmed.

Just about that time, automobile racing—and Formula One in particular—was beginning to flourish, especially in the Grand Prix races of Europe, where dashing, handsome drivers went speeding through the twists and turns of romantic places. The occasional fatality only seemed to enhance the aura of the sport as drivers like Juan Fangio, Stirling Moss, Jimmy Clark, and Jack Brabham became the new swashbucklers. In the sixties, the Grand Prix touched down at Watkins Glen in New York, and the CBS *Sports Spectacular* covered it. I remember only the awe I had of these daring drivers making all those gear changes, speeding through all those turns, the charm and good looks of Graham Hill, and the death-defying ride behind a police escort down the hill to the airport.

In my final year at CBS, I was assigned the twenty-four hours of Le Mans, a race that only the French could bring off. It admits several different classes of cars, all racing at the same time. For the spectators, it is a literal carnival; for one full day and night the race continues unabated while a fair featuring a giant ferris wheel and sideshows keeps pace. As dawn breaks and the neon lights begin to pale, another Le Mans emerges as mass is said inside the circuit and the faithful pray for the safety of the drivers.

There have been many changes to the racing circuit at Le Mans over the years, but one section has remained the same. The English call it the Mulsane, the French call it Les Hunaudieres. It is the longest straight on the course, and the place where the cars go the fastest. There is a Hotel Restaurant at Les Hunaudieres that in 1981 was owned by Monsieur Maurice Ginnisel. Monsieur Ginnisel had seen every Le Mans; the race began in 1923, and in 1928 Maurice's father bought the hotel on the Mulsane. Maurice remembered the old days when the cars did not go so fast; people would sit at tables by the side of the road in front of the hotel and eat and drink and watch the cars race by. The drivers would see a spectator being served his soup, then, several laps later, his entree, and, finally, dessert. At that point the driver would know it was time for a pitstop.

Today there are more sophisticated ways of getting the cars into the pits, and because of the tremendous speeds it is forbidden for safety reasons to sit by the side of the road. There is an ugly but effective fence that separates the road from the Hotel's entrance and the garden. There is, however, one tradition that was still being observed in 1981; Jackie Icyx was the winner that year and, on Sunday evening after the presentation ceremony, he drove down to Les Hunaudieres and had dinner with Maurice.

There was a fatal accident that year, which sent up another round of debates about automobile racing. It is an unending debate, and will be with us as long as men and women want to go ever faster in automobiles. All automobile races are loud, but Le Mans has its own special sound. It is a French, nasal, whining, screeching, screaming sound that fills the head and penetrates to the bones for twenty-four hours without letup. If Joan of Arc had been in Le Mans on race day instead of down the road in Orleans, she could never have heard those voices and the history of France might have been quite different.

The noise at the Grand Prix in Monte Carlo has an abundance of decibels, too, as the Formula One cars slither their way up and down the hills and around the streets of this fascinating town. The race is over in just a couple of hours, though, and the silence descends like a benediction over the eclectic crowd that ranges from the champagne group on the terrace of the Casino and on the yachts in the harbor, to the picnickers on the hillside with their babies, blankets, and cheese.

In 1982, I experienced another one of those cultural shocks that make the broadcast life so intriguing. We left the seductive background of the Monte Carlo Grand Prix and went directly to Indianapolis for the Indy 500. Going from the Hermitage Hotel in Monte Carlo to the Airport Sheraton in Indianapolis is to cross not just the better part of two continents but two different ways of life. The Grand Prix of Monaco is so European, the Indy 500 so American. Americans and Europeans approach the automobile with different attitudes: The American takes his car for granted, the air conditioning, the automatic shift, the CD and tape deck, the phone; the European treats his car with great passion, and the manner of driving is reflected in these attitudes. Most Americans are accelerator, brakes, and horn, while Europeans drive as if they were Walter Mitty being Mario Andretti. I shall never forget driving in Italy on the Autostrada between Milan and Verona one evening in fog so thick that the visibility was only about ten yards. I kept being passed on both sides by cars going seventy and eighty miles an hour.

Indianapolis in 1982 was in the flowering of the Cosworth V-8 age and the beginning of the Penske team's dominance. That year, for the first time, the purse passed the two-million-dollar mark. The Old Brickyard had become one of our glittering sports palaces, on a par with Yankee Stadium and Madison Square Garden. Since it was purchased by Tony Hulman in 1947, it had grown into one of the most famous racing plants in the world, and the race had become one of the world's most important. It was also the keeper of the history of American racing, from Ray Haroun's 1911 Marmon, through Wilbur Clark's Maserati and Maurice Rose's Offys to the present, all located in the land of Booth Tarkington, Phil Harris, and Chris Schenkel. Basketball may be the Hoosier religion, but the Indy 500 is its soul.

Producer Bod Goodrich had assigned me a few sidebar stories. We visited the luxury boxes on Turn Two and contrasted them with the gang at Turn One. The world of Turn One at Indy is an experience of almost extragalactic dimensions. The fans there are like no others; if you took the cheeseheads of Green Bay and crossed them with the profane and demanding Philadelphia Eagles' fans you wouldn't even be close. These are the fundamentalists of racing fans and their little conclave on Memorial Day weekend would have made Hogarth a happy man.

I also had a role in the opening of the show: ABC technicians had perfected a tiny TV camera, which they were able to install in the back of the pace car. The camera was aimed backwards to where the field of thirty-three cars would be following in qualifying order as they made the first lap around to the starting line where the race would begin. It is called a *rolling start*, and as the cars near the starting line, the drivers begin to accelerate and the pace car ducks into the pit lane.

I was to be in the back of the pace car, describing the scene as we sped around the course with the thirty-three Indy cars getting closer all the time, while our tiny camera showed them coming on practically at ground level. This was going to make a dramatic shot and we were all excited about it. Excited and apprehensive: Several years before, Chris Schenkel had ridden in the pace car and as it swerved into the pit area to allow the race cars to go by, it struck the photographers' stand, collapsing it and injuring several people, including the intrepid Mr. Schenkel. A person could get hurt in the pace car.

I was aware of that as I walked out on the track to the Chevrolet Camaro Z-28 that would waltz me around the speedway, but it was such an exciting time that my apprehension disappeared. I watched the Purdue Band leave the track as the last strains of "Back Home in Indiana" were drifting across Gasoline Alley. They fitted my microphone on and checked the communications among Bob Goodrich, Jim McKay, and myself. I shook hands with the pace-car driver; that year, the honor went to Jim Rathman, who won the Indy 500 in 1960 and was a veteran campaigner over the course, and I immediately felt better. I climbed into the small back seat of the Camaro. The door closed. We heard those rousing words, "Gentlemen, start your engines!" The thirty-three racing machines began clearing their throats.

In an instant we were off and rolling the straight to turn one, picking up speed with every moment. Around the quarter-mile turn we sped, now going well over 110 miles an hour. Jim McKay cued me and I began talking about the feeling of speed and what it was like to barrel over this famous racing grounds with thirty-three of the best drivers and machines in the world giving chase. Then I looked out the back window and realized that the thirty-three cars were nowhere in sight. The back stretch of the Indianapolis Speedway was as empty as an interstate in Montana at three in the morning. Then Bob Goodrich was yelling in my ear to throw it back to Jim McKay.

There had been a collision in the first two rows as the cars began to move into the rolling start. The front row that year was composed of Rick Mears in the pole position, Kevin Cogan in the middle, and A. J. Foyt on the outside. As the cars began to roll, Cogan slammed into Foyt's car, and then was rammed from behind by Andretti, who was in the second row. All but Mears were penalized by the accident. An irate Foyt finished nineteenth, a fuming Andretti thirty-first, and Cogan next to last. Rick Mears went on to duel with Gordon Johncock and lost by just 0.16 seconds, the closest Indy 500 finish in years. That made up for the messy start, but our exciting pace car opening became a casualty, along with Foyt and Andretti.

My second visit to the Indy 500 was memorable for quite another reason: It was the occasion of one of my more egregious gaffes.

My most flagrant mistake happened on October 8, 1956 at WCAU-TV in Philadelphia. I was doing a ten-minute sports show in the 11–11:30 news slot, sandwiched between the weatherman and Ed McMahon's *Five Minutes More* variety segment. I was sponsored by Felton-Sibley, a Philadelphia paint company. There were two live commercials I had to perform during the ten-minute segment; these were demonstrations crafted to show, in the words of the company's slogan, that Felton-Sibley "Dries to a hard, durable finish."

On this particular evening, I had to take a roller dripping with Felton-Sibley paint and cover a piece of particularly ghastly wall-paper, all green and red cabbages and roses. I remember saying to myself, as I walked over to the commercial area, what a horrible piece of wallpaper it was. I dipped the roller into the paint, rolled it over the wallpaper, turned to the camera and said clearly, "You see, Felton-Sibley dries to a HORRIBLE FINISH."

There was a gasp from several of the crew members and a sti-fled giggle or two as I stammered, "I mean, of course, to a hard, durable finish." I was shaken to the core. That was the evening of the day Don Larsen had pitched a perfect game in the World Se-ries against the Brooklyn Dodgers, and Robin Roberts of the Phillies was my guest that evening to talk about the game and the Series. I walked back to the desk still in shock after my blunder. I turned to Robbie and asked, "Well, Rob, what did you think of the Series?" And Robin Evan Roberts, the pride of Michigan State, ace of the Phillies staff, winner of 286 major league games, even-tual Hall of Famer, smiled and said:

"Jack, I thought it had a horrible finish."

Now there were hoots of laughter from all over the studio. The two cameramen were doubled up, the stage manager, John Het-herton, was shaking with uncontrollable mirth, the lighting man, everyone was guffawing and giggling. I managed a weak smile and signed off saying something to the effect that it had been nice working at Channel Ten and that this was probably my last night on the air. And it almost was. Two things saved me: Robin's per-fect line at the right time, and the fact that on the following day Felton-Sibley sold a lot of paint. Women, especially, were buying gallons of the stuff so 'that nice young man won't lose his job.'

At Indianapolis, my blunder was almost as blatant. I was doing an essay on the impact of the Indy 500, how it was the continuing love story between America and the automobile, how it had contributed to the safety of the cars we drive. I ended by quoting one of the best known lines in all of sport, "Gentlemen, start your engines!" Only I said, "Gentlemen, start your motors." I didn't realize what I said for several moments and then I was mortified. I looked around the announcing booth, but no one would make eye contact. There was no Robin Roberts to give me a lift with a funny line, no little old ladies to buy a gallon of paint. I was alone with my misery, and I left the Old Brickyard feeling just as shaken as I felt forty-five years before, returning to the studio in Pottsville after the midget auto race. The taste of a mistake never changes. It is always bitter.

A Matter of Perspective

"Remember, it's an adventure."

In 1969, I took my wife, Bert, and our six children on a skiing trip to Italy. The children ranged in ages from five to eighteen and, before we left, I sat down with them and explained what a different experience it was going to be, how the language and food would be different, that the bathrooms would not be quite the same as the ones at home, and how much fun it was going to be. "Remember," I concluded, "it's an adventure."

Our destination was Cervinia, up near the Swiss border. The mountain is called *Cervino* in Italy; it's the Matterhorn in Switzerland. My heart dropped when I saw the size of the rented Fiat I would drive from the airport in Milan to our hotel. Somehow we were able to cram all six children and our baggage in and began the drive. I had a lot of trouble with the gear shift, and the car was not responding well to my clumsy shifting. The road up the mountain was a nightmare of hairpin turns, no guard rails, and hundred-foot drops on either side. I was scared and every time Bert or one of the children would say something I would yell and tell them to shut up. Finally, we made the last turn and entered the village of Cervinia. There, halfway up the main street, the Fiat expired. The engine just stopped. At that very moment, a snow plow with a blower on the top passed us going the other way and dumped a half-ton of snow over our stalled Fiat. A silence more icy than the Arctic descended in that little station wagon. Finally, after about five seconds, before I could open my mouth, from the back of the car came the voice of my daughter Mary Beth: "Remember, Daddy, it's an adventure."

And that's what it's been for me from my first days in radio to the present. An adventure where good and bad things have happened. Those years were played out against the background of the assassinations, urban riots, Vietnam, and racial conflicts that still stalk us. Those immense changes in American life have been mirrored in sports. The baseball strike of 1994 blew away that last vestige of the romantic notion my generation had that sport was still an ingredient of professional games. My generation was raised in the Depression and formed by World War II; if you were able to get through those two experiences without being maimed physically or psychologically, then the world was yours. We survivors were fortunate to find an America that was expanding and prosperous. Today our generation is appalled and bewildered by gangsta rap, TV talk shows, and multimillion-dollar salaries to surly, weak hitters, perhaps the way our mothers and fathers were appalled and bewildered by swing bands and jitterbugging.

The changes in sports since I first sat down in front of a TV camera have been enormous, but a few things never change. Champion athletes over the years have two enduring qualities, the desire to win and the discipline to work hard. One early morning in Jimmy Weston's restaurant in New York, Frank Sinatra told me a story about Benny Goodman that every performer of any kind should know. During World War II, all the big dance bands were gathered together in Chicago to put on a show to sell war bonds. This was at the time when Frank was becoming nationally known through his stint as the male singer with the Tommy Dorsey Orchestra.

"I came into this large building where we were rehearsing," said Frank. "And the first person I see is Benny over in the corner practicing the scales on his clarinet. I had never met him, so I went over and introduced myself. We chatted for a while, and then I asked him why he, one of the greatest clarinetists in the world, was practicing the scales. Benny looked at me and said, 'If I didn't practice every day, I would only be good, I wouldn't be great.' And from then on," said Frank, "I vocalized every day."

No matter how much or how little talent we have, we must hone it every day. One year I was doing a story on Jim Otto, the often-injured Hall of Fame lineman on the Oakland Raiders. Our last location was at the team's practice facilities, and when we were finished it was getting dark, practice was over, and everyone was heading for the clubhouse. George Blanda pulled me over and pointed down the field. There in the gathering dusk was Fred Biletnikoff all by himself, running his pass patterns. "He'll work there for another hour," said George, smiling with admiration.

On another California evening, I watched Tom Kite on the putting green at Pebble Beach practicing by the light that spilled from the drug store windows. That was on Friday evening. On Sunday, he won the Open. All the great ones work hard and make it look easy.

That is true today as it was fifty years ago in spite of the vital changes that have occurred in sports.

One of the most difficult things in reporting on sports over the years has been to keep perspective. This became increasingly difficult as the money grew bigger and the hyped-up publicity screamed at us that this fight, this game, this golf tournament was the best in history. My two favorite statements of perspective are Coach John McKay's admonition to his USC football team before a big game against UCLA, "Remember," he said, "800,000,000 Chinese don't even know this game is being played," and the words of Andy Sidaris, an ABC director of great force and wit who would always say to everyone, seconds before we went on the air, "Remember, we're not doing brain surgery on children."

It seemed indecent to me to be concerned about who was playing football on that last weekend in November of 1963, or what the Rangers and the Knicks did the night after Martin Luther King was shot. Life goes on, but there should be a time to pause and reflect.

We are also bombarded with references to clutch shots, clutch hits, clutch everything. Performing well under pressure is uplifting, but sinking a foul shot for the Final Four championship or sinking a ten-foot putt to win the Masters is not on the same pressure level as raising a large family on a small income. Whenever I hear the word *clutch* now I think of Hymie Haas, a man I never heard of until 1994.

That was the year of the fiftieth anniversary of D Day and the invasion of Europe in World War II. I had landed on Omaha Beach on D Day plus 3, the ninth of June. Except for an occasional artillery shell, our landing was uneventful. The beach was churned up and you could tell there had been a lot of activity. We did not see a single dead American, and we walked calmly up the path from the beach to the bluff and camped in a field near the village of St. Laurent-sur-Mer. Fierce fighting lay ahead, but on June 9, 1944, Omaha Beach was busy and peaceful. I was to learn fifty years later that this was due in large measure to Hymie Haas.

I wanted very much to do an essay for ABC News on my expe-

thesis: The Masters, Final Four, Super Bowl,
won on the beaches at Normandy.

Professional sport has grown into a voraciou
all proportion to reality. If it continues on its p
devour itself. Still, I would not hesitate to recor
sportscasting or sports writing to any young
about the games themselves and the English la
fers a marvelous opportunity for creative express

The world of professional sports seems sadly
that will change, probably by an economic brea
val the 1929 stock-market crash. In the meanti
good people in that world: athletes and coach
give back to their communities. For several year
with Ken Venturi a TV show called the *Arete*
Greek term that means a human performance i
of being the best you can be in the pursuit of
Arete Awards Show is for courage in sports and
Venturi's courageous win in the 1964 U.S. Op
nearly overcome by heat stroke.

The recipients have included a blind sailor
school gymnast, a ninety-three-year-old swimmer
records, a college woman who one year after a li
her basketball team to victory. The stories of th
overcame handicaps, sickness, and age and fou
through sports is welcome testimony to the pu
never leave the *Arete Awards Show* without feelin

There is a price to be paid for a career in bro
will be a lot of missed birthdays, anniversarie
which can affect family relationships and marri
can handle those problems, they are more than
by the impressions that remain long after the
scores have disappeared onto the floppy disks of

I would tell young people about early morni
track with the rising sun making long shadows

rience for their D Day program, of how we heard the unending drone of aircraft at about eleven at night in our billet in Dorset on June fifth, and, shortly after, getting the order that we were moving out in the morning. I wanted to tell of the people who lined the narrow English roads and cheered us as we rode in the two-and-a-half ton trucks that took us to Weymouth; of how the staging area there had the latest movies, and steak and ice cream for dinner, the first since we had been in England. I wanted to describe what the harbor at Weymouth looked like, filled with ships of all shapes and sizes and stretching as far as you could see. It seemed to me that you could walk across their decks to France.

I wanted to tell of the ship that took us over, a posh channel steamer that could have been the set of a Nöel Coward play, its finery dimmed, its black-tied, evening-dressed characters now replaced by G.I.s in full battle dress. I wanted to see if I could express the chilling, thrilling fear that clutched us that day as we began the biggest adventure of our young lives. Much to my surprise and regret, ABC was not interested in my little part in the invasion of Europe, and I resigned myself to watching the celebrations on television.

Then an old friend and colleague from my WCBS days called. Jim Jensen asked me to tell my story on a show he was doing on the D Day anniversary. We taped the interview, and afterward Jim mentioned that WCBS was taking a house in Normandy for the celebration and offered me a room. I accepted gratefully. I had been back to France many times since 1944, but I had never gone to Normandy to see the invasion beaches or the American cemetery that sits on the bluff above Omaha Beach in the same field we camped in on June 9, 1944. Now that field is a beautifully groomed green carpet with rows of short, white crosses. They say survivors feel guilty, and I guess that's true because when I walked among those crosses in 1994 and read the names and units and the dates of death of those buried there, I began to cry uncontrollably. Many buried there had been killed at Omaha Beach, but

others had fallen in the battle of the he
through at St. Lo. It was at the latter p
wound that took me back to Englan
capricious life is.

Jim Jensen and his WCBS crew had
story that to me has epitomized D Day,
some extent my generation. The first
Omaha Beach at 6:30 A.M. on June 6th
plete command of the beach from pill
dred feet above. At 7:30 A.M., the seco
find a scene of chaos and blood. The
down, unable to move up from the bea
was close to being a disaster. In that sec
with a thirty-seven mm. recoilless rifle n
colonel came running up to him implo
damned pillbox. Hymie backed his ha
that he had a view of the German po
tance of about 200 yards and 100 feet
see the pillbox that was doing most of t
of that pillbox was about one foot high
fired and the shell found the aperture.
the beach was secured, and the invasio
sands of other Americans were able to v
beach two days later without danger.

Hymie and his comrades were hono
Laurent-sur-Mer on June 6, 1994 with
burned-out pillbox. On that day, Hyr
worker from the Bronx, wondering what
ter all, all he did was obey orders. But to
mans and to me and all the survivors
hero. He hit a target a foot high and six
dred yards and one hundred feet below
letes perform wonders; Hymie performe

What we have here is a revision of t

---

coming off the horses and the banter of the grooms up and down the shed row, and of the morning works at the Curragh in Ireland as the horses move over the ground and a relaxed gait, moving almost to the rhythm of the country. I would tell them of the works on the Downs at Lambourne in England where some of the stables are in the village, and of the cloppity sound the horses' shoes make on the cobblestone streets.

I would tell them of winter sports and of standing on a mountain top in the morning after a fresh snow when the whole world looks clean and white, and of Saturday afternoons in the autumn glory of Palmer Stadium in Princeton, or any other college stadium, before the leaves have fled and the grass is still green.

I would like them to know the feeling of being at the ball park before the start of the first World Series Game—the red,white, and blue bunting fluttering in the breeze and the excitement that is impossible to disguise.

They should know, too, the happy congress that occurs on the practice tee at a golf tournament, the gossip and the repartee that mingle with the serious work at hand, and of the stimulation that occurs at the four Major championships.

And I would tell them that, sooner or later, another Nicklaus, another Secretariat, or another Michael Jordan will come along and light up the sky. They always do and it is great to be a part of it. And what a marvelous thing it is to travel and learn the world. You discover a new appreciation of the United States, and at the same time realize that people everywhere react the same way in certain situations and that we are more alike than we think we are.

Sports cannot end wars, erase racism, or end poverty, but properly guided, they can be a more positive force in these areas than they are now. To help with that guidance seems a worthwhile challenge for a new generation of sportscasters and sportswriters. All they must remember is that it's an adventure, not brain surgery on children.